PELICAN BOOKS

A548

GEOGRAPHY OF WORLD AFFAIRS

Born in Sydney, Australia, in 1928, John Cole
has lived almost all his life in England. He was
educated at Bromley Grammar School, Kent,
and then read Geography at Nottingham University, where he is now a Lecturer in the
Geography Department. After graduating in
1950, he spent a year with a British Council
Scholarship at Pavia University, Italy. Since then
he has spent some months in Peru, working on
a study of Greater Lima for the National Planning Office, and in 1961 visited twelve Latin
American countries. He is also interested in the
geography of the Soviet Union and is joint
author, with Mr. F. C. German, of *A Geography
of the U.S.S.R.* He is married and has two sons.

There are, at the present time, two great nations in the world which seem to tend toward the same end, although they started from different points: I allude to the Russians and the Americans. Both of them have grown up unnoticed; and while the attention of mankind was directed elsewhere, they have suddenly assumed a most prominent place among the nations; and the world learned their existence and their greatness at almost the same time.

All other nations seem to have nearly reached their natural limits, and only to be charged with the maintenance of their power; but these are still in the act of growth; all the others are stopped, or continue to advance with extreme difficulty; these are proceeding with ease and with celerity along a path to which the human eye can assign no term. The American struggles against the natural obstacles which oppose him; the adversaries of the Russian are men; the former combats the wilderness and savage life; the latter, civilization with all its weapons and its arts: the conquests of the one are therefore gained by the ploughshare; those of the other by the sword. The Anglo-American relies upon personal interest to accomplish his ends, and gives free scope to the unguided exertions and common sense of the citizens; the Russian centres all the authority of society in a single arm: the principal instrument of the former is freedom; of the latter servitude. Their starting-point is different, and their courses are not the same; yet each of them seems to be marked out by the will of Heaven to sway the destinies of half the globe.

Extract from *Democracy in America* by Alexis de Tocqueville
First published in 1835

To be more precise about international tension, it is obvious that everything in the end revolves round the relationship between two countries – the U.S.S.R. and the U.S.A. To illustrate this figuratively, one can say that just as you would have to tear the leaves from a cabbage gradually, one by one, to discover the heart, so if you were to remove one by one all the various undecided or disputed questions among countries then the heart of the matter would turn out to be the contradictions between our two countries, the U.S.A. and the U.S.S.R.

Khrushchev on International Tension (*Pravda*, 10 May 1957)

J. P. COLE

GEOGRAPHY OF WORLD AFFAIRS

PENGUIN BOOKS

Penguin Books Ltd, Harmondsworth, Middlesex, England
Penguin Books Inc., 3300 Clipper Mill Road, Baltimore 11,   d, U.S.A.
Penguin Books Australia Ltd, Ringwood, Victoria, Australia

—

First published as a Penguin Special 1959
Reprinted 1960
Reissued in Pelican Books 1963
Reprinted 1964
Third edition 1964
Reprinted with a Postscript 1965
Reprinted 1966

—

Made and printed in Great Britain
by Hazell Watson & Viney Ltd,
Aylesbury, Bucks
Set in Linotype Times

CONTENTS

Contents

LIST OF FIGURES

List of Figures

FOREWORD

The reader is asked to bear in mind that the rapidity with which important developments are occurring in world affairs makes it impossible to be up to date with everything in this book. What is more, since many parts of the world lag behind in the publication of figures it has been impossible to obtain reasonably complete sets of figures for a year or two immediately preceding the period of revision, which means that some statistical data will be a few years old by the time the book is read. In most cases, the substitution of the latest figures would not appreciably alter the conclusions drawn from the material.

The author wishes to thank Professor K. C. Edwards, M.A., PH.D., F.R.G.S., and his other colleagues in the Department of Geography, Nottingham University, for their many helpful suggestions during the preparation of this book. He is especially grateful to Dr R. H. Osborne for advice at various times on Eastern Europe. He has further been encouraged by the interest shown by the students of the Department in many of the questions discussed in it.

For this third edition, the revised version for the second edition has been left virtually unchanged, but an additional chapter has been added to allow the inclusion of a discussion of important developments in world affairs in the early 1960s. In addition, some space has been devoted to a consideration of the question of planning the location of new industries in the United Kingdom itself. The reader is asked to forgive any discrepancies that may have arisen as a result of the revision.

*

In the 1965 reprint, a postscript has been added, bringing up to date some of the statements and figures found elsewhere in the book, without however attempting to make alterations in the text of the second edition published in 1963. Some sets of recent figures for thirty-five countries have been used in conclusion, to illustrate a way in which correlations may be tested by statistical methods with some precision.

LIST OF ABBREVIATIONS

Benelux	Belgium, Netherlands, Luxembourg
Br.	British
C.	Central
C. Afr. Fed.	Federation of Rhodesia and Nyasaland
Comecon	Council for Mutual Economic Assistance (U.S.S.R. and East Europe)
E.	East
E.C.S.C.	European Coal and Steel Community: France, Italy, West Germany, Belgium, Netherlands, Luxembourg
E.E.C.	European Economic Community
E.F.T.A.	European Free Trade Association
Fig.	figure
Fr.	French
H.E.P.	hydro-electric power or project
I(s)	Island(s)
kwh.	kilowatt hours
L.A.F.T.A.	Latin American Free Trade Association
m.	million
N.A.T.O.	North Atlantic Treaty Organization
Neth.	Netherlands
N.	North
S.	South
S.E.A.T.O.	South East Asia Treaty Organization
sq. ml.	square mile
t.c.e.	tons of coal equivalent
Un. of S. Africa	Union of South Africa, now Republic of South Africa, referred to in this book usually simply as South Africa
U.S.S.R.	Union of Soviet Socialist Republics, or Soviet Union
U.K.	United Kingdom of Great Britain and Northern Ireland
U.N.	United Nations
U.S.(A.)	United States (of America)
W.	West

Chapter 1

INTRODUCTION

I. INTRODUCTORY

To appreciate the significance of problems and events in world affairs, the student of the subject, professional or amateur, must have some knowledge of the scope and content of a number of disciplines. In particular, he must know something about the history of different parts of the world, at least during the last few centuries, and of the geography of different parts of the world at the present day.

Professional geographers are not in complete agreement about the extent of the field covered by their subject but it would be unfair to drag the non-geographer into a discussion of the nature of geography. Here it is sufficient to point out that geography is not merely the accumulation of innumerable facts about where places are and what they produce, though naturally the more of these a geographer knows without having to look them up, the more quickly he will be able to work at his subject, at least when he is concerned with the study of regional geography. Geography is about the Earth's surface, and naturally, since man during the last few millennia has played a great part in shaping this, the geographer appreciates the close relationship between the physical environment and human activities. An important part of geography therefore is man's economic, social, and political life in space (i.e. on the surface of the world) in the same way that history is concerned with human activities in time. Thus, the contribution of the geographer to the study of world affairs is an understanding of the influence of the physical environment and of the significance of distributions and space relationships.

The present book is intended to provide a brief geographical background to the study of world affairs for the reader who has no special training in geography and who might hesitate to refer to textbooks written by and prepared for trained geographers. Technical terms have therefore been avoided as much as possible and explained where indispensable. The amount of detail is, of course, limited by the space available, and at times the reader may feel that insufficient evidence has been assembled to justify controversial conclusions. An attempt has been made to keep a balance by devoting to each major problem and each region of the world the share of the space available that, in the opinion of the author, its particular significance merits.

Chapters 1–4 are devoted to general considerations and deal with some terms and misconceptions, the spread of European influence over the world since the fifteenth century, the question of dividing the world into regions, and some aspects of population and production. Chapters 5–7 include an outline of the physical environment, population, economic life, and main geographical problems of each of twelve regions into which the world has been divided for the purposes of this book. Chapters 8–10 are concerned with the balance of power in the world at present. Particular attention is given to the U.S.S.R. and the U.S.A. Although the topics are arranged in sequence, each chapter can be read independently of those preceding or following it. At the end is a list of selected publications to enable the reader to study in greater detail many of the subjects dealt with in this book. The figures (maps and diagrams) are placed as near as possible to the page or pages they illustrate. They are a vital part of the book and should be consulted whenever they are referred to in the text, as they are intended to show processes, distributions, and viewpoints.

The rest of this chapter is mainly devoted to a consideration of certain misconceptions and prejudices about world affairs.

II. PROJECTIONS AND MAPS

Most people will agree that maps are useful in the study of world affairs for showing where places are. Not so many are aware either of the many advantages that may be derived from a fuller application of maps or of the snags that arise from representing the surface of the spherical globe on the flat surface of a map.

There are many ways in which a map can be useful in the

study of world affairs. It is often important to know not only where a place is but also where it is located in relation to certain other places. Too often a map merely shows a country or a district, without indicating in which part of the world it is located or what neighbours it has. There is, too, a tendency to use maps merely for showing such features as boundaries, towns, and railways. The blank background on which these are mapped might be mountain or lowland, desert or forest, good cropland or poor pasture. Many important distributions can be shown by means of maps. In addition, a process or a viewpoint may be better understood by a glance at a map than by the study of many pages of text.

Turning now to the difficulties connected with the construction of maps and the representation of material on them, the reader should appreciate that on any map showing a sizeable part of the earth's surface (a continent, for example) there must be some distortion. Just as it is impossible to flatten a large piece of orange peel without tearing it or pulling it out of shape, so a part of the Earth's surface, when represented on the flat surface of a map, becomes distorted, whatever projection (the method of converting) is used. Area, distance, shape, and direction – all, or some of these must be sacrificed. The distortion is negligible when an area like Cornwall or Caithness is shown on a map, but it becomes appreciable for an area the size of Europe, and enormous when the whole world is represented on a flat surface. On some projections area is shown correctly (a projection of this kind is called equal area), but for this to be done, shape must be distorted. On other projections shape is preserved (orthomorphic projections) but area must be sacrificed, and some places will be much larger than they should, which means that the scale will be reasonably true only for a part of the map.

Fig. 1a, Mercator's projection, shows a map of the world familiar to many people. On this projection, shape is represented correctly, but area is greatly exaggerated towards the poles, because the scale increases away from the equator. Although Greenland appears to be as large as South America, in reality it is not much more than one-tenth the size. Fig. 1b

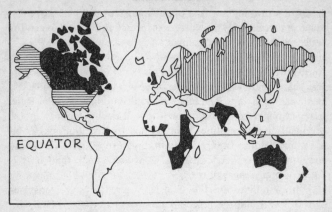

1a. The world on Mercator's projection. Key to shading on figs. 1a, 1b, and 2. Black: British Empire in the 1930s; horizontal lines: U.S.A.; vertical lines: U.S.S.R.

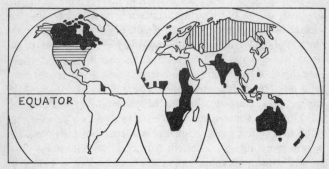

1b. The world on Interrupted Mollweide's homolographic projection.

shows the world on Interrupted Mollweide's homolographic projection. On this projection area is correct (compare Greenland and South America now) but shape is distorted, especially towards the poles.

On both these projections the equator is a straight line running across the map from one side to the other. A world map with the equator in this position is useful when the purpose of the map is to show how temperatures decrease away from the equator towards the poles. It also serves admirably to show how climate, vegetation, soils, agriculture, and even types of building and clothing are related to latitude, because all these are related to temperature. In the study of world affairs, however, it is often more important to know how various places are located in relation to one another than how they are located in relation to the equator. The best way of finding out this is to consult a globe. One of the worst ways is to refer to a projection of the kind shown in Figs. 1a and 1b. It is not possible to sell a collapsible globe with this book, but fortunately there are other projections of the world that are more useful for the study of world affairs than the type already discussed, though they are not so good as a globe. The globe, of course, is not without disadvantages, and one is that it is never possible to see more than part of the Earth's surface on it at a time.

Fig. 2 illustrates Bartholomew's regional projection, which has been used for several world maps in this book. Neither the shape nor the scale of the continents is more than slightly distorted. The projection is constructed by 'peeling' the globe from the south pole and flattening the pieces produced. The oceans, of course, are hopelessly distorted, and Antartica is divided into several parts. Another drawback of the projection is the fact that the Bering Strait (only about 50 miles wide at its narrowest), which separates the U.S.A. (Alaska) from northeast U.S.S.R., has been stretched by the process of 'peeling'. In this book an attempt has been made to remedy this by showing the area twice on some maps. In spite of all these drawbacks the arrangement of the continents is much more realistic than it is on Mercator's projection or other projections of that kind.

The reader should appreciate that the world or parts of it can be shown on many different projections. Every projection is a compromise, but that does not mean that an attempt should not be made to find the most suitable compromise for any particular purpose. Familiar projections (such as Mercator's) are often used to illustrate such topics as world strategy when other projections would be far more suitable.

Just as we recognize the world, or large parts of it, only when

17

we see them on certain projections, so also are we accustomed to seeing continents and countries only from a certain viewpoint. Doubtless the custom of putting north at the top of maps has advantages, though there is apparently no top and bottom to the universe and therefore no top and bottom to the world.

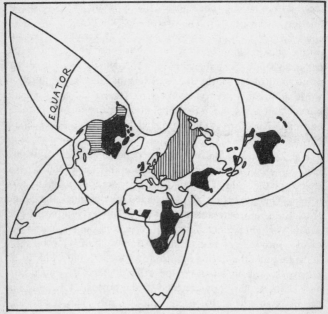

2. The world on Bartholomew's regional projection (this projection is reproduced in various figures in Chapters 1–4 with the kind permission of John Bartholomew and Son Ltd).

We are accustomed to seeing north at the top and the Arctic Ocean as the 'roof of the world', because when a globe is put on a stand, north and not south (or any other point) is put near the top. We are erroneously applying our idea of gravity, or up and down in relation to the surface and centre of the earth, to the universe as a whole. At all events, north–south meridians (lines of longitude) and east–west parallels (lines of latitude) are used for the location of places on the earth's surface and, unless otherwise indicated, north is assumed to be at the top of a map. Obviously, it is pointless to put south or west-north-west or any other compass point at the top merely to be different. But as there is no rule about putting north at the top, there is no reason why another compass point should not be put there if a more useful map is produced by so doing. Incidentally, though this hardly affects the argument, it is in fact impossible to put north at the top on a map with the North Pole at the centre.

This book is not the place to go at length into the arguments for putting other compass points at the top of maps instead of north, but a few of the advantages of an occasional change may be noted. One result of always putting north at the top of the map is that we tend to think of some countries and towns as being above others and of each country as having a right way up and a particular shape. This leads to what might be called north–south thinking. We are so accustomed to looking at various parts of the world in one particular way that we are reluctant to turn a map round another way and thus may miss the chance of seeing completely new relationships between places and obtaining new ideas on particular problems by doing so.

One important reason for turning a map round or, better, drawing the whole map with some other compass point at the top is that we can more easily see and appreciate something that happens along a direction running roughly from the bottom to the top of a page in front of us than in any other direction. This is of course why routes such as those provided for motorists usually have the starting point at the bottom and the destination at the top whatever the general direction of the route. Where north is does not matter in the slightest to the motorist, but to be able to hold his route in front of him with the turnings on his map as they are on the road in front is an obvious advantage.

Likewise, it may be useful to do the same for a larger area. A map showing the territorial growth of the U.S.A. in the nineteenth century ought to have the west (the Pacific coast) at the top since this was the direction in which the pioneer settlers were moving. Russian expansion, on the other hand, has been most spectacular eastwards, and a map showing this should have east (also the Pacific coast) at the top. Nor is it asking too much to suggest that if a comparison were being made, the two might be put side by side and neither would have north at the top. So, in the same way, to give another example involving smaller areas, a comparison of the ports of London and Hamburg and of their respective estuaries, the Thames and Elbe, would be much easier and clearer if the rivers were arranged parallel to one another and east put at the top for the Thames, north-west at the top for the Elbe.

It is hoped that from what has been said the reader will appreciate how without any drastic mental effort one can achieve a more flexible and realistic outlook on world affairs by remembering that the choice of north as the top of the map is arbitrary and that there can be many viewpoints. These viewpoints can be found more easily on a globe than in most atlases.

Incidentally, it should be appreciated that the northern and southern, eastern and western hemispheres (half spheres) are not the only possible ones, and also that these and any other hemispheres (for example, the one with the most land in it) can be represented in various ways, not necessarily with north at the top.

III. VIEWPOINTS AND VIEWS

Each individual who studies world affairs is bound to have his own viewpoint and views. The viewpoint is partially determined by the locality (in space) and the period (in time) in which he lives. His views are influenced by his environment, by the particular language he speaks, by the customs and traditions of his country and compatriots as well as by what he hears and reads. It is probable, however, that his own particular world outlook may not differ greatly from that of his contemporaries in the same part of the world. The British, for example, tend to have a collective, Anglocentric (or Britannocentric), outlook towards the world. Our outlook is bound to differ from that of the Mexicans or Persians or Australians. After living in another part of the world for some time, a person may of course begin to acquire a world outlook similar to that of the people among whom he is living.

Not surprisingly, there is a tendency for people to feel that what they are accustomed to in their own district or country is normal and that everywhere else in the world there are only varying degrees of abnormality. But there is no justification for thinking that conditions in Britain (or anywhere else, of course) are any more normal than those in other parts of the world. Indeed, we should bear in mind that such a highly industrialized and urbanized trading community as Britain is something very unusual both now and in the past.

The tendency for people to consider that what they are accustomed to is normal can easily be accompanied by another, more dangerous, tendency. This is for people to think that they, their compatriots, and their way of life are superior to others. They may base their claim to superiority on their superior military strength, on the numbers of cars or telephones they have per hundred inhabitants, on the light colour of their skin, or on the fact that they belong to a certain religious faith or have a particular type of political organization.

The idea that one's own group is not merely different from all others, but also better, is widespread. It is reflected in the rivalry between individual communities and between tribes in simple societies, between towns and regions in civilized countries, and between nations and even continents on a world scale.

Owing to the strong influence that Europe has exerted on the rest of the world during the last few centuries, Europeans have developed a tendency to consider the world and world affairs with a collective or Europocentric viewpoint. Our thinking is consequently affected by various features of this viewpoint. In particular, the Europeans have imposed Europocentric place terms on the rest of the world. The *Near*, *Middle*, and *Far East* are only near, middle, and far in relation to Europe. The Far East is the centre of the world for the Chinese and Japanese. It is the Far West for people living in California and British Columbia. Likewise, the terms *Old World* and *New World* are misleading. If America was a new world for the European explorers who arrived there towards the end of the fifteenth century, it was the Old World for the tens of millions of people whose ancestors had already been living in the continent at least for a few thousand years. The terms *West*, *Western World*, and *Westernization* are also unfortunate. The West is a vague term widely used in world affairs, but we should remember that if it is west of the East, the East is also west of the West. If we must use these and other Europocentric terms we should not allow them to prejudice our thinking. Other examples of the acceptance by all or much of the rest of the world of European place and time terms are the labelling of the meridian of Greenwich as 0 and the use of the Christian calendar (Sunday, of no significance in non-Christian countries, is still kept as a rest day).

There are many viewpoints as individual viewers and as many collective viewpoints as groups of viewers with some collective interest and consciousness of their collectiveness. If we appreciate this fact we begin to be more critical of some of our own views and more sympathetic towards the views of others while remembering, of course, that these are just as biased as our own. Certainly we cannot afford to ignore what other people say and do, whether they are allies or enemies. Indeed, if they are more powerful, it often pays to do what they say.

Failure to consider the aims and aspirations of others leads to misunderstandings. Something might have been done to prevent the Second World War if certain countries had taken seriously what was said in others. What is more important, a third world war might be avoided if people in power spent more time trying to understand the views of others and less in broadcasting their own.

Failure to appreciate the impact on others of one's own statements and actions can also lead to misunderstandings. Politicians are frequently unable to anticipate reactions to their speeches and policies, because they have very little idea of what views other people are likely to hold. It is easy to build up a dream world about the history of one's own country and to be self-righteous about its actions and aspirations. It should be appreciated, however, that other countries do not necessarily agree. There is no better example than Britain itself. In the 1770s it unsuccessfully attempted to prevent its American colonies from gaining their independence. In the 1820s, on the other hand, it was helping the Spanish colonies to free themselves from Spanish colonial rule (one reason, no doubt, was because it could trade more easily with them when they were free). Throughout the nineteenth century, however, it was building up its empire in South Asia, and in the last decades of the century took part in the scramble for Africa. Yet by 1935, when the Italians set out to annex Abyssinia, the last large territory in Africa remaining outside European control, Britain had again changed its attitude towards colonialism, and opposed Mussolini. However brutal the Italians were towards the Abyssinians in this campaign it is hard to deny their claim that the British were hypocrites. It is easier to disclaim responsibility for the actions of our compatriots of one or a few generations ago than to explain, let alone justify, an inconsistent policy of this kind to others.

Excessive preoccupation with one's own views and viewpoints can also lead to a misanthropic attitude in world affairs. The Soviet Communist Party professes to sympathize with the workers of the world, yet its party newspaper, *Pravda*, is not the only Russian publication to include articles anticipating an economic depression and gloating over working days lost in strikes and high unemployment figures in capitalist countries, however much inconvenience and misery these bring to the workers themselves. Many U.S. publications are no less jubilant about bad harvests, shortfalls in industrial output, and rumours of unrest in the U.S.S.R., even if the ordinary Soviet citizens, rather than the members of the Communist Party, are likely to suffer the consequences. We in Britain have the misanthropic habit of lamenting industrial progress in Germany and Japan, yet this results in better conditions for the Germans and Japanese. After all, we can hardly blame the Germans for losing the war; they did their best to win it.

Introduction

The large number of vague terms and terms that lend themselves to imprecise thinking and talking makes it easy to become hypocritical and misanthropic in connexion with world affairs. Terms like *the capitalist world* or *the free world* are vague and difficult to define. Then there are many partners, such as *information* and *hostile propaganda, partisan* and *terrorist, bandit* or *counter-revolutionary*. The *free world* of the U.S. press is everywhere outside the Communist bloc, yet it includes countries governed by powerful monarchs and military dictators as well as colonies governed by European powers. The *capitalist powers* of the Soviet press include not only the U.S.A., where the Post Office is the only large civil enterprise run by the Federal Government but also the U.K. and Italy, where many branches of the economy are state-owned. Numerous other ill-defined terms confront the student of world affairs. Among them are democracy (but several countries with a Communist regime style themselves democracies) and Communism; aggression and justified armed intervention; satellite and ally; indoctrination and education.

We may blame politicians and journalists for introducing, distorting, and disseminating terms of this kind, but we too are responsible if we continue to use them, at least without endeavouring to decide what they really mean in any particular context. Only when escape words of this kind are abandoned or defined, and personal views put aside, can world problems be studied with impartiality.

IV. RACE

Since the question of race is connected with so many world problems some pages are now devoted to this subject. Although numerous publications have been prepared on the subject for the non-specialist reader, many people with strong views on race, and particularly on skin colour, appear to be completely ignorant of the most elementary scientific principles concerning the classification of human beings.

For many people, racial groups coincide with cultural groups – political units or linguistic, religious, and other groups. If there are Swedish and Portuguese nations and languages there must be Swedish and Portuguese races. Certainly all the members of some nations (and of other groups of this kind) have many features in common, but it would be more difficult to be satisfied about a Swiss race than a Portuguese one, and the reader who hoped to prove the existence of an Indian or Brazilian or even a U.S. race would come across many difficulties.

Many other people are aware that race is generally accepted by scientists as referring to the measurable physical characteristics of human beings (e.g. height, blood group) and not to cultural features (e.g. language, religion) nor even to mental capacity (ability in intelligence tests) which is, of course, quite different from volume of brain, a feature that can be measured objectively. But they assume that skin colour (which depends largely on the quantity of the pigment melanin in the outer layers of the skin) is the most important distinguishing characteristic. Since much of the prejudice concerning race is based on this assumption or connected in some way with skin colour, this question deserves our consideration. Many Europeans and people of European origin assume that a darker skin is connected with inferior mental and moral standards. This assumption can easily lead to the argument that *if* people are dark-skinned they must be inferior, and even a stage farther to the idea that *because* people are dark-skinned they are bound to be inferior. But why do so many people attach much more importance to skin colour than to other characteristics?

The earliest attempt by Europeans to classify human beings into races, after they had explored most of the world in the fifteenth to seventeenth centuries, was the classification (still at the back of many people's minds today) into white (European), yellow (East Asian), black (African), red (North American Indian), and brown. This early classification was probably based on skin colour for two main reasons. Firstly, before the long-distance movement over short periods of large numbers of people since the sixteenth century, skin colour was (with exceptions) reasonably uniform among the inhabitants of large regions (e.g. the tropical Africans were all dark-skinned by

European standards) and it was therefore easy to associate a certain skin colour with a certain part of the world. Secondly, vision is in many ways the most powerful of our senses, and skin colour is one of the first features that strikes us, especially as it is a feature that affects the whole body, if only 'skin deeply'. One wonders if a blind person would attach such importance to skin colour as to some other characteristics. Perhaps dogs classify human beings by their smells.

At all events, it must be appreciated that skin colour is only one of many physical characteristics by which human beings can be classified, and is not necessarily any more useful in this respect than others, such as type of hair (according to its cross-section), shape of head (breadth measured against length), and so on. Indeed, with the rapid growth of the study of characteristics of human blood, anthropologists are coming to doubt more and more the usefulness, at least at this stage, of earlier ways of measuring physical characteristics of human beings and of the race classifications evolved. While the study of blood groups has had to wait until recently for sufficient data to make any appreciable progress, blood is a simpler and more easily understood kind of feature than many other characteristics since, unlike most, it is passed on through one gene pair and the manner in which it is inherited is simpler. In view of the present controversial nature of race classification, even though based on numerous and accurate measurements, it is safe to say that it is not known whether or not any of the many inheritable physiological characteristics affect the mental capacity of individuals and groups and make them inferior or superior. If any do, skin colour seems one of the least likely.

It remains to be proved scientifically, then, that the view held by many Europeans that light skin is connected with racial superiority is anything more than a tragic example of illogical inference. Certainly it is easy to point to the material advances made by Europeans during the last few centuries and to their present generally high living standards where they are scattered about the world today and to infer that light-skinned people must be superior at least in mental capacity, and perhaps even morally. Yet a thousand years ago most Europeans were living in agricultural communities differing little in their economic and social organization from those found in Africa a hundred years ago, and, presumably also to be found in Africa a thousand years ago. In contrast, China was then civilized (even though most of its inhabitants were rural dwellers). Were the Chinese therefore superior racially at that time?

Why such remarkable material advances have been made in Europe (and by Europeans outside Europe) in the last few centuries is a difficult matter to decide. Some argue that European 'stock' possesses special qualities. Others suggest that the physical environment of Europe, perhaps the changeable weather, stimulating mental activity, has been responsible. Both may be right – or neither. The development of the modern machine age in Europe may be nothing more than the result of a number of accidents producing a cumulative or snowball effect, each discovery and invention leading on to others. What matters most in world affairs is that some centuries ago Europeans emerged with the most effective way of demonstrating their racial superiority over the rest of the inhabitants of the world – the firearm.

Many current problems are a result of the reluctance of Europeans to mix with non-Europeans and of their reluctance even in the face of modern investigations regarding race to relinquish their superior position and their prejudices. Perhaps that is largely why there is a widespread idea that white people cannot perform physical work in the tropics (though Negroes work very well in cool climates). If they found they could, there would be less justification for relying on the natives.

In conclusion, two points should be considered by the reader. Firstly, when the general level of intelligence of members of different racial groups is compared (e.g. that of non-whites and whites in the U.S.A.) the tests suggest that differences in level may be entirely due to inequality of opportunity, particularly lack of educational facilities for the members of the underprivileged group or groups. Tests also suggest that where members of different races have been brought up in comparable living conditions, with similar educational facilities, their level of intelligence is also comparable. In other words, the generally poorer standards of intelligence and living conditions among non-Europeans in societies in which Europeans and non-Europeans live together results from their generally underprivileged social and economic position, not from their racial inferiority.

Secondly, in connexion with the mixing of races, and particularly of persons with different skin colour, many people consider that mixing produces degenerate half-castes. But perhaps the degeneration is psychological rather than physical, and the responsibility lies with the people still of pure race on both sides, but particularly on the European side, who maintain a prejudiced attitude towards mixing. And why object so strongly to the mixing of people with different skin colour without also objecting to the mixing of people with different shaped heads, different types of hair, or different types of blood? (Here, indeed, there is sometimes a good reason for advising against marriage.)

These problems are social rather than racial, but for various reasons it has been useful for politcans and others, even if aware of the findings of scientific investigations, to exploit the widespread ignorance of most people regarding race. The Nazis are one example, the Europeans in South Africa another. The question is, even if it were proved conclusively that there is no such thing as racial superiority, would people change their attitude to the matter if it did not suit them to do so?

We might remember that at one extreme there is only one race of mankind – the human species (or, according to some anthropologists, human genus); at the other, there are as many races as individuals, for no two persons (not even 'identical' twins) are identical down to the last detail.

V. ON THE USE OF STATISTICS

In certain chapters of this book a considerable number of population, production, and other figures are quoted. As far as possible, statistics are for the years 1959–60. The principal source has been the *United Nations Statistical Yearbook 1960*.

Many other publications have also been consulted, and a few are listed among the selected references at the end of the book. Although most of the figures will be two or three years old by the time this revised edition is published they will not usually differ significantly from current figures.

Statistical material varies greatly in its reliability. Some countries have already for some decades been publishing figures that are accurate or reliable to within only a small margin of error. Others have few or no facilities for collecting accurate statistical data, and many parts of the world have never even been covered by a census of population.

Some countries, especially the U.S.S.R., are thought to publish false sets of figures, but there is good reason to suppose that most sets of absolute figures published by Communist countries are reasonably accurate. This view is held by several experts working on the U.S.S.R.

Errors may occur during the collection and preparation of any material for publication, and in more popular publications one or two noughts may even be inadvertently omitted or added without anyone noticing. But although it is difficult for these reasons to trace population and production changes from past periods up to the present and often impossible even to make accurate comparisons between different parts of the world at the present day, world problems can only be appreciated if there is some quantitative basis, however approximate it is, from which conclusions may be drawn.

Throughout this book round numbers have been used. When most numbers are only approximate anyway, it is absurd to put such a precise figure as 179,323,175, the population of the U.S.A. on 1 June 1960, according to the census taken that day, alongside a figure of 21,800,000 for Ethiopia in 1959, a pure 'conjecture' (United Nations definition) not based on any census at all. For our purposes it is quite sufficient to know that the figure for the U.S.A. was about 180 m. in 1960 and that it is increasing at present by about 3 m. per year.

Figures are often presented in such a way that their significance is difficult to appreciate. Frequently absolute figures are given where comparative figures would mean much more. To know that China has about 700 m. inhabitants is less useful than to know that it has about fourteen times as many people as the U.K., or between one-fifth and one-quarter of the total population of the world. Unless something is provided against which absolute figures can be measured they may mean nothing at all to us. It has been estimated that some £40,000 m. will be spent during the next decade by world oil companies (outside the Communist bloc) on expansion, but very few people would stop and question £4,000 m. or even £400 m. if one of these had been given as the result of a misprint.

In this book an attempt has been made to present figures so that they may be measured against others. In this way the significance of absolute figures may more readily be appreciated. Not infrequently figures are shown for production per inhabitant (*per caput*). The following example illustrates the difference between total and *per caput* figures. In 1960 France and China each produced about 15 m. tons of steel, but China has about fifteen times as many people as France and therefore output *per inhabitant* in France (300 kilograms) was fifteen times higher than in China (20 kilograms).

Chapter 2

THE SPREAD OF EUROPEAN INFLUENCE

I. THE PROCESS OF EUROPEANIZATION

MANY current problems in world affairs are in some way related to the spread of European influence over the world in different forms and in varying degrees of intensity during the last five centuries. This process, which might be termed *europeanization* rather than *westernization*, has been accompanied since the War of American Independence (1775–83) by a parallel, but reverse, process of de-europeanization, by which European political influence has already been shaken off in most parts of the world.

Europe is the north-west corner of the great triangular-shaped land mass of Eurasia. It is broken into a number of peninsulas and islands by seas penetrating far towards the interior, while its continuity is further interrupted by high mountain ranges. The present generally accepted limits of the continent of Europe are the Ural Range and River Ural in the east, and the River Araks (in Transcaucasia), the Black Sea and the Mediterranean in the south. The limits of the Europa of the Ancient World and of medieval Europe were certainly not so definite as this. Even so, what is important in a consideration of the effects of European influence on the rest of the world is the concept of a part of the world known as Europe, rather than the exact boundary of the region. The Empire of Alexander the Great, the Ottoman Empire (and now modern Turkey), and the Russian Empire (and now the U.S.S.R.) are three examples of empires which, according to the current definition of Europe, were or are partly inside and partly outside the present precise limits already mentioned.

The fifteenth century was a critical period for Europe in several ways. Three developments, in particular, greatly affected its subsequent relations with the rest of the world. Firstly, the Ottoman Empire, having expanded from a small nucleus in Anatolia, was gaining control of the trade routes between south

31

Europe and Asia and making it more and more difficult to import various commodities into Europe from south and east Asia, thus cutting Europe off from supplies of certain tropical plant products, such as spices, which could not be grown in Europe's climate, and from supplies of a number of luxury manufactures from the East. Secondly, in Europe itself, a number of sizeable states, some of which had already been in existence for a considerable time (e.g. England and Portugal) and some of which were just emerging (e.g. Spain), were developing a strong consciousness of their nationhood. In this respect, the introduction at this period of printing, which facilitated the dissemination of literature in national languages, must have been a powerful influence. Thirdly, it was becoming widely appreciated that the world is a sphere and, therefore, that its surface, the exact size of which was not of course known then, is finite in extent. This was believed for a time in the Ancient World, but not demonstrated by circumnavigation of the globe. The first globe was constructed in 1492, and in 1522 Magellan's expedition successfully completed the first voyage round the world, though Magellan himself died in the Philippines in 1521.

These three apparently disconnected developments together played a great part in starting off the process of europeanization. As a result of the expansion of the Ottoman Empire astride the old routes to the East, new ways of reaching south and east Asia were sought. Portuguese navigators were already exploring the western coast of Africa in the fifteenth century. Modern Spain, formed by the union of Aragon and Castile (which became effective in 1479) and by the final expulsion of the Moors (in 1492) started later, and, unable to challenge Portugal in Africa, backed the idea of a spherical world and supported Columbus and other explorers who set out westwards across the Atlantic to find Asia in that direction. Subsequently, England unsuccessfully sought yet other possible routes to the East, the north-east and north-west passages. During the sixteenth century, therefore, a number of emerging European nations were already competing to extend their influence over the globe by exploring the oceans of the world. Portugal was the first modern European nation to penetrate by sea far beyond the limits of Europe, Spain the second. England, France, and later Holland, followed suit.

From eastern Europe another state, the Principality of Muscovy (Moscow), the nucleus of modern Russia, began to expand beyond the limits of the continent of Europe. But, unlike the nations of western Europe, it carried its influence by land, not by sea, and expanded across the great land mass of northern Asia. To what extent the empire-building of Russia can be compared with that of the western European nations is a difficult and debatable question. In this book, Russia is considered to be one of the active participants in the process of the europeanization of the world during the last five centuries. Russia of the Tsars (and now the European part of the U.S.S.R.) is considered to be part of Europe. In the West, students of Russian history seem less prone than previously to stress Asian influences on Russia. The Russians themselves consider that they are European if not Western in the current political sense. Turkey also has strong connexions with both Europe and Asia, a small part of modern Turkey actually being in Europe, but most in Asia. Turkey has been more strongly influenced from the east than Russia has, but in recent decades Turkey has set out to westernize itself, and is now in transition.

Returning now to the question of European influence on the rest of the world, it is important to bear in mind the great significance of the appreciation in the fifteenth and sixteenth centuries that the world is a sphere and its extent therefore measurable. Until it was established that the earth is a sphere and therefore finite, it was impossible to know where, if anywhere, the land and sea ended.

A few decades ago some European explorers discovered a group of about 300 Eskimos (the Polar Eskimos), living in the vicinity of Smith Sound, in the north of Greenland. These Eskimos believed themselves to be the only inhabitants of the universe. They had been isolated from other groups of Eskimos for some generations and knew of no other men except by legend.[1] Why, after all, should they be expected to know how

1. See Weyer, E. M. *The Eskimos*, New Haven, 1932.

large the earth is or what form it has? Similar in some ways, though it refers to a much larger group of people, is the story of how Alexander the Great wept when he thought there was nowhere else for him to conquer. Even if he had heard of China, he certainly could not have known of the existence of civilizations in America or, for that matter, of America itself. The Incas, who built up a large empire in the Andes of South America, had no evidence that their civilization was not the only one in the world. Genghis Khan's empire covered an enormous part of Asia and Europe but still *terra incognita* lay beyond all its frontiers. For all these empire builders the world might have been any size and shape and (the problem was being debated in Europe in the Middle Ages) there might even have been other worlds like this one. When talking about the past we should think of the world not as we know it today, but as it was known or imagined to be by the inhabitants of the world at the particular period or periods to which we refer.

The situation changed completely around 1500. In 1494 (two years after the first voyage of Columbus to America) it was established by the Treaty of Tordesillas that Portugal should have any lands it acquired to the east, and Spain any to the west, of a meridian passing 370 leagues west of the Cape Verde Islands (this meridian, near 50° W., happens to pass close by the mouth of the Amazon). Some decades later, by the Treaty of Saragossa in 1529, a demarcation line was drawn on the other side of the world (about 145° E.). In this way the whole world was for the first time (but not the last) divided in principle between two powers. Not much of it had of course actually been visited by Europeans at that time. Nevertheless, some decades after this, in 1581–1640, when Spain and Portugal were temporarily united, Spain did control most of South and Central America, as well as much of the coast of Africa and south Asia, thus encircling the globe with its possessions and their spheres of influence. What is important in world affairs is the fact that since the sixteenth century, any power or group of powers preparing to dominate the whole world or finding itself doing so unintentionally, whether militarily or economically, or in any other way, has been able to know the limits of the world.

The Process of Europeanization

Hardly a corner of the world has not by now felt the influence of Europeans in some way. Some regions, like Australia and the U.S.A., have been transformed by them; other regions, such as the Congo and India, have merely been modified by their occupation; while such countries as China, Tibet, and the Yemen have until very recently hardly felt the impact of European culture at all.

In the sixteenth century the Europeans already had certain advantages over the rest of the world. Most important by far was the development by this period of reasonably effective firearms, which, as in the conquest of the Aztec and Inca empires, helped small numbers of Europeans to overcome and control large numbers of non-Europeans. The cannon was being developed in Europe in the fourteenth and fifteenth centuries and hand weapons, the pistol and the musket, were also being developed, although with greater difficulty.[1] Another instrument, which was vital in navigation in oceans, as opposed to seas, was the magnetic compass. This, also, was being used in Europe in the later Middle Ages. Printing, gunpowder, and the magnetic compass were, ironically, used in east Asia before they were used in Europe.[2]

The rivalry between European nations, both in Europe itself and elsewhere, acted as a further stimulus to explore the world and to acquire territories. Colonial territories became a matter of prestige as well as a source of wealth. The rivalry was strengthened by the Reformation and the desire of the different religious groups in sixteenth-century Europe to Christianize non-Europeans in their own particular ways.

The process of europeanization did not follow the same pattern everywhere. Each nation had its own approach, which itself changed with time. Broadly speaking, however, the following process took place. Explorers and traders set up footholds on the coasts of newly discovered areas (or in the case of the

1. Not only firearms but also the crossbow played an important part in the conquests of the time.
2. The magnetic compass, and gunpowder for military purposes, in China in the twelfth century, and the first book in movable type in Korea in the early fifteenth century.

Russian land empire in Siberia, at the meeting-place of natural routes, such as rivers). If and when the footholds were consolidated and expanded by the annexation of appreciable pieces of territory, soldiers and administrators, including some representative of the crown (such as a viceroy) followed, and forts were set up. With these came men of religion to maintain their creed among Europeans and, frequently, to convert the non-Europeans. In the colonies of Spain and Portugal, a class of ambitious Iberians (inhabitants of Spain and Portugal) made up of the original conquerors, as well as of later settlers, were given large estates in conquered lands. In many parts of the world the Europeans came to form a ruling class dependent for its existence on the non-Europeans it ruled, a superstructure of largely non-productive members of the community.

In complete contrast were the settlers who left Europe to undertake some form of manual work in colonial territories. Some of the earliest of these were religious minorities persecuted in Europe, who went to North America. Not until the eighteenth century did appreciable numbers of Europeans of this kind settle outside Europe, and the great migration of settlers, when hundreds of thousands of emigrants left Europe each year, began only in the nineteenth century, with the introduction of the steamship and the development of railways.

Yet another type of settler, though not a voluntary one, was the non-European forced to move from his own homeland to another part of the world. Africa was the main source of slaves and America the destination of most who survived the journey.

More recently, European influence has been extended, especially during the period of the Industrial Revolution, by the adoption by non-Europeans of European techniques and institutions. Japan, for example, was never a colony of a European power and never received European settlers, yet it has voluntarily adopted many features of European culture. China is now doing the same, modelling itself at present mainly on the U.S.S.R.

The participants in the process of europeanization over the last five centuries include Portugal, Spain, Russia, England, and France, all of which were active from the fifteenth or sixteenth centuries; Holland, which began early in the seventeenth; Germany, Italy, and Belgium, which started in the nineteenth century; and Denmark and Norway, which, however, only played a small part. Modern empire builders outside Europe include the U.S.A. and Japan, the former inhabited largely by people of European origin and the latter with industries run on modern European lines.

Fig. 3a shows the world in about 1500. Europe has hardly yet started to influence the rest of the world. The Ottoman Empire is pushing north-west towards the heart of the continent, and peoples of recent Asiatic origin inhabit the southern and eastern parts of what is now European U.S.S.R. Outside Europe there are extensive parts of the world which may also be called civilized because urban life is developed and empires and other large administrative units are to be found. Elsewhere there are thinly peopled lands inhabited by simple societies. These depend in some areas on plough or hoe cultivation, in other areas on the herding of domesticated animals, while in parts of the world they still maintain a precarious existence by hunting or gathering what is offered by nature. The distribution of the simple types of economy in Fig. 3a is based on a map in Professor C. Daryll Forde's very interesting book *Habitat, Economy, and Society*.

Fig. 3b shows where European influence has extended after about two centuries. Spain and Portugal have concentrated on the tropics and between them hold almost all of South and Central America (though by no means all has been explored) as well as many coastal areas in Africa and south and southeast Asia. Russia, in contrast, has colonized lands lying in cool temperate latitudes, some of them even within the Arctic Circle (see Section I in Chapter 8 for a more detailed account of the growth of the Russian Empire). England, France, and Holland nowhere hold such extensive territories, though France controls the important Mississippi–St Lawrence axis, dominating the interior of North America, while Holland, following in the footsteps of the weakest European empire builder, Portugal, has established a formidable chain of trading stations and forts between Europe and the East Indies. Little impression has yet

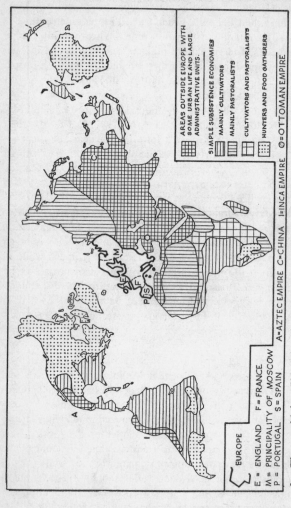

3a. The world in 1500. The distribution of simple subsistence economies is based, with the kind permission of the author, on a map 'World distribution of dominant economies' in Professor C. Daryll Forde's work *Habitat, Economy, and Society*, London, 1934.

EUROPE

E = ENGLAND   F = FRANCE
M = PRINCIPALITY OF MOSCOW
S = PORTUGAL   S = SPAIN

A = AZTEC EMPIRE   C = CHINA   I = INCA EMPIRE   O = OTTOMAN EMPIRE

AREAS OUTSIDE EUROPE WITH SOME URBAN LIFE AND LARGE ADMINISTRATIVE UNITS.

SIMPLE SUBSISTENCE ECONOMIES

MAINLY CULTIVATORS

MAINLY PASTORALISTS

CULTIVATORS AND PASTORALISTS

HUNTERS AND FOOD GATHERERS

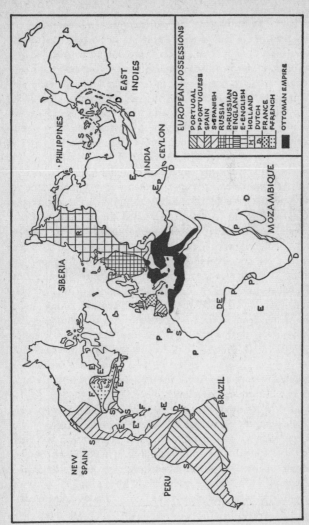

3b. The world in 1700, showing the extent of European influence.

been made by Europeans on Africa, and no impression on Australasia, while Russia has been the only European power to acquire more than a foothold on the mainland of Asia.

Before the eighteenth century, relatively few emigrants left Europe to settle in non-European lands. In 1700, for example, the English colonies in North America had fewer than 300,000 British settlers. By about 1820, after three centuries of Spanish colonial rule, the colonies of Spain in America had only about $3\frac{1}{4}$ m. whites, and most of that number was due to the natural increase of population after its arrival.

The trade between the European colonial powers and their various possessions was in goods that were of high value in relation to their weight. Obviously the limited cargo-carrying capacity and speed of vessels restricted the amount of trade that could be carried on. Among the products entering Europe from the colonies were precious metals and stones, furs, spices, tobacco, dyes, and special types of wood, and, most important of all by 1700, sugar and sugar products. Cane sugar cannot be cultivated economically in Europe, and beet sugar was not cultivated commercially until the nineteenth century. Many of the slaves taken from Africa to America worked in the sugar plantations of north-east Brazil and the West Indies. Neither perishable goods, such as tropical fruits and dairy produce, nor bulky goods such as cereals and coal, could be transported economically over long distances until the nineteenth century, when steamships were developed.

Much less territory was acquired by European powers outside Europe in the eighteenth century than in the preceding two centuries. Spain, France, and England spent much of their energy in frequent wars with one another, and Russia, seeking footholds on the Baltic and Black Seas, was more concerned with expansion in Europe itself than with pushing south from Siberia into central and east Asia. During the eighteenth century the Russian Empire did, however, expand across the Bering Strait into North America, Holland extended its control over the East Indies, and the English possession of eastern North America and India was assured, while the first European (English) colony was established in Australia in 1788. On the eve of the French Revolution the French Empire consisted only of Haiti and some smaller islands and trading posts.

Between the 1780s and 1820s a reverse process, that of de-europeanization, took place in America, when most of the English colonies in North America and almost all of the Iberian colonies in Latin America gained their independence from Europe. In America, therefore, only Canada (English), Alaska (Russian), Cuba and Puerto Rico (Spanish), and some less important islands in the West Indies and footholds in Central and South America remained under European control. This did not mean, of course, that the cultural or economic influence of Europe was suddenly everywhere weakened. Britain, France, and other European nations merely replaced Spain and Portugal in the trade with Latin America. The U.S.A., on the other hand, soon rose to the rank of a major world power. The former ties between America and Europe were maintained by the migration of many millions of people from all parts of Europe to the new daughter states. The result was that each of the former colonies began to be influenced by several European nations instead of merely by the particular power that had previously held it as a possession. It is significant that it was the people of European origin and not the indigenous population (the American Indians) who were largely responsible for shaking off the control of Europe.

Towards the middle of the nineteenth century there began a second great period of empire-building by European powers. This time Spain and Holland took very little part, but three younger nations, Belgium, Italy, and Germany, participated.

A comparison of Figs. 3b and 3c shows the areas colonized by Europeans between about 1700 and 1914 as well as the areas in which political, if not economic and cultural, influence was lost during this period. Almost all Africa was occupied during the second half of the nineteenth century, and most of the leading European powers of the time carved out a share. British colonization proceeded in Canada, Australia, and New Zealand. In Asia, Russia pushed south across the Caucasus into the northern lands of the Ottoman Empire, south-east into central Asia and into the Lower Amur Valley, while, in south

NEW ZEALAND

AUSTRALIA

PHILIPPINES

JAPAN

CHINA

INDIA

RUSSIAN EMPIRE

ABYSSINIA
Ital. Prot.
1889-96

UNION OF
SOUTH AFRICA

ALASKA

CANADA

LIBERIA

Africa

U.S.A.

REPUBLICS OF
LATIN AMERICA

EUROPEAN NATIONS

COLONIES OF EUROPE

BRITISH DOMINIONS

FORMER COLONIES OF EUROPE

LANDS NEVER HELD BY
EUROPEANS IN THE LAST
500 YEARS EXCEPT IN
SMALL LOCALITIES

1 TURKEY
2 PERSIA
3 AFGHANISTAN
4 ARABIA
5 SIAM

3c. The world in 1914, showing the extent of European influence.

Asia, Britain further strengthened its hold on the Indian Empire, and France annexed part of south-east Asia (Indo-China). By 1914, therefore, only two main areas had not been colonized by Europeans: east Asia, where the Chinese Empire and Japan had resisted European territorial expansion, and south-west Asia, where the Ottoman Empire had retained its hold after losing its African and most of its European territories to European powers.

That is not the end of the process of europeanization. Being on the losing side in the 1914–18 war, the Ottoman Empire was dispossessed of almost all its territories in south-west Asia outside the heartland of Turkey itself, and Britain and France were able to make south-west Asia their sphere of influence. In 1935, Italy invaded Abyssinia, the only extensive area in Africa by then still free from European colonization.

In addition, two nations outside Europe, the U.S.A. and Japan, began to expand towards the end of the nineteenth century. Japan was able to annex and dominate extensive densely populated territories in East Asia through having evolved its own version of the European Industrial Revolution.

Turkey (since the 1920s) and more recently China (only seriously in the last decade) have followed the example of Japan and adopted many features of European culture. In this way, very few parts of the world have escaped some form of European influence. Indeed, we are now witnessing what may turn out to be the last scramble for territory, at least on this planet, the exploration of Antarctica, with no permanent inhabitants, and no temporary inhabitants until a few years ago.

Finally, since 1945 a further stage has begun in the process of de-europeanization. Colonies held by Europeans but inhabited by non-Europeans (as against people of European origin) have been granted or are still striving to achieve political independence. India, Indonesia, and Angola are examples. (See Fig. 3e.)

II. THE RESULTS OF EUROPEANIZATION

Fig. 3d is an attempt to represent the broad outlines of the complex end product of more than four centuries of european-

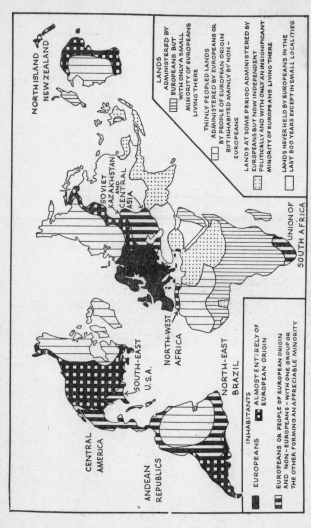

3d. The world in 1957, showing the results of europeanization.

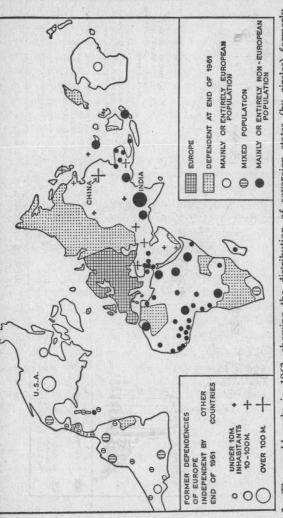

3e. The world early in 1962, showing the distribution of sovereign states (by circles) formerly colonies of Europe. Note: For convenience Israel is considered as having a non-European population. During 1962–3 the following new states gained sovereignty: in 1962 Rwanda, Burundi, Jamaica, Trinidad and Tobago, Algeria, Uganda; in 1963 Kuwait became a member of the United Nations, and Zanzibar and Kenya became independent.

45

ization. The intensity of shading varies according to the intensity of europeanization. Apart from Europe itself (shaded black) there are lands such as north-east U.S.A., Argentina, and Australia where the indigenous population has been reduced (in some cases by a deliberate policy of extermination, in others by the large numbers of European immigrants) to an insignificant proportion of the total population. Secondly, there are parts of the world where Europeans or people of European origin live alongside non-Europeans, and where one or the other group forms a significant minority. Examples are south-east U.S.A. and South Africa. Thirdly, there are colonies such as Kenya and Mozambique, held by European powers but with only an insignificant proportion of Europeans living there – a superstructure of administrators, teachers, doctors, and so on. Fourthly, there are independent countries, such as India and Indonesia in Asia, and the Sudan and Ghana in Africa, which have been European colonies for some time but which have not been settled by Europeans. Finally, there are countries that have never been possessions of Europe. Some, such as Japan and Turkey, have adopted many features of European culture, while others, such as the Yemen and Tibet, have until very recently attempted with almost complete success to keep Europeans and European ideas out of their countries.

Fig. 3e shows the large number of present-day sovereign states that have at one time been colonies of Europe or at least closely controlled by Europe in some way. There are 22 in America, 15 in Asia, 28 in Africa, and 2 in Australasia, a total of 67 compared with only 27 in Europe itself and 14 outside Europe (shown by crosses) never seriously controlled by Europe.

What are the results of European influence on the rest of the world, and how do they affect present-day world problems? Firstly, there are the past actions of Europeans against non-Europeans. Contemporary Europeans may try to forget these or disclaim responsibility, but the memory cannot be wiped out in a few generations. Secondly, there are the present problem areas where Europeans and non-Europeans live in the same regions and where the non-Europeans are politically underprivileged and economically in an inferior position.

The Results of Europeanization

It is naïve to think that some European nations have behaved better than others towards non-Europeans. It is a mistake also to think that Europeans have treated non-Europeans more harshly than they themselves have been treated in the past by non-Europeans. Another point to remember is that European nations have also treated each other just as harshly as they have treated non-Europeans. Finally, it should not be forgotten that Europeans have, on many occasions, brought benefits to non-Europeans. All this does not prevent most non-Europeans from harbouring resentment of some kind or other at unpleasant treatment received from Europeans, and understandably, too, for on the whole the story of europeanization is a dismal one. The key to it is the possession by Europeans of superior arms, assuring them of military superiority in other parts of the world.

Spain completely disorganized the economic and social structure of the Aztec and Inca Empires. Throughout Latin America the Spaniards and Portuguese virtually enslaved the American Indians. When and where there were too few of these to work for them, the Europeans imported or purchased from other European traders Negro slaves from Africa. The Portuguese were the first modern Europeans to take slaves from Africa, but when in the seventeenth and eighteenth centuries a large-scale trade in African slaves was established it was the English who had the largest share most of the time. The French, Dutch, Spaniards, Portuguese, and, in the eighteenth century, also the Danes, all participated. The slaves were sold and used in America by the Spanish, Portuguese, English, and French colonists. European conquest in Asia was no more praiseworthy, but thanks to the much larger indigenous population there than in America there was little actual slavery.

The period from about 1500 to 1800 was a great age of colonial expansion for Europe and few people pretended then that a colony was anything more than a piece of territory to be exploited in the quickest possible way on behalf of the mother country. Even the success of most of the colonies in the Americas in gaining independence around 1800 did not greatly change the European attitude, and conquest by Europeans continued elsewhere, as well as conquest by the former Europeans in the new countries that had freed themselves from Europe.

The Spread of European Influence

In the nineteenth century many primitive tribes in different parts of the world were exterminated or reduced in numbers and relegated to the poorest lands by the large number of settlers emigrating from Europe. In North America, Argentina, and Australasia there were conflicts in which the indigenous population was greatly reduced in numbers or even systematically exterminated, as in the campaign against the American Indians in the Argentinian pampa (1878–83) or in Tasmania, where the few thousand natives, who were living in Old Stone Age conditions, have disappeared. The last stages of the process by which the Europeans (mainly British) in North America reduced the American Indians from at least several million before they discovered the continent to their present number of a few hundred thousand have been immortalized in the Western films so popular in Europe and America.

During the last decades of the nineteenth century almost all of Africa, more than one-fifth of the world's land area, was overcome by European powers and divided among them. The continent, which had survived with only European footholds for nearly four centuries was conquered even more rapidly and efficiently than Latin America by Spain or Siberia by Russia. The nineteenth century also saw a revival of Russian activity in Asia, and their military superiority enabled the Russians to occupy large areas in central Asia long settled by Asian nomads and cultivators. Nor was European influence confined to territorial conquest; for economic reasons non-Europeans were treated unfavourably. For example, during the rubber boom in the Amazon basin, people of European (mainly Portuguese) origin brutally exploited the primitive tribes of South American Indians, and in the Congo the same was done to the Africans.

During the present century the Soviet Communists 'collectivized' or 'denomadized' the Kazakhs and other nomadic peoples in Central Asia; the Italian Fascists invaded Abyssinia, using modern arms, including gas, against Africans with primitive arms; and the Nazi Germans endeavoured to exterminate the largest group of non-Europeans in Europe – the Jews.[1]

1. See *The Scourge of the Swastika*, by Lord Russell of Liverpool, London, 1954.

The Results of Europeanization

These are but a few examples from the tragic and squalid record of europeanization. Nothing would be more wrong than to say that all Europeans have treated all non-Europeans badly. For example, during the sixteenth century Spanish and Portuguese men of religion were preoccupied with the material well-being, as well as the souls, of the American Indians, and, ever since, Christian missionaries of many denominations have striven to help non-Europeans. In the nineteenth century it was the English, for whom until then the slave trade had been very profitable, who first seriously objected to it and began to take measures to suppress it.

The European attitude to non-Europeans has undoubtedly been improving since the Second World War; the granting of self-government to many colonies by France and Britain is an example. Nevertheless, there are still uneasy regions in the world, and relations are most strained in the areas named in Fig. 3d, where Europeans and non-Europeans live in the same regions. A note follows on each of the more important of these problem areas.

In the U.S.A. over 10 per cent of the population is classified as 'non-white'.[1] This consists mainly of Negroes and persons with some Negro element, but also includes American Indians and other groups such as Japanese. Most of the non-whites still live in south-east U.S.A. (the old 'South'), the former area of slavery in which cotton was widely grown and is still cultivated; here in some districts non-whites are as numerous as whites. Many non-whites have moved north into industrial centres such as Chicago, Detroit, and Cincinnati. Here they usually occupy certain districts within the towns.

The non-whites are generally worse off economically than the whites living in the same areas. In the U.S.A. as a whole the median income for a white family is about $5,300, for a non-white family only $2,700. A larger proportion of non-whites than of whites are labourers of one kind or another, or domestic servants, and this disparity, which is shown also by the low average annual *per caput* income in the states of the south-east having a large non-white element, is, of course, due to the fact

1. In 1800 the proportion of Negroes was higher: 1 m. out of 5 m.

that in a few generations the descendants of former slaves have not generally had the opportunity to train and enter the classes of skilled workers and professional persons. Although being below the general level in the U.S.A. they are still many times better off than the Negroes of Africa.

What is more serious is that as well as being mostly in the poorer classes, the Negroes in south-east U.S.A. are politically underprivileged and socially segregated. Although almost a hundred years have elapsed since the Civil War, the Negroes in the southern states are still not fairly represented in the U.S. government. The persecution of Negroes still continues in certain forms. When 10 per cent of its population is thus underprivileged, the U.S.A. can hardly expect its teaching of democracy, equality of opportunity, and freedom of the individual to have the appeal it might otherwise have among non-Europeans. What is more, there appears to be no answer to the problem of the Negro in the U.S.A. By the clearcut division into white and non-white there is no ladder up which the non-white can climb socially into the respectable category of white, whereas in Latin America the system is more flexible, the transition gradual and in the last resort people who are nowhere near white can even define themselves as white in a census. Even so, some attempt is at last being made to improve the position of the U.S. Negro, and it is a mistake to pick on isolated examples of the persecution of Negroes and imply that they are typical.

In the republics and the colonies of tropical Latin America there is almost everywhere a mixture of races. In some areas (e.g. Argentina), people of European origin predominate; in other areas (e.g. much of Mexico and the Andes), American Indians are in the majority; while in some parts (e.g. Haiti, Jamaica, and parts of north-east Brazil) Negroes are the predominant element. The Europeans (Spaniards and Portuguese) who settled in tropical Latin America are generally darker-skinned than the northern Europeans who predominate in North America, and the American Indians are mostly somewhere between the Europeans and the Negroes in skin colour. The sharp distinction drawn in the U.S.A. between white and non-white does not exist, therefore, but there is a distinction between varying degrees of darkness of skin colour.

Although it is difficult to assess (as can be done with reasonable precision in the U.S.A.) the difference in living standards, privileges, and opportunity between the different races, it is safe to say that the landowning and professional classes, and the office workers of Latin America are generally of European origin. This, of course, is not true in a country such as Haiti, where very few Europeans settled. Here, however, the lighter-skinned people, with some admixture of European characteristics, dominate the pure or almost pure Negroes. In countries such as Mexico, Ecuador, and Bolivia, where the inhabitants are mainly American Indians, Spanish, or mixed, the agricultural workers, miners, and more recently the factory workers, are mainly American Indian or mixed, while the more wealthy citizens are mainly Spanish or mixed. Everywhere in Latin America, as, indeed, also in the U.S.A., there are exceptions to the generalizations so far made.

In South Africa the situation is different again, for here the Negroes (Bantus) are in the majority and the Europeans in the minority, whereas there is no state in the U.S.A. with more non-whites than whites. The situation is further complicated by the fact that although most of the people of European origin are from Holland, an appreciable minority is English. In addition, there are settlers from Asia (mainly India) as well as the Cape Coloured, who are mixed African and European. Whereas the Federal Government in the U.S.A. is endeavouring to bring the status of the Negro closer to that of the white settler, the government in South Africa is clearly attempting to consolidate the present socially, economically, and politically privileged status of the European fifth of the population. The non-Europeans are mainly farm labourers, miners, and factory workers. Their standard of living is far below that of the people of European origin, though admittedly their living conditions are in certain ways superior to those of most African natives living outside South Africa. This is a doubtful compensation for being virtually the slaves of a prosperous European minority, and if and when they obtain better economic conditions and superior educational facilities it seems unlikely that the present situation can survive.

In certain other parts of Africa there are also problems connected with European settlement. In Southern Rhodesia there is an appreciable minority of people of English origin, and even in Kenya, where the Europeans form less than 1 per cent of the population, racial problems occur. In these parts of Africa the Europeans include permanent settlers owning land, as well as temporary residents engaged in various kinds of professional duties.

In the North Island, New Zealand, there are areas in which the indigenous population (Maoris) live alongside European (almost entirely British) settlers. The Maoris are in the minority, but although they undoubtedly suffered as a consequence of the impact of European civilization, and had lands confiscated, their economic and social position in New Zealand is now more favourable than that of almost any other non-European minority living among people of European origin anywhere in the world.

In Algeria, and to a lesser extent in Tunisia and Morocco, European settlers form a small but influential minority – more than 10 per cent in Algeria, but less than this in Morocco and Tunisia. While Morocco and Tunisia achieved independence from France without much friction between the European settlers and indigenous population, Algeria has been one of the problem areas of the last few years. The actual differences in racial (physical) characteristics are not so great as elsewhere in Africa and the problem is more closely connected with the economically privileged situation of the Europeans than with any fear of loss of purity of race. The Europeans own much of the best farm land and have much of the better-paid employment. In an independent Algeria with equal political representation for both Europeans and Moslems the Europeans would immediately have a minority position.

In the U.S.S.R. about 80 per cent of the total population consists of Russians, Ukrainians, Belorussians, and other smaller European groups (e.g. Latvians). The remainder of the population is Asian (Transcaucasia being considered as non-

European by many Russians, if not by the Transcaucasians themselves). The original inhabitants of most of Siberia were few in number, considering the great size of this territory, and their economic and social organizations were mainly simple. There appears to have been relatively little friction here between these peoples and the Russian and Ukrainian settlers who moved out in large numbers along the Trans-Siberian Railway after about 1900. In contrast, in Transcaucasia and Central Asia (lands that have been civilized longer than Russia itself) many social problems have arisen since the Russians conquered them in the last century. Before 1917 the Russians settled these territories in relatively small numbers and largely constituted a class of administrators and professional workers. These colonies were important principally as a source of raw materials, particularly cotton.

During the Soviet period, the intensity of Russian influence has increased greatly. Republics have been formed round the more important peoples (really language groups), but their independence is theoretical and they are dominated politically by the Communist Party and economically by Soviet all-union planning. Non-Russians have, of course, been given important posts in the Party but at the same time Russians and Ukrainians have been moved in not only as teachers and technicians but also to settle permanently as farmers. Table 1 shows clearly how between 1926 and 1959 the proportion of Russians has increased greatly in the non-European republics.

TABLE 1

	Russians as percentage of total population	
	1926	1959
Kazakhstan	20	43
Uzbekistan	6	14
Kirgizia	12	30
Azerbaijan	10	14
Georgia	4	11
Turkmenistan	8	17
Tadjikistan	1	13
Armenia	2	3

While the way of life of these Asian subjects of Russia was little modified before 1917, the Soviet policy has been to transform it in many ways. In agriculture, for example, nomadism has been suppressed and the pastoralist farmers collectivized. The language and traditions have been respected, but the Moslem religion is discouraged, and the Russian language, the only language in which many publications on technical matters are available, is widely taught. The Soviet policy may well be to 'russify' the Asians of the U.S.S.R. by settling a certain proportion of Russians in every region and by eventually replacing the native language by Russian.

It will be appreciated from the foregoing examples that the racial and social problems resulting from the presence of Europeans and non-Europeans in the same area differ from region to region. It might be suggested that the greatest hatred arises where the skin colour contrasts are greatest and miscegenation prohibited or discouraged. This occurs where people of north European origin (Scandinavians, Dutch, Germans, and British in particular) live in the same area as dark-skinned people (especially Negroes). Fortunately, many of the worst aspects of europeanization, such as the slave trade and the deliberate extermination of primitive peoples, no longer exist. Even so, Europeans or their descendants are a privileged section of the community in many regions of the world. It should be remembered that their claim to this privilege rests largely on their initial military superiority, and that to this day the French in Algeria, the Russians in Central Asia, and, for that matter, the British in all their dependent territories maintain themselves at their own invitation. Rarely in the last five centuries have Europeans been invited by the indigenous population to annex, colonize, and govern their lands.

III. THE SHIFT OF POWER IN EUROPE

To conclude this examination of some of the main features of European colonization there follows a brief study of events in Europe during the last five centuries. The competition to colonize different parts of the world to some extent reflected the struggle for power within Europe itself. While the process of europeanization outside Europe was in progress a process was taking place in Europe by which the centre of power gradually shifted eastwards across the continent.

In the sixteenth century Spain was undoubtedly a powerful nation in Europe, although the data necessary to measure its strength with any precision are lacking. After its union with Portugal in 1581, it had territories in the Netherlands, central Europe, and the Mediterranean, as well as almost all of Central and South America and numerous footholds in Africa and south-east Asia. The defeat of the Armada in 1588 and the secession of Portugal in 1640 were setbacks for Spain in Europe and overseas, for the Portuguese colonial possessions, like their mother country, were lost to Spain in 1640.

While the economic basis of Spain's power weakened in the seventeenth century, France, agriculturally a more prosperous country, was challenging the strength of Spain. After a series of wars in the eighteenth century in which Spain, France, and England were frequently involved, France emerged the strongest land power in Europe, and was not conclusively defeated until 1814–15, when England, Prussia, and Russia had all taken a hand in assuring its downfall. At this stage Russia, with its superiority in manpower and in the production of arms, might have taken over the role of dominant military power in Europe. By this time, however, it was behind western Europe technologically, and in the nineteenth century most of its leaders were unwilling to consider any of the social changes necessary to modify the antiquated economy of the country. Serfdom was at this time undoubtedly a great obstacle to progress, and Russia fared badly compared with western Europe, where the French Revolution and subsequent wars had caused many changes. At this point, Britain, where many of the innovations of the Industrial Revolution had been applied for the first time, was gaining a powerful position in the world, and between about 1850 and 1870 was producing about half of the world's pig iron, a rough measure of its great industrial expansion. The final emergence of the German Empire in 1871 and its decisive defeat of France established Germany as the strongest single land power in Europe, larger in population than Britain or France and by then well in advance of Russia industrially. The final shift of power followed the defeat of the German armies in the U.S.S.R. in 1943–5 and resulted in the emergence of that country as the leading land power in Europe.

The centre of power has thus shifted gradually from Spain, at the height of its power, perhaps, in the 1580s, to France, which controlled much of Europe around 1810, and then to Germany, which in 1942 held even more of Europe than France had done at the beginning of the previous century, and finally to the U.S.S.R. which itself occupies half of Europe and, in Communist East Europe, controls another tenth.

Although the U.S.S.R. had become the leading land power of Europe by 1945, the U.S.A. was already the leading world power from both a military and an economic point of view. The tension and rivalry between so-called West and East is no more than a continuation of the struggle for power between European nations. The U.S.A. is an offshoot of Europe now backing West Europe against the U.S.S.R., the strongest single power on the continent.

How long the struggle between U.S.A. and the U.S.S.R. will continue to dominate world affairs or whether the assumption that it does is even valid now will be discussed in Chapter 10.

During this period of conflict between the nations of Europe, England's role in European affairs has been to oppose the leading land power. Indeed, the part it has played in bringing about in turn the decline of Spain, France, and Germany has by no means been insignificant (though frequently magnified in British history books). Surely the next step for Britain and its former rivals is to collaborate in some form of union more solid and lasting than the North Atlantic Treaty Organization to balance the growing economic and military strength of the U.S.S.R.

Chapter 3

A REGIONAL DIVISION OF THE WORLD

SEVERAL reasons may be suggested why the traditional division of the land areas of the world into a number of continents is in many ways unsatisfactory and misleading in the study of world affairs. One is that the distribution of European settlers and the intensity of European influence outside Europe itself (see Fig. 3d, Chapter 2) bear little relationship to the continents as we know them, and vary greatly from one region to another within them. Another reason is that the U.S.S.R. and Turkey, each of which is a political and economic unit, lie partly in Europe, partly in Asia, and would have to be artificially divided to keep the two continents intact. Yet another reason is that there is a tendency for us to assume that countries in the same continent must have something in common. But such areas as Siberia, Syria, Indonesia, and Japan, all of which happen to be in Asia, differ so greatly both in their physical conditions and in their economic life that it would be difficult to find four more different areas in the world.

Perhaps the most important reason why the present major divisions of the land areas of the world are unsatisfactory for many purposes is the fact that the continents are improvised and arbitrary. Whether the reader recognizes only five continents or prefers to divide America into North and South or even raises Antarctica [1] to the rank of a continent, he should appreciate that the names of some of the continents are of relatively recent origin, while others were only used vaguely before the world was explored by Europeans in the fifteenth and sixteenth centuries. The word Europe was employed in Ancient Greece, and both Asia and Africa were in use in the Ancient

---

1. Recent exploration in Antarctica shows that parts of the Antarctic ice-cap (which covers almost all of the 'continent') reach below sea-level and therefore rest not, technically, on land, but on the sea bed. There may therefore be no compact land mass in Antarctica, but a land broken by many inlets, or even an archipelago.

World. Asia referred to an undefined part of the world split up more precisely into such areas as Arabia and India, while Africa was merely the name of a small part of the Roman Empire in what is now North Africa and what was then Libya. The word America did not come into use until about 1500, while the island of New Holland only became Australia after British settlement began there in 1788. The terms Australasia (literally South Asia) and Oceania, alternatives for the Australian continent and the islands of the south-west Pacific, are of even more recent origin. The application of the term Africa to the whole of the African land mass is also a relatively modern development.[1]

It is not surprising, therefore, that although textbooks on regional geography still deal with the traditional continents, many geographers and other students of the world and world affairs regard these as over-simplified. That is why the world has frequently been divided for various purposes into groups of countries bearing little or no relationship to the traditional continents. One interesting example is the choice of cultural divisions in *Culture Worlds*, by R. J. Russell and F. B. Kniffen (New York, 1951). Their 'worlds' (subdivided into realms) are: Polar, European, Dry, African, Oriental, Pacific, and American.

For the purpose of breaking down statistics the world has also been divided in many different ways. Fig. 4a shows the traditional five continents and Fig. 4b is an example of a set of regions used in a statistical publication of the United Nations (*United Nations Statistical Yearbook, 1960*) for world energy production and consumption (see caption for explanation).

Fig. 4c (p. 61) shows twelve regions of the world chosen for use in the present book in the consideration of world population and resources, and for descriptions of different parts of the world. The regions are shown again in Fig. 5, this time on the

1. In this connexion, the following lines from *A Compendious Geographical Dictionary, etc.* . . . (London, 1795, p. 28) are interesting: 'Geographers generally reckon four continents, or very large portions of land, each containing many countries; namely Europe, Asia, Africa, and America; and also the continents near the poles'. The Arctic area, of course, is a deep ocean partly covered with floating ice.

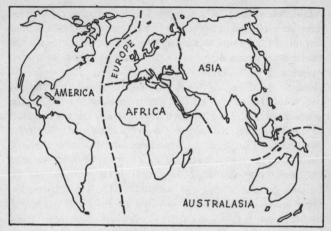

4a. The five continents.

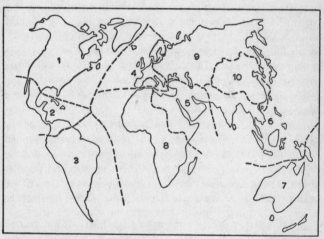

4b. The world divided into ten areas for a table showing world energy production and consumption in the *United Nations Statistical Yearbook, 1960*. 1 North America, 2 Caribbean America, 3 Other America, 4 Western Europe, 5 Middle East, 6 Far East, 7 Oceania, 8 Africa, 9 U.S.S.R. and East Europe, 10 China.

projection, mentioned in Chapter 1, which gives a better idea than the more familiar world projection in Fig. 4c of the relationship of the land masses to one another. Once again the reader is reminded that a globe should constantly be consulted by students of world affairs.

There are obviously too many individual political units in the world for each to be considered separately, while, at the other extreme, the five continents are too few. For the purposes of this book, therefore, the world has been divided into twelve regions. The regions have been chosen with the following considerations in mind: to respect as far as possible the limits of the five existing continents; to respect *de facto* political boundaries (one reason why this is essential is that often statistics are available only for whole countries, not for parts of them); and to produce compact groups of countries, with no detached portions in other regions (the British Commonwealth could not therefore be a region). Although the countries in each region may have certain features and problems in common, it is not suggested that the regional boundaries are the only possible ones or that the regions have any particular geopolitical unity or significance. It was very difficult to decide in which region certain countries could best be included. Moreover, boundaries can be altered at any time as the result of political changes, while the regions themselves can be subdivided or grouped together for different purposes.

The choice of the regions was made by the author when the book was first being planned in 1957 and had to be determined before the book was written. Subsequently various people have offered criticisms of the divisions, both of the fundamental choice and of details. The basis was the acceptance of the existence of the 'Communist bloc' of states (Socialist camp in Soviet publications) and the assumption that this was surrounded by a fringe of relatively small but usually densely populated non-Communist states in which many of the trouble spots of the post-war world were to be found. Beyond this, at a greater distance from the Communist bloc were a number of larger but less densely populated land masses more distant from Communist influence.

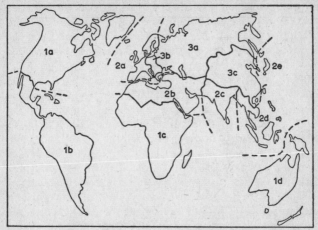

4c. The world divided into twelve regions for the purposes of this book. See Fig. 5 for greater detail, and text for explanation.

Some changes have been made in the regions in the present edition but the three main groups of regions have been maintained since, in the view of the author, they are satisfactory for the purpose of this book, even though there is obviously also a strong case for making a threefold division into the West, the neutral countries, and the Communist countries. This is not so viable as the basis used, however, since West, neutral, and to some extent even Communist (e.g. Cuba) are mixed in some parts of the world, and compact regions could not be achieved for the purposes of description in Chapters 5–7.

The reader who is familiar with the concepts of the late Sir Halford J. Mackinder regarding world geopolitical problems and the pivot area (later the Heartland) will find some familiar features in the division used in this book.[1]

1. The reader will find much of interest in Mackinder's paper 'The Geographical Pivot of History' in the *Geographical Journal*, April 1904, Vol. XXIII, No. 4. Although so many political and technological changes have taken place since the paper was published, some of the ideas are still worth consideration. Later ideas of Mackinder will be found in *Democratic Ideals and Reality*, first published London, 1919.

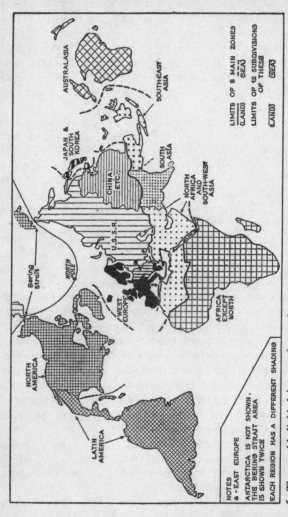

5. The world divided into twelve regions for the purposes of this book. See text for explanation. Projection: Bartholomew's regional.

A Regional Division of the World

The three main divisions are broken into the following twelve regions (Antarctica might be considered a thirteenth), numbered in Fig. 4c and named in Fig. 5:

1a *North America.* This is everywhere in America north of Mexico and the Gulf of Mexico. The author would prefer Anglo-America for this region but the term, widely accepted in the U.S.A., causes confusion in people's minds in Britain.

1b *Latin America.* This region is the rest of America, including twenty republics and a number of small colonial territories. Here Spanish or Portuguese (languages of Latin origin) is the official language of all the more important countries.

1c *Africa except the North.* Northern Africa has been separated from the rest of the continent because a number of countries have most of their population close to the Mediterranean and are separated from countries further south by the Sahara Desert. Culturally, too, they differ appreciably from Africa south of the Sahara, and at present their strongest ties appear to be with South-west Asia, on account of the current move towards Arab unity. The rest of Africa includes the Sudan, Ethiopia, and Somalia, which are to some extent a transition area between South-west Asia and central Africa.

1d *Australasia.* Australia and numerous islands of various sizes form the fourth region. Here it might be argued that the island of New Guinea, as well as some smaller islands, should be included with South-east Asia. Until 1962, however, New Guinea was shared by Australia (eastern half) and the Netherlands. Now the Netherlands half is to become part of Indonesia, and therefore of South-east Asia.

2a *West Europe.* This consists of all countries in Europe without a Communist regime but unless otherwise indicated (in some tables) does not include Yugoslavia (in East Europe) or Turkey (in South-west Asia).

2b *North Africa and South-west Asia.* This area is almost entirely Moslem but only partly Arab. Non-Arab Turkey, Iran, and Afghanistan have been included partly because they have more features (if not interests) in common with the rest of the area than with any other adjoining regions. Algeria is still associated with West Europe but now fits more conveniently into region 2b.

2c *South Asia.* South Asia is former British India with bordering Nepal and Bhutan but not Burma.

2d *South-east Asia.* Non-Communist countries from Burma round to Formosa, and including Indonesia.

2e *Japan and South Korea.*

3a *The U.S.S.R.*

3b *East Europe.* This is a useful and widely adopted, if somewhat inaccurate, term to cover the eight Communist countries between West Europe and the U.S.S.R.

3c *China.* For convenience, Communist-dominated North Korea, North Vietnam, and the Mongolian People's republic are included in this region.

These twelve regions, several of which, unfortunately, have unwieldy titles, are used in Chapters 4–7 in various maps, diagrams, and descriptions. Other regions may also be referred to – for example, South America as opposed to the whole of Latin America, or South-west Asia, instead of South-west Asia with North Africa.

An interesting tendency may be noted in connexion with the regions chosen (or, for that matter, with any division of the world of this kind). A crisis in any country immediately affects neighbouring countries in the same region (or in an adjoining region just across a regional boundary), soon arouses interest in adjoining regions, and only more slowly attracts attention in regions that do not adjoin it. The Israeli invasion of Egypt in October 1956 is an example. This attack immediately brought reactions from such neighbours as Syria and Jordan, and from the U.K. with its vital interest in the Suez Canal and a foothold (Cyprus) in the region. Neighbouring regions, the U.S.S.R., South Asia, and West Europe were quick to issue threats or to offer opinions on the matter. Reactions were slower in more distant regions. U.S. diplomats were taken by surprise, China finally offered to send military aid to Egypt, while in Latin America, particularly in Venezuela, oil exploration was gradually speeded up and production boosted as a result of the closure of the canal, an event that demonstrated the vulnerability of the supply of South-west Asian oil for Europe.

Similarly the Cuban revolution has aroused very strong feelings both in nearby Latin American countries and in the U.S.A., whereas one feels that although it has received much publicity in the Soviet press the Russians are really much more concerned about countries nearer to themselves such as Finland, Yugoslavia, and China.

Nevertheless, major events in world affairs do eventually have repercussions throughout the world. As the world 'shrinks' with the improvement of communications, so news, politicians, troops, and supplies can be carried more and more quickly over great distances. As time goes on, then, each significant event will surely tend to have stronger and stronger repercussions all over the world, a tendency already appreciated by H. J. Mackinder more than fifty years ago: 'From the present time forth (1904) ... we shall ... have to deal with a closed political system and ... it will be one of world-wide scope. Every explosion of social forces ... will be sharply re-echoed from the far side of the globe, and weak elements in the political and economic organism of the world will be shattered in consequence' (op. cit., footnote p. 61).

A student of world affairs may specialize in the study of a certain part of the world and he may not be interested in other parts. But he must know a little about every region of the world to understand the full significance and consequences of major world events, wherever they occur. The world is like a jig-saw puzzle, the pieces of which can be carefully studied without revealing much until all have been fitted together to give a complete picture.

Chapter 4

WORLD POPULATION AND PRODUCTION

I. THE TECHNOLOGICAL REVOLUTION

No less important as a background for the appreciation of world affairs than the process of europeanization discussed in Chapter 2 is an appreciation of the technological revolution, which has made such a profound impact on the world already and yet may still be only in its early stages. It has made possible the incredible material progress achieved in certain parts of the world over the last century or so, it lies at the root of many modern sociological problems, and it is responsible for the precarious position in which humanity at present finds itself as a result of the evolution of nuclear weapons. Technology is used here to include any advance made by man to utilize the resources of his environment, whether for constructive or destructive purposes; and by this definition the first technological advances were already made by early man, who used, for example, stone implements and fire, and who practised agriculture. In many different parts of the world at different periods considerable progress was made in various ways: for example in the Chinese Empire several centuries ago, in the Roman Empire about 2,000 years ago and in the civilizations of Central and Andean America before the coming of the Europeans. The technological revolution of West Europe has, however, been far more rapid and profound than any other and has, moreover, made an impact on the whole world, not just one part. Its basis has been a rapid and continuing increase in the utilization of inanimate sources of power.[1]

The Agrarian and Industrial Revolutions are widely accepted terms for the technological revolution in Britain beginning in the eighteenth century (if not before) but they do not give a

1. See Carlo Cipolla, *The Economic History of World Population*, for a concise study of the revolutionary implications of this trend and the accompanying explosion of population.

complete picture of this revolution. Most advances in technology have been applied either to improving the forces of production or to improving transportation facilities, or in some cases (e.g. the steam engine) to both at once, although admittedly advances in such fields as destructive weapons and medicine do not fall clearly into the two categories suggested. Technological advances applied to production would have been only of limited use without parallel advances in transportation, since more efficient production in farming, mining, and manufacturing activities implies specialization in certain things in particular areas and the movement of goods over considerable, often very great, distances. The purpose of the rest of this section is to give some recent examples of the impact of technology on means of production, transportation, and destruction.

Agriculture has on the whole been less easy to improve with modern techniques than industry, but although it tends to be overshadowed by non-agricultural activities in the leading industrial countries, it is ultimately quite as important, especially in view of the rapid increase in the population of the world. Improvements both in the quality of plants and livestock and in the soil itself by the application of fertilizers, deeper ploughing, and so on, have led to a fairly steady increase in yields per unit of area in many countries of the world (e.g. Japan, Denmark, the U.S.A.) but by these 'conventional' methods progress has not been so spectacular as in industry. At the same time the introduction of more and more complicated farm machinery and of suitable vehicles to work this have meant that mechanization has in some parts of the world greatly increased output per farm worker. The result has been a widespread decline in the percentage of the total labour force engaged in agriculture, though in some areas such as India and China the change has so far been slight. Thus an Australian or American wheat farmer may produce twenty or thirty times more grain than a rice-growing farmer in South-east Asia. Obviously there is scope for the further application of improved farming methods in many parts of the world. But the most spectacular progress is still being made, ironically, in the more advanced countries. Thus, for example, the study of trace elements has enabled farmers in Australia, by applying often only a very small quantity of one particular element lacking in the soil of a district, to increase the quantity of fodder from pastures many times. By using new types of seed, farmers in the maize-growing region of the Middle West in the U.S.A. have achieved yields of grain *several times higher* than the average. The yield of around 40 bushels per acre, which is already good by world standards, but which has only increased gradually in the last few decades, has been increased suddenly to as much as 160 bushels per acre. The incentive has been Government policy restricting the maize acreage to keep down production. Yet another example of a revolutionary technique for agriculture comes from Israel, a small but relatively advanced country, in the form of a very cheap way of distilling sea water to make it suitable for irrigation. This naturally is of particular interest to Israel itself, with a desert area near the coast, but is also of interest to other countries with arid conditions such as Australia, Chile, and many African countries. Instead of having exhausted the possibilities of improving agriculture by new techniques, it appears that the serious agrarian revolution is only just beginning and has to await advances in other fields.

In mining and industry, impressive advances have been made for many decades now but even so there is no lack of further progress. Indeed, automation, as opposed to mechanization, is only in its infancy. Some examples show what kind of progress has been made in the 1950s. In the U.S.A. a giant excavator worked by a few men has been built capable of extracting about 2 m. tons of coal per year; as many as several thousand men would be needed to mine this coal in a conventional coal mine. A new machine for cutting and moving out coal from the seams is due to be applied soon in Britain and this could revolutionize deep coal mining, reducing the labour force underground enormously and putting coal in a stronger position to compete with oil. More revolutionary is the possibility of using atomic energy to produce explosions under the ground both to release oil from oil shale deposits (there is, for example, a very large deposit of these in Colorado, U.S.A.) and to pulverize metallic ores under the ground, enabling them to be brought to the surface by suction through suitable shafts, without underground workers being needed.

In manufacturing industry there have been some impressive achievements too. For example in Japan in 1958 a tanker of more than 100,000 tons, the largest in the world, was built in less than six months. In Sweden a shipyard is under construction to build ships of up to 140,000 tons on assembly-line methods.

No less important has been progress in transportation in the last 120 years or so, following the major breakthrough, the application of the steam engine to rail and sea transport. From the first transatlantic steamers of 1–2,000 tons with paddle and sail of the 1840s to the Queens of the late 1930s of around 80,000 tons and, perhaps the last of these giants, the French 'France', in service from 1962, the progress in moving passengers and goods in greater quantities and at greater speeds has been incredible when compared with progress over preceding centuries. If sea and rail transport can now be improved only by using more efficient methods of traction and types of power within the framework of existing equipment, there is still great scope for improving road and air transport. A possibility for the future in road transport is the replacement of wheeled vehicles by vehicles 'gliding' on a thin film of compressed air. As far as the transportation of goods is concerned, air transport is only at a very early stage at present, but there is talk of evolving suitable jet aircraft to carry cargo across the Atlantic even within the next few years, while aircraft for carrying cargo over shorter distances are also being evolved. As for passenger travel by air, the progress towards higher speeds has been unbelievably rapid recently. It took several decades to reach a speed of around 300 m.p.h., but only a few years to double this with large jet aircraft. Now an airliner with a speed of around 2,000 m.p.h. is being considered. Given the size of the world, a greater speed than this hardly seems worth bothering about. No less impressive has been the increase in the distance over which electricity can be economically transmitted. From a few miles in the 1890s, the distance has increased steadily to several hundred miles at present, using alternating current. But it seems that a new advance is on the way and this will make it possible to take electricity three or four times the distance by changing the alternating current to direct current for transmission and then back to alternating for consumption.

Much more ominous are the increase in destructive power and the improvements in delivering weapons of destruction. So great has been the change that it seems not to have penetrated the imagination of many people. Between the complete firing power of the entire British navy early in the nineteenth century and the power of a thousand bombers in the Second World War is an enormous gap, but one 20-kiloton atom bomb dropped on Hiroshima in 1945 by one aircraft did more damage than a particularly massive British blitz on Hamburg lasting several nights in 1943, while a modest 1-megaton H-bomb evolved in the 1950s could do many times more damage than the Hiroshima bomb, and the Russian weapons of 1961 of around 50 megatons far more still. The world is so small that even a few of these, suitably placed, would ruin our civilization of today.

Some examples of the technological revolution have been quoted to give an idea of trends in the post-war world. The general conclusion one must reach is that in many forms of technology the ceiling to advances is so far away that it cannot even at present be visualized, while in some instances the progress achieved since the Second World War has been much greater than all advances together before this. For a country like Britain, poorly endowed with natural resources, considering the size of its population, technology seems not merely the best but perhaps the only resource left to exploit. Even the coal reserves, which together with the application of technological innovations enabled Britain to move ahead in the earlier stages of the Industrial Revolution, are a doubtful asset now, and certainly some oil or natural gas would be more useful at this stage.

More than seven-tenths of the surface of the world is covered by water. Of the remainder, part, including Antarctica, Greenland, and many smaller areas, is permanently (or at least has been for thousands of years) covered with snow or ice. Without Antarctica the earth's land surface occupies roughly one-quarter of the total surface area. North America, Latin America, and the U.S.S.R., the three largest regions suggested in Chapter 3, each account for slightly less than one-sixth of this, while Africa and Australasia together cover more than one-quarter. Europe and Asia, excluding the U.S.S.R., occupy the remainder but together contain more than two-thirds of the total population of the world.

The political divisions of the world vary enormously in area. In addition to the U.S.S.R., which is more than $8\frac{1}{2}$ m. sq. mls. in area, Canada, China, Brazil, the U.S.A., and Australia each cover 3–4 m. sq. mls. Countries such as France (213,000 sq. mls.) or New Zealand (140,000 sq. mls.) are very small by comparison, yet still far larger than minute but administratively separate (and, in their own particular ways, by no means insignificant) units such as Monaco, the Vatican City State, or Bermuda (the first two measured in acres rather than square miles). The great difference in area between the largest and the smallest political divisions of the world is one of several reasons why it is difficult to compare countries.

When assessing the importance of different countries, it is necessary to bear in mind not only their area but also their population. Owing to the very uneven distribution of the world's population over the habitable land, the density of population varies greatly from one part to another. Although Australia is nearly 15 times the size of France, France has more than four times as many inhabitants. In Australia there are about 3 persons per square mile, in France about 200. The extremes of density are much farther apart. In Greenland there are about 40 square miles per person, while England and Wales have 760 inhabitants per square mile, and many urban areas in different parts of the world, of course, have tens of thousands of persons per square mile in the more crowded sections.

The great difference in the number of inhabitants between the most populous and the least populous political divisions of the world is a second reason why it is difficult to compare countries. The largest countries are not necessarily the ones with the most people. In Table 2 the ten largest and the ten most populous countries are listed side by side in order of importance.

TABLE 2

Area	Per cent of Total World Land Area*	Population	Per cent of World Total (1960)
1 U.S.S.R.	16·3	1 China	23·0
2 Canada	7·4	2 India	13·5
3 China	7·3	3 U.S.S.R.	7·1
4 Brazil	6·3	4 U.S.A.	6·0
5 U.S.A.	5·8	5 Japan	3·1
6 Australia	5·7	6 Indonesia	3·0
7 India	2·4	7 Pakistan	2·9
8 Argentina	2·1	8 Brazil	2·2
9 Sudan	1·9	9 West Germany	1·8
10 Congo (ex-Belg.)	1·7	10 U.K.	1·7

* Excluding Antarctica

Only five countries appear in both columns. Certain countries with large populations, such as Japan, Germany, and the U.K., would come far down on the list of countries arranged in order of area, if it were continued, while Canada and Australia would be low on the population list. Two important points should be borne in mind in connexion with the density of population. Firstly, countries with a high density are not necessarily over-populated. Secondly, within countries, especially the larger ones, there are great variations in density from one part to another, just as there are over the world as a whole. In both Australia and Brazil, for example, more than four-fifths of the total population is concentrated in less than one-fifth of the total area.

Fig. 6 shows the main features of the distribution of population over the world in the 1950s. Each dot stands for approximately 10 million inhabitants and in most cases, of course,

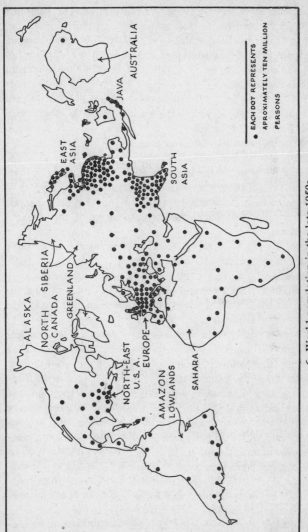

6. World population in the late 1950s.

represents 10 m. people living in a much larger area than that
actually covered by the dot itself.[1] The fact that Madagascar,
for instance, has no dot, does not imply that it is uninhabited.
The dot on the mainland opposite represents the $4\frac{1}{2}$ m. inhabitants of Madagascar, as well as $5\frac{1}{2}$ m. of the inhabitants of
Africa itself.

It is obvious from the map that there are three main concentrations of population in the world: East Asia, South Asia,
and Europe. Two smaller concentrations stand out: north-
east (or industrial) U.S.A., and Java. In contrast, vast areas are
clearly uninhabited or only thinly populated. They are: the
coldest parts of the northern hemisphere, including Alaska,
Greenland, most of Canada, and Siberia; the driest parts of
the world, including the Sahara, the interior of Asia, and much
of Australia; and the dense tropical forest of the Amazon
lowlands.

East Asia (China, Japan, Korea, Formosa) has rather more
than one quarter of the world's population, South and South-
east Asia, slightly less than a quarter, and Europe, including
European U.S.S.R., about a quarter. At the other extreme, the
more empty half of the world's land area accounts for less than
2 per cent of the total population.

To appreciate world problems it is necessary to consider
changes of population as well as present distribution. The
number of inhabitants in any given part of the world is constantly changing. We tend to think of the change only in terms
of population increase, and there is some justification for this,
for Ireland is probably the only country in the world of any
size that has fewer inhabitants now than 150 years ago. On the
other hand, although before the last 200 years or so there were
fluctuations in different parts of the world, with increases in
one area, decreases in another, there was probably never an
increase everywhere at the same time. At present, on the contrary, there is an almost world-wide increase of population,
although small areas, as, for example, parts of the French Alps,
have lost population in recent decades.

1. The dot is placed as near as possible to the 'centre of gravity'
of the 10 m. people it represents.

Area and Population

To have a reasonably accurate idea of population changes, all that need be considered are the number of live births and of deaths and the number of people immigrating and emigrating during a given period. If a country had 1,000,000 inhabitants at the end of 1960 and 1,020,000 at the end of 1961 its population must have increased by 2 per cent during 1961. In many parts of the world today population is increasing at about this rate.

What happens to a population of 1,000,000 people in 1960 if it continues to increase annually by 2 per cent for some decades? The increase is 20,000 in the first year, bringing the total to 1,020,000. The increase in the next year is 2 per cent of 1,020,000, which is 20,400, not 20,000. 20,400 is added to 1,020,00, and the next figure is 2 per cent of 1,040,400. Instead of increasing at simple interest rate, which would be by 2 per cent of the original 1,000,000 per year, the increase takes place at compound interest rate and the effect is cumulative. The country of 1,000,000 would double its population not in 50 years but in less than 35 years. This is almost exactly what has happened in recent decades, for example, in Costa Rica, which in 1920 had about 420,000 inhabitants, in 1952, 850,000. At this rate of increase, due almost entirely to the excess of births over deaths, the country would have 1,700,000 inhabitants in 1985. Estimates in the 1950s suggest in fact that now the rate of increase is not 2 per cent each year but 4 per cent; the 1959 figure was 1,120,000 and at this rate 1,700,000 would be reached by about 1970. Of course there is no guarantee that present trends will continue.

It is calculated that the population of the world as a whole has been increasing by 1·7 per cent each year during the 1950s (*United Nations Demographic Yearbook, 1960*, Table 2). The total in 1959 was 2,907,000,000 and should be about 3,060,000,000 in 1962, an increase of 50 m. persons per year. If present trends continue, then by the end of this century the world should have about 6,000 m. inhabitants.

The rate of increase of population varies considerably from one country to another (and even within countries from one region to another). The way things were going before the 1950s it looked as though the rate of increase was diminishing in the countries with the highest standards of living, such as the U.S.A., the Scandinavian countries, Britain, and France. But there is undoubtedly now a move towards larger families in some of the more prosperous countries, not least the U.S.A., and the rate of increase is at present higher, for example, in France (0·9 per cent per year), Switzerland (1·2 per cent), and the Netherlands (1·3 per cent) as well as the U.S.A. itself (1·7 per cent), than in certain poorer countries, including Italy (0·5 per cent) and Spain (0·8 per cent). Even in Japan the rate of increase is now only 1·1 per cent per year. The increase is, of course, generally much higher still in so-called underdeveloped areas: for example 2·1 per cent in Indonesia, 2·8 per cent in Communist China, and well over 3 per cent in parts of Southwest Asia, Africa, and Latin America.

How can this world-wide increase of population be explained? Obviously it can only take place if more and more food and other items of consumption become available as well. During the last 150 years or so the world production of food has increased for two main reasons. First, new lands have been brought into use for farming for the first time (mainly by people of European origin) and secondly, new techniques (e.g. the widespread use of chemical fertilizer) have made it possible to obtain higher yields in existing farming areas. At the same time the development of various branches of science, and in particular medical science, has helped to eliminate or lessen the effects of many diseases, to reduce the proportion of stillbirths, and to enable more babies to survive into childhood and more adults to reach old age, while there is still a hangover from the time when people had as large families as they could because the chance was that most children would not survive long.

Merely to maintain present living standards production must be raised to satisfy the needs of more than 50 million additional people each year. For more than 150 years now there have been gloomy forecasts that eventually population will increase more rapidly than production. At the same time the opposite idea of material progress and constantly improving living standards has become the theme of economic development and the election promise of many political parties in almost every region of the world.

The example of the British Isles shows that the forecast of the pessimists has already come true in one part of the world. With some 20 m. inhabitants, it was more or less self-supporting in food and raw materials 150 years ago. As the number of inhabitants increased in the nineteenth century, home-produced food became sufficient to feed only part of the population. The pressure of population on the land in Ireland was relieved largely by emigration to North America. Population continued to increase in the rest of the British Isles, and the pressure on resources here was relieved largely by the expansion of manufacturing, which has enabled Britain to import from overseas an appreciable proportion of the raw materials and food it consumes, although, as from Ireland, millions have emigrated as well. Emigration and the export of manufactures to buy food and raw materials are satisfactory measures to deal with overpopulation as long as other parts of the world are prepared to receive immigrants or have surpluses of food and raw materials that they wish to exchange for manufactures. Through being early starters in the development of industry, West Europe and to a lesser extent Japan have achieved a privileged position which they may gradually lose as other areas use surpluses of products that they at present export to industrial countries.

Clearly, only a limited number of countries can rely on the export of manufactures to import raw materials and food. At present Japan and most countries of non-Communist Europe do so. Both the U.S.A. and the U.S.S.R. are doing the same thing, though at present foreign trade is less vital to their economies than it is to the smaller industrial countries. It seems improbable that India, China, and other overpopulated countries of Asia will be able to solve their demographic problems by exporting manufactures on the same scale that Europe has been doing, while it is very unlikely that other parts of the world will be prepared to absorb more than a very small proportion of their constantly increasing populations. Other ways must be found.

In spite of its precarious economic position we might be reluctant to consider the U.K. as overpopulated, even if its density of population is very high. This is largely because the U.K. has important trading connexions with English-speaking parts of the world. Similarly, although living standards are low, for example, in Bolivia or Thailand, we should again hesitate to call countries such as these overpopulated. There may be pressure on present farmland, but both countries have areas in which cultivation and grazing can be extended and both could obtain higher yields in existing farming areas. On the other hand, there are countries such as Egypt and Haiti in which the possibilities of increasing food production are much more limited, yet population is increasing rapidly. Mexico is another interesting example. This country has about 35 m. inhabitants. It already imports some food, but manages with great effort at present to increase its food output to cater for the 1 m. new people each year. In twenty years' time, if the present rate of increase of population continues, there will be far more than 1 m. new people to feed each year, yet it is becoming more and more difficult and costly to raise food output because all the better-quality farmland is already in use. Perhaps Mexico is a better example of an overpopulated area than Britain.

Broadly speaking, there are two ways in which the problem can be, and is being, solved. It is possible to slow down the rate of increase of population,[1] and it is possible to raise production by developing new resources and techniques. We may ask why the rate of increase of population has already been reduced in some parts of the world (and more in some sections of the community than in others). There are many different ways of doing this, ranging from outright infanticide and the deliberate neglect of weaker babies to more refined methods of prevention of birth and to the custom of marrying only a considerable

1. Incidentally, the idea that modern wars have greatly affected population changes is a misconception. In the six years of the Second World War, between 20 and 30 million people lost their lives as a direct result of the conflict. That represents less than one year's increase of the world's population.

length of time after reaching the age of puberty. In most societies, shortage of food has in the past been a formidable means of causing and regulating population changes. The practice of having small families so that each child can benefit from a large share of the family budget seems to have become widespread mainly in the industrial countries of the world, which, at the same time, are the countries with the highest living standards and the largest proportion of urban dwellers. In these countries it may not have been government practice to encourage the spread of knowledge about birth-control methods, but usually no serious obstacles have been put in the way. On the other hand, in poorer countries with large rural populations there are several reasons why modern methods of birth control can be applied only with great difficulty. Apart from governmental and religious objections there are the enormous problems of manufacturing contraceptives, distributing them, explaining their application (and to be effective they must be properly applied, for a miss is as good as a mile). Then there is the question of persuading and enabling people who have not enough money to buy food or who receive no true wages, to purchase or acquire them at all. These conditions prevail, perhaps, among three-quarters of the population of the world. It may well be a matter of decades before modern birth-control methods could be universally adopted. Even then it is unlikely, and indeed, hardly desirable, that there will be any compulsory limitation of the size of families. In the meantime, it is of great importance to ensure that production is increased, particularly in the poorer countries. To appreciate the possibilities of achieving increased production it is essential to have some idea of the world distribution of resources and their utilization.

III. PLANT AND ANIMAL PRODUCTS

When considering the resources of the world and their utilization it is useful to have in mind a broad twofold division of raw materials into plant and animal on the one hand and mineral on the other. While most of the world's land surface, as well as extensive sea areas, are put to some use for farming, forestry, and fishing purposes, the distribution of economic minerals (any minerals utilized by man) is much more limited, and their extraction is usually confined to small districts. The contrast is further emphasized when it is remembered that whereas good conditions for farming and suitable conditions for forest growth are to a considerable extent confined to areas with certain types of climate, the distribution of minerals bears (with a few exceptions) no relationship at all to present-day climatic conditions.

Farming is by far the most important single form of employment in most countries of the world, but good-quality farmland, like population, is very unevenly scattered over the earth's land surface. In certain favoured land areas of the world, such as the plain of the Ganges in India and the Middle West maize belt of the U.S.A., enough food can be produced on one square mile of land to feed several hundred people. In contrast, many millions of square miles produce no food at all. In Fig. 7 an attempt has been made to show which parts of the world are most intensively used for farming and which are of little or no use, or are little used at present. Three categories are distinguished:

A. Lands that are used relatively intensively for cultivation or grazing. Not by any means all the area shaded black is intensively farmed, but on this scale little detail can be shown. For example, the Alps and Pyrenees could not easily be distinguished as areas only partially used for farming.

B. Lands that for various reasons are only partly used for farming. This includes the grazing of comparatively small numbers of animals on large areas and the cultivation of small, scattered zones, in some cases intensively (for example, the sugar plantations of Queensland, Australia).

C. Lands that at present are used for farming very little or not at all. This category includes very small cultivated clearings in the Amazon and Siberian forests, the reindeer herds that are grazed in northern Siberia, and the livestock grazed in small numbers in arid areas.

Without doubt there are or will be possibilities of increasing agricultural output in all three types of land. In the black

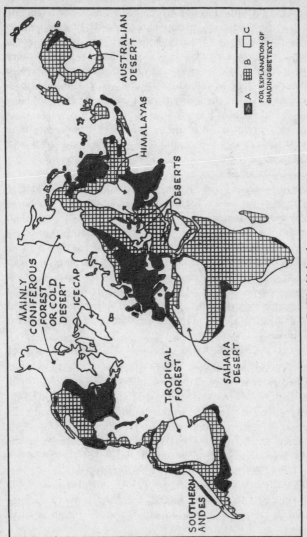

7. World land use.

regions the possibilities of extending the area of farmland are not great, but in many parts yields could be increased appreciably. In the shaded regions there is greater opportunity for extending cultivation, while many areas could be utilized much more intensively than they are at present. In the white regions it will be difficult to extend cultivation and grazing until considerable advances have been made in agronomy and other branches of science.

In any consideration of the possibilities of increasing farm production, the following limitations, set by natural conditions, should not be forgotten. Firstly, many mountain areas are too rugged to be utilized without great difficulty. Slopes are steep, and soil, where it forms, is easily removed. Secondly, owing to low rainfall (or, more precisely, precipitation) many parts of the world are too arid for plant growth without irrigation.[1] Thirdly, there are extensive regions in which temperatures are too low for the growth of vegetation or in which the shortness of the growing season greatly limits the range of plants that can be cultivated. These regions include most of the northern hemisphere north of latitude 60° and high mountain areas closer to the equator than this.[2] Finally, there are large tracts of tropical forest which, at present, anyway, can be cleared only with great difficulty.

About 20–25 per cent of England is arable land and much of the remainder is good or moderate-quality grazing land. For anyone accustomed to seeing an intensively utilized farming landscape of this kind it is difficult to appreciate how different most of the rest of the world is from Britain. In Brazil, for example, only about 2 per cent of the total area is crop-land, while it has been estimated that only a few hundred square miles out of more than one million in the Brazilian Amazon region are cultivated. Only 1 per cent of the total area of Australia is crop-land, though much of the remainder is used for

1. The effectiveness of a given amount of rainfall increases, of course, away from the equator, with the reduction of evaporation.

2. Because temperature decreases with altitude as well as towards the poles.

grazing. Even in such a populous country as China, only about 10 per cent of the total area is farmed intensively.

The amount of farmland available per inhabitant is far greater in some countries than in others. The U.S.A., for example, can produce enough food to provide each inhabitant with an average of 3,000–3,200 calories per day and could produce even more.[1] India only grows enough food to supply each Indian with little more than half that number of calories daily. Total farm production in the two countries is therefore roughly comparable in quantity, because India has more than twice as many people. In the U.K., Japan, and other small densely populated countries the amount of farmland available per inhabitant is very limited but is efficiently used.

At the risk of over-simplifying matters it is useful to classify the countries of the world into three groups with regard to food production. The first group consists of those in which home-produced food is abundant and some food is even available for export. It includes the U.S.A., Canada, Australia, New Zealand, Argentina. The second group covers countries which could produce all the food they require, but in which, for various reasons, some shortage occurs. In this category are most of the countries of Latin America, many African countries, Southeast Asia, and the U.S.S.R. The third group comprises countries such as the U.K. and Switzerland which provide only part of the food they need, but which can afford to import food without difficulty, and countries such as China and India in which by any standards the bulk of the population is underfed, but which are unable to import large enough quantities of foodstuffs to increase food supplies substantially.

The world production of food and agricultural raw materials can be increased in two main ways. Higher yields can be obtained in existing areas of cultivation and grazing, or new areas can be farmed for the first time.

Higher yields can be obtained in existing farming areas by

1. It does, of course, import certain foodstuffs and beverages, which it cannot produce at home because it lies outside the tropics. On the other hand, it exports cotton, cereals, and other farm products.

many different methods. Chemical fertilizers, at present available in abundance only in a limited number of countries, might be manufactured and used much more widely. The widespread application of trace elements where these are deficient offers great possibilities to farmers. Sometimes the introduction of new types of plant or new breeds of animal into a region helps to raise yields there; in particular, there is room for experimentation with pasture grasses and other fodder plants for livestock in many parts of the world. Improved strains of plants and breeds of animals are constantly being evolved. Many weeds and insect pests may eventually be eliminated. There is good reason to be optimistic about the possibilities of producing more food in existing farming areas.

The introduction of farm machinery, and in particular, of tractors, does not necessarily result in higher yields in areas of intensive cultivation, but machinery does release farm workers from the land and enable them to take up other occupations. It may also become economical with tractors to plough extensive tracts of country where natural conditions make high yields unlikely. This has been done in parts of the U.S.A. and Australia but, as a result, soil has been blown or washed away and land rendered useless. The same thing is now being done in the U.S.S.R., where poor steppe lands and even semi-desert areas have been ploughed by machinery in an attempt to grow more grain.

The expansion of agriculture into lands that are not at present utilized for farming brings with it many problems and risks. The tropical forest lands of South America, Africa, and many of the islands of South-east Asia, have so far hardly been utilized at all for farming. One problem here is the difficulty of clearing the trees, together with their stumps and roots; another is the danger of soil erosion and loss of soil fertility. Once the forest has been cleared, however, there seems little danger of soil erosion if suitable pasture plants are grown and the land grazed, and, of course, provided suitable types of livestock (probably cattle) are available. The coniferous forests, which cover much of Canada and Siberia, present another set of problems. In many areas the water in the subsoil is permanently frozen and only the uppermost layer thaws during the short warm season. The topsoil formed in these coniferous forests is usually deficient in plant foods and frequently rests on a hard layer which cannot be penetrated by the roots of smaller plants. There are farms in clearings in the coniferous forest zone of Canada and Siberia, but they occupy only an insignificant fraction of the total area, and the soil requires the application of fertilizer to be productive.

In semi-arid and arid areas further problems occur. Special drought-resisting plants have been evolved for use in semi-arid areas where the rainfall is not very effective but does allow some plant growth, while dry farming methods, which enable the crops to make the best possible use of the moisture available, are practised. There is a tendency at present for cultivation to retreat from some semi-arid areas of the world. In Australia, for example, the wheat acreage now tends to be smaller than it was in the 1930s, though yields are higher. The rainfall in semi-arid areas is often unreliable, varying greatly in amount from year to year, and there is the constant danger that winds may remove soil from areas exposed by the plough.

Both in semi-arid and in arid zones in certain parts of the world there are possibilities of extending the irrigated area. This depends at present largely on the availability of water carried by rivers with their headwaters in more humid regions (usually mountainous). Irrigated land can be extended in certain parts of the U.S.S.R., Australia, Egypt, Iraq, Peru, and elsewhere. Expensive works of construction, including dams and channels, are generally necessary. It is possible that in the not very distant future it may not be too costly to pump distilled sea water from any coast into nearby areas of semi-desert and desert where soils are suitable for cultivation but rainfall inadequate.

Two other activities relating to plant and animal resources, forestry and fishing, although, strictly speaking, not farming, have many features in common with cultivation and grazing.

Although the forests of the world have hitherto largely been exploited without being replanted, there is a growing tendency in different countries for land that has been cleared for its timber to be reafforested. The cultivation of trees, or silviculture, is becoming a branch of farming. In many parts of the world, including most European countries, the U.S.A., the U.S.S.R., Japan, Brazil, and New Zealand, extensive acreages have been planted with various species of tree.

The U.S.S.R. and Canada have the most extensive reserves of softwood in the world, while most of the hardwood forest is in South America, central Africa, and South-east Asia. For various reasons softwood forest is usually easier to exploit, and its timber has a greater number of uses, than hardwood forest. Countries that have small stands of forest in relation to their total population include China, Japan, and most countries of South-west Asia, as well as the U.K. and certain other industrial countries of Europe. *Per caput* consumption is so high in the U.S.A. that although that country still has considerable reserves, timber products now form a large item of import.

Commercial fishing is largely confined at present to a limited number of relatively shallow sea areas in temperate and even cold latitudes. This generalization does not, of course, take into account the locally important fishing industry in many lakes and rivers as well as in certain tropical seas, nor the whaling industry in the oceans of the southern hemisphere. Fish is a significant item of diet only in a few countries, including Japan, where it is the principal form of protein food, Norway, and the U.K.

At present, fishing is comparable rather with the hunting of wild land animals than with the grazing of domesticated ones. So far, only small-scale attempts have been made to breed and rear fishes, but it is possible that, in the future, shallow sea areas may be isolated and used for raising fish. Meanwhile, with a few exceptions, the seas and oceans of the world remain little utilized but possibly a vast potential source of food.

IV. MINERAL PRODUCTS

Economic minerals, like good-quality farmland (but mainly for different reasons), are very unevenly distributed over the earth's surface and, what is more, the minerals in some areas have already been extracted or heavily worked, whereas those in other parts have not been touched. Most of the land area of the world, including, of course, Antarctica, as well as much of Africa, South America, and Asia, has not yet been explored systematically for economic minerals. An illustration of the uneven distribution over the world of production of minerals is the fact that the U.S.A., with little more than one-twentieth of the total land area of the world, has about one-third of its oil production.

Broadly speaking, minerals are either sources of fuel and power or raw materials to be manufactured into something. The division is not, of course, rigid. Coal, for example, is largely used as a source of fuel and power, but many materials are made from it as well. At present, three minerals are of outstanding importance in the economy of all important industrial countries: coal, oil, and iron. Many others, including for example aluminium, copper, manganese, and tin, are no less vital, though they are used in smaller quantities. One important feature of the utilization of minerals is the fact that most are consumed today almost entirely by a limited number of industrial countries.

Of the minerals that are used as sources of fuel and power, coal and oil are by far the most important. World coal consumption has always been higher than world oil consumption even when the greater calorific value of a ton of oil is taken into consideration, but world oil output is expanding more rapidly than coal output and now the two are very close. Other sources of fuel and power, not all mineral, of course, include nuclear fuels, natural gas, peat, wood, and dung, as well as wind, falling water, and animal and human energy. It should be appreciated that most of the electricity produced in the world is generated by coal, oil, and other fuels and not by water, although in certain countries, including Japan, Italy, Canada, and Brazil, more hydro-electricity than thermal electricity is generated. At all events, it is probably best to think of electricity as a means of distributing energy, rather than a source, and only hydro-electric power as a source of energy distinct from other fuels.

World Population and Production

Coal [1] is still the basis of many branches of modern industry in the leading industrial countries of the world. One of its main uses is the smelting or refining of metallic ores. In particular, most of the world's pig iron is produced by the smelting of iron ore by certain types of coal that can be made into coke. The U.S.A. and the U.S.S.R. have the largest reserves of coal in the world. The reserves in Germany, China, the U.K., Poland, South Africa, Canada, and Colombia are satisfactory, and many other countries have enough to last at least some decades at present rates of production. Proved deposits are small or insignificant in most parts of Latin America, Africa, South-west and South-east Asia, which is one reason, though not every-where the most important one, why there has been little indus-trial development in these parts of the world.

The international trade in coal is less important both rela-tively and absolutely than it was earlier in the present century. The main reasons appear to be the greater ease with which oil can be transported, and its higher calorific value, which makes a ton of oil worth more than a ton of coal. This means that most of the coal mined in the world is consumed in the coun-tries in which it is extracted, while much of the oil produced in certain countries is consumed elsewhere. Another feature of the coal industry is the decline in absolute production over the last two or three decades in certain countries. The decline is most marked in the U.S.A. In many respects this is the most advanced country industrially, and oil and other sources of power are now replacing coal in many branches of industry.

A striking feature of the oil industry is the fact that a con-siderable proportion of the oil produced enters world trade. Several of the world's leading producing countries consume only a small part of their output. At present there are four principal producing countries or groups of countries, shown in Table 3. These have less than one-sixth of the population but account for 84 per cent of the world's oil.

1. This includes brown coal, or lignite, which is much lower in heating value than ordinary types of coal. Where figures are given for coal production and consumption, allowance has been made for this fact by reducing lignite to its coal equivalent.

Mineral Products

TABLE 3

	Production in 1963 (millions of metric tons)	Percentage of World Total
U.S.A.	373	29
South-west Asia	344	26
Venezuela	170	13
U.S.S.R.	205	16
World	1,305	100

Venezuela and the oil-producing countries of South-west Asia (Kuwait 98 m., Saudi Arabia 81 m., Iran 73 m., and Iraq 55 m. are the chief) export almost all of their output. West Europe is by far the largest importing area in the world since it only produces about 18 m. tons but consumes nearly twenty times this amount. East Europe (from the U.S.S.R.), Japan, and Australia are other considerable importers while the U.S.A. although being the largest producer, also imports large quantities. In China, India, and many African countries not only is the production of oil very small, but imports also are limited, since oil only plays a negligible part in the economic life.

In addition to the main oil-producing areas of the world, listed above, there are many regions in which it is thought that extensive oil deposits may be found. Large reserves have already been proved in the Sahara and western China, while parts of the Amazon lowlands in South America are promising.

Natural gas is a source of energy of rapidly growing importance in certain countries. It is generally but not always associated with oil and is easy to extract and transport (by pipeline). The U.S.A. is by far the largest producer but rapid progress is being made in the U.S.S.R., while Canada, Romania, Mexico, and Italy depend to some extent on natural gas.

Although other sources of fuel and power may be of great significance locally, only sources of atomic energy seem likely to rival coal and oil in importance in the future. It is difficult to say at present which countries have the best reserves of nuclear fuels. Producers include the U.S.A. and Canada, Australia, the Congo, East Germany, Czechoslovakia, and the U.S.S.R.

The second group of minerals, those which are not sources of fuel and power, is much more numerous than the first. It includes iron ore and the ores of various ferro-alloys such as manganese, chrome, and tungsten, which are associated with steel production; important non-ferrous metal ores, such as copper and aluminium, lead and zinc; silver, gold, platinum, and precious stones; minerals such as phosphates, nitrates, and potash, which form the basis of fertilizers; limestone for the smelting of iron ore and the manufacture of cement; and hundreds of others of varying degrees of importance. With advances in technology fresh uses are constantly being found for minerals, and new minerals are being used for the first time.

Almost always, minerals have to be processed in some way before they are of commercial use. The processes are rarely simple and the necessary equipment is often costly to install and complicated to run, while large amounts of power are frequently required. For these reasons it is the older and larger industrial countries that possess most of the installed capacity for the smelting and processing of minerals, either at home or in non-industrial countries where they have set up processing establishments.

Many minerals occur in large quantities only in a very limited number of localities. Not surprisingly, therefore, the production of a certain mineral in commercial quantities may be confined to a few countries only. Tin is an example. It is produced in small quantities in many countries, but outside the Communist bloc Malaya accounts for more than one-third of the world's production, Indonesia and Bolivia each for about one-sixth. Most of the remainder comes from the Congo, Thailand, and Nigeria. It is the industrial countries, however, which consume most of the minerals produced in non-industrial countries, even if these countries buy back their own minerals later in some manufactured form. Chile, for example, exports almost all its copper, Venezuela its iron ore as well as its oil, and Indonesia its tin.

One mineral, iron ore, has been of outstanding importance throughout the period of modern industrial development and, indeed, throughout the Iron Age, which has lasted much longer. The absolute production of pig iron (almost all of which is made into steel) or of steel in a country is a good measure of its significance as a world power, while the amount of steel consumed per inhabitant in any country over a given period is a useful though very approximate indication of the standard of living there. Table 4 shows the leading steel-producing countries in 1960 and 1961 (provisional).

TABLE 4

	Production in millions of long tons		Percentage of world total	Percentage of world
	1960	1961	in 1960	population
U.S.A.	89	88	27	6
U.S.S.R.	64	70	19	7
W. Germany	34	33	10	2
U.K.	24	22	7	2
Japan	22	28	7	3
China	18	15	5	23
France	17	17	5	2
Belgium and Lux.	10	10	3	under 1
Italy	8	9	2	2
Poland	7	7	2	1
Czechoslovakia	7	7	2	1
World	335	352	100	100

Other countries producing more than about 3 m. tons are Canada, Australia, E. Germany, Sweden, and Austria. (The figures have been kindly supplied by the British Iron and Steel Federation.)

V. INDUSTRY

Industrial capacity is distributed far less evenly among countries than is agriculture. Modern industry is almost unknown in many parts of Africa and Asia and has affected much of Latin America only slightly. In spite of considerable progress in China, India, and some smaller under-developed countries recently, nearly all the capacity is at present to be found in North America, Europe and the U.S.S.R., and Japan. Although it is possible to compare total capacity or volume of output of different countries, the method is so complicated that for the purposes of this section two more straightforward if less com-

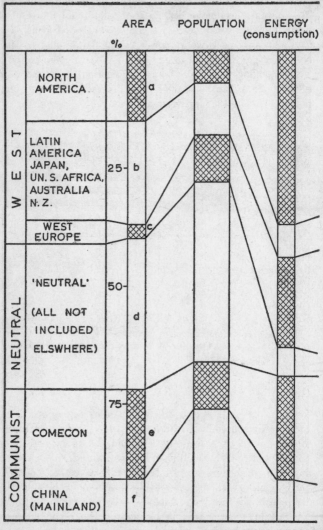

8. World share-out around 1960.

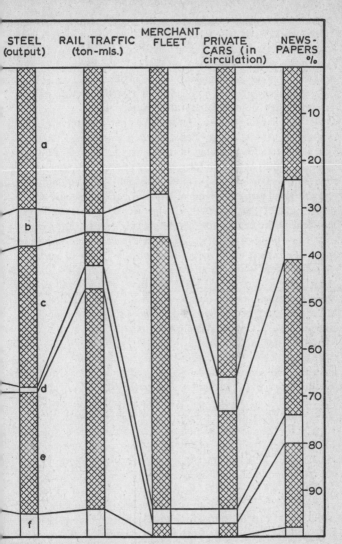

See text for explanation.

plete ways of measuring the industrial strength of different parts of the world have been taken : the consumption of all forms of energy (converted to coal equivalent) and the output of steel. The position is summarized in Fig. 8. The share-out of rail traffic, merchant shipping, private cars in circulation, and newspapers is also shown; each of these in a particular way reflects the level of economic or cultural development.

In Fig. 8 each column represents the world total of one particular item and is divided according to the percentage of the world total to be found in each of six groups of countries. The main purpose of the diagram is to show at a glance how unevenly the various items chosen are distributed among these six groups. Thus, for example, North America has only about 7 per cent of the population of the world, but consumes 37 per cent of the energy and has nearly two-thirds of the private cars in circulation. If everything were shared out according to population, then the divisions on the six columns to the right of population would be at the same place as they are on the population column. In reality the three principal industrial areas of the world, North America, West Europe, and Comecon,[1] with only about 30 per cent of the population of the world, have 75–90 per cent of the other items, as the dark shading brings out at once.

Each set of figures must, of course, be explained and qualified, but the general picture given by this diagram would not be fundamentally altered by reservations made on account of the data used. Energy, for example, is put to different uses in different areas. Obviously, much of it is used in the U.S.A. merely to keep the sixty million cars in circulation whereas in, say, India or China, it is used for more basic purposes. But this does not alter the fact that consumption of energy in the U.S.A. in industry is still many times greater than in these two countries.

In any study of industrial development in the modern world some knowledge of the main features of distribution, production, and movement of raw materials is essential. In this chapter

1. The U.S.S.R. plus the Communist countries of East Europe excluding Yugoslavia.

attention has been concentrated on the consideration of the availability of farmland and on three of the basic ingredients of industry and trade, coal, oil, and steel. The reader should not underestimate the importance of numerous plant and animal products, textile fibres (such as cotton and wool), hides, vegetable oils, wood, and so on; nor the role of numerous minerals, which are of ever-increasing necessity to the expansion of industry. In particular, the *per caput* output of cement serves as a useful guide to the capacity of the building industry of a country, while the *per caput* output of such products as superphosphates and nitrogenous fertilizers is an indication of the progress made in obtaining higher yields in agriculture. No less important are questions of technical education and skilled labour, the organization of industrial establishments, government policy towards trade and economic planning, and many others.

It is by no means easy to assess precisely the industrial capacity of a country. Owing to great variations in the size, population, resources, and production, as well as in the level of education and consumption in different parts of the world, it is even less easy to compare the industrial strength of two or more countries. Take Switzerland and Italy as an example. In value (but the meaning of this is misleading as a result of complications and contradictions in exchange rates) Italy's industrial production is several times as high as Switzerland's. On the other hand, there are ten times as many people in Italy. Italy turns out about half a million cars and lorries per year; Switzerland has no motor-vehicle industry. On the other hand, Switzerland makes many precision instruments and machine tools not produced in Italy. Both produce manufactured goods for export, but the export market is much more vital to Switzerland than to Italy because it has to import half its food while Italy produces most of its food requirements at home. These are just a few of the complications that make comparison difficult. A comparison of the U.S.S.R. with the U.S.A. is even less easy to make owing to the different economic systems in capitalist and Communist countries.

In a study of the distribution and development of industry

it is useful to distinguish two main types.[1] The first type is heavy industry, producing capital goods such as girders, factory machinery, and railway locomotives, used for construction, for the manufacture of other goods, for transport purposes, and so on. The second type is light industry, producing consumer goods such as clothing, furniture, and household appliances. It is of course impossible to make the division rigid. In the U.S.A. private cars are regarded as consumer goods, while in the U.S.S.R. all motor vehicles except motor-cycles are classified as capital goods (Group 'A').

This twofold division of manufacturing industry into heavy and light helps us to classify the countries of the world into three groups, according to their industrial development and production. Some, of course, are on the borderline between one group and another. The countries of the world fall into the three groups as follows:

1. Those that produce both capital and consumer goods and are therefore in a position to expand their own industries with relatively little outside help. This includes the U.S.A. and the U.S.S.R., which are probably the most independent of all; the U.K., Germany, France, Italy, and other manufacturing countries of non-Communist Europe; Poland and Czechoslovakia in Communist East Europe; and Japan. Even these countries depend on each other for some capital goods. The U.K., for example, imports various kinds of machinery and equipment from the U.S.A. and Germany, but exports textile machinery and other equipment to many industrial countries.

2. Those that satisfy most of their consumer goods requirements but produce few or no capital goods and therefore depend on countries in the first group for their machinery and equipment as well as for technical assistance in the running of factories. China, India, Brazil, Canada, and Australia still come into this category to some extent but they are all beginning to produce capital goods in appreciable quantities and

1. This applies to industry in the more limited sense of *manufacturing* industry, but does not cover industry in a broader sense, which can include processing, mining, and even farming, fishing, and forestry.

are therefore on the way into the first group. Others that have made progress in manufacturing consumer goods include Mexico, Colombia, and Argentina.

3. Those that have little or no modern industry at all. Among these are the smaller republics of Latin America, most European colonies and ex-colonies in Africa, and many countries in Asia, including Pakistan, Indonesia, and Thailand.

The extent to which a country can be industrialized on modern lines depends on many factors, including the resources of the country and the size [1] and standard of living of its population. The importance of size of the 'home' market for industrial products is now widely appreciated and is one reason for the formation of economic unions in various parts of the world. The chances are that a large underdeveloped country (e.g. India, Brazil) can build up a wider range of industries than a small underdeveloped one (e.g. Cambodia, Paraguay, to take extreme examples).

As already stressed, industrial capacity is at present distributed over the world much more unevenly than food production. Obviously, a given number of people require a certain number of calories, without which they would perish, whereas almost all manufactured goods are luxuries rather than necessities, at least by the lowest standards. Nevertheless, in almost every country of the world today efforts are being made to establish and expand at least some branches of manufacturing on modern lines, and the production of many manufactured articles is much less the monopoly of a few countries than it was a hundred years ago, or even thirty. In the leading manufacturing countries, however, new products are constantly being evolved (the manufacture of jet aircraft engines and atomic power stations are examples), and for decades they can expect to remain the only producers of these. The future

1. Only in countries with a large population can certain industries be run economically. Switzerland is without a motor-vehicle works not because it lacks the technicians, nor even the capital, to establish one, but because its internal market of 5 m. people is too small to make one worth while and because it can make other things more profitably.

prosperity of West Europe and Japan, in particular, depends on their ability to keep ahead, technologically, of as many other parts of the world as possible. For the U.S.A. and the U.S.S.R. this is not so vital since they depend less on selling their manufactured products to other parts of the world.

VI. CONSUMPTION AND LIVING STANDARDS

The uneven nature of the world share-out of agricultural, mineral, and industrial production results, not surprisingly, in great differences in standards of living between one country and another and even from one region to another within countries (e.g. in Brazil, Turkey, Italy). Although, however, it is obvious that the U.S.A. is more prosperous than India, and Switzerland richer than Paraguay, it is no easy matter to compare them with accuracy. The standard of living in a country could be measured roughly by dividing total production (by all branches of the economy) plus imports, minus exports, by the total number of inhabitants. Looking at it in another way, it could be measured by assessing what an average family might expect to purchase and consume during a given period, although in reality the average family (or inhabitant) is a myth, created for the convenience of statisticians, and in poorer countries particularly there is usually a small number of families enjoying a relatively high standard of living and a large number that can only hope to possess somewhat less than the average family.

Since many world problems are closely related to differences in living conditions, and therefore to production per inhabitant, it is necessary to have some idea of the extent of the differences between extremes of prosperity and poverty, and to be able to rank the countries of the world approximately according to their living standards. To illustrate the first point, conditions are compared in three sample countries: the U.S.A., Argentina, and India (Table 5). To show the second point, all countries in the world with more than 5 m. inhabitants have been arranged in Table 6 according to *per caput* consumption of energy. *Per caput* national income would perhaps give a more accurate picture but figures are not so readily available nor so comparable as consumption of energy.

Table 5 compares some features of the U.S.A., Argentina, and India in the 1950s. In most respects (but by no means all) the U.S.A. has a higher standard of living than any other country in the world. India, without any doubt, comes among the poorest countries. Somewhere between is Argentina, a country with good conditions for farming over an appreciable part of its total area and a certain amount of modern industrial development.

The fact that most of the figures in Table 5 are only approximate need not prevent us from making a comparison on

TABLE 5

	U.S.A.	Argentina	India
Food: calories consumed per day per inhabitant	3,200	2,800	1,800
Rooms per 10 inhabitants	10	4*	2*
Kilograms of cotton yarn per inhabitant per year	10	4	2
Doctors per 100,000 inhabitants	120	70	20
Dentists per 100,000 inhabitants	50	20	2
Percentage of population over 10 years of age literate	*Almost* 100	87	18
Students enrolled in higher educational establishments per 10,000 inhabitants	150	40	12
Copies of daily newspapers published per 1,000 inhabitants	340	155	8
Radio receiving sets per 1,000 inhabitants	750	140	2
Motor vehicles per 1,000 inhabitants	390	33	1

* Very approximate figure.
NOTE: The figures can only be compared in a horizontal direction.

these lines merely through lack of accurate data. In addition to the items included in the table, many others could be shown: opportunity to travel for pleasure, availability of entertainments, of books, of modern cooking and heating appliances, and so on. In every case the average U.S. family is better off than the average Argentinian or Indian family. Another item that is even more urgent than food, namely domestic water supply, should not be forgotten. In most poorer countries an abundant supply of good water is assured only to a small part of the community.

An important point is brought out in Table 5. While the ratio of food consumption in the U.S.A. and India is about two to one, the ratio of the availability of radios and motor vehicles, which in India are luxuries, is several hundred to one. Air, domestic water, and food are essential anywhere, and a certain amount of shelter and clothing is desirable almost everywhere. There is clearly a downward limit below which the consumption of calories could not descend without the consumer dying. There is also an upward limit beyond which the consumer would become ill or fail to digest all the food consumed.[1] In contrast, people can go on living without any of the numerous products of our modern machine age, and just as happily, probably, without them as with them, though in less comfort.

Any classification of different parts of the world according to living standards is bound to be to some extent subjective. Even if figures were available to measure production and consumption in all branches of the economy of every country in the world it would be impossible to reach agreement as to how much importance should be attached to each particular branch.

Food consumption per inhabitant is no doubt a useful measure of living standards, especially when the actual content of the food (e.g. the proportion of protein) is taken into account.

1. The lower limit must be somewhere in the vicinity of 2,000 (otherwise half of the population of the world would die) although about 2,750 calories has been suggested as the desirable minimum. The upward limit might be about 4,000–5,000, but there are so many variables to be considered that rigid limits cannot be set. The amount required by each individual varies. A baby needs fewer calories than an adult, a large man more than a small one, an Eskimo more than an inhabitant of the tropics (but not many more, perhaps), and a person doing physical work more than one lying down all day. The average American is larger than the average Indian and lives (mostly) in a cooler environment. On the other hand the Indian is probably obliged to perform more physical work.

Unfortunately, figures are not available for many parts of the world, while, as already shown in the case of the U.S.A. and India, the range is relatively small between the countries with the highest and lowest *per caput* consumption (see *United Nations Statistical Yearbook, 1960*, Table 127).

The range in *per caput* consumption of energy (see Table 6) between countries of the world is far greater than that of food consumption or even national income, but it is not suggested that the U.S.A. is nearly a thousand times more advanced or better off than Ethiopia because *per caput* consumption of energy is about 8,000 kilograms compared with 10.

Energy figures allow a wide spread of countries from the poorest to the most prosperous and are available for every country. The different categories, based on position above or below the world average of approximately 1,400 kilograms

TABLE 6

Per caput consumption of all sources of energy (in kilograms of coal equivalent) in 1959 in all countries with over 5 m. people.

	Americas	Europe and Africa	Asia and Australia	Communist	
5,600	U.S.A. 7,830 Canada 5,610				5,600
2,800		U.K. 4,590 Bel./Lux. 3,850 W. Germ. 3,270 Sweden 3,000	Australia 3,680	Czecho. 4,590 E. Germ. 4,390 Poland 3,000 U.S.S.R. 2,940	2,800
1,400	Venezuela 2,510	Neth. 2,680 South Afr. 2,500 France 2,370 Austria 1,960 Switz. 1,690		Hungary 2,180	1,400
		(World average)			
	Argentina 1,030 Mexico 820 Chile 790 Cuba 780	Italy 990 Spain 830	Japan 970	Romania 1,250 Bulgaria 1,180 Yugoslavia 790	

Table 6 (*continued*)

	Americas		Europe and Africa		Asia and Australia		Communist	
700								**700**
	Colombia	470	Rhodesias	560	Taiwan	500	China	510
			Greece	400				
			Portugal	360				
350								**350**
	Brazil	330			Iraq	340		
	Peru	320			Iran	330		
			Egypt	240	Turkey	250		
			Algeria	240	Malaya	240		
					S. Korea	210		
					Sa. Arab.	190		
175								**175**
					Philipp.	150		
					India	150		
			Morocco	140	Indonesia	140		
			Ghana	90	Ceylon	100		
			Br. E. Afr.	80	Thailand	70		
			Congo	70	Pakistan	60		
			Sudan	50	S. Vietnam	60		
			Nigeria	40	Burma	50		
			Ethiopia	10	Afghan.	20		

Source: *United Nations Statistical Yearbook, 1960*, Table 121 1960 figures for important countries were: U.S.A. 8,013; Mexico 1,012; Brazil 372; U.K. 4,920; W. Germany 3,651; France 2,402; Italy 1,186; Japan 1,164; U.S.S.R. 2,847 (revision of coal-equivalent of low-grade coal); China 600; India 140.

per caput are made merely for convenience. A few important features should be noted. The U.S.A. is far ahead of any other area, West Europe and Comecon are mostly above average, and Australia (also New Zealand) is high. Latin American countries are spread over a wide range, whereas apart from South Africa and Rhodesia all African countries are very low. Only Japan (and Israel) stand fairly high in Asia (apart from Asiatic U.S.S.R.) but China is coming up fast.

Table 6 should be used only for making broad comparisons between different countries, but the picture it gives does not differ greatly from that conveyed by *per caput* steel consumption or national income. Countries with a *per caput* consumption above average (1,400) all have reasonably high living standards except Venezuela; those between about 1,400 and 700 are by no means entirely poor or underdeveloped; but most of those below about 700 have a long way to go. They also contain about three-fifths of the population of the world.

Bearing in mind the great difference in output and in consumption per inhabitant between the countries in the highest and lowest groups, might we not question whether in reality there is any possibility that the poorer countries will ever catch up the more prosperous ones? Living conditions in the U.S.A. and India were closer 150 years ago than they are now. The gap has *widened* over that period, not *narrowed*, because India's economy has long stagnated and any recent increase in production has been absorbed by increasing population, whereas the standard of living has increased many times in the U.S.A. in spite of the great growth in population. There is much evidence to show, in fact, that the gap between the more prosperous and the poorer countries is continuing to widen at the present day. Nor is this confined to the capitalist world, for present trends show clearly that in twenty years' time, unless China produces some economic miracle, the gap between the living standards of the average Russian and Chinese citizen will be much greater even than it is now. Similarly, India and the U.S.A. might both double their *per caput* national income in the next two or three decades but this would mean an increase from $50 to $100 in India, from $2,000 to $4,000 in the U.S.A.

We, as Europeans, or people of European origin, are obsessed with the idea of material progress, and have witnessed remarkable examples of it in both peace and war in Europe, North America, and more recently the U.S.S.R. It is thought to be merely a matter of time before the underdeveloped countries of the world (and these contain between 60 per cent and 70 per cent of the world's population, depending where the line is drawn) achieve a standard of living for all their inhabitants comparable with the present standard in North America and north-west Europe.

On the other hand, some people in advanced countries question whether material progress is even desirable in the poorer areas of the world. People who take this view are usually well provided for, themselves, and certainly have not spent any time in areas of the world where conditions are bad, They have not seen homeless, underfed populations with few or no medical or educational facilities, but often with large families and little prospect of any employment. The problems of our affluent society such as juvenile delinquency, mass entertainment, new forms of psychological and physiological illness, may be widespread, but at least their impact is reduced by a reasonable level of comfort for most, if not all, of the community, and they are unquestionably preferable to the problems of really poor areas.

However, even if it is desirable to raise the economic standards of the poorer countries there seems little prospect of this happening quickly. This is partly because almost everywhere population is growing rapidly and tends to absorb what material improvements are made. On the other hand the increase is much slower in West Europe and Japan, where the level of development is already high. It is about average in North America and Comecon, but these areas are well endowed with resources, compared with their population, and material production is increasing more quickly than population. Although a later starter than West Europe or the U.S.A., Russia was already an industrial country of some importance early in this century. Elsewhere the prospects are not at present very bright, either because population is large compared with resources (India, China) even if organization is progressing, or because organization is lacking (Africa, much of Latin America) even if the resources are there.

Any advance in the poorer countries requires either the organization of the economy to accumulate capital within the area, or financial aid from outside, or both. The earliest countries of the world to industrialize on modern lines (Britain, France, Belgium, Germany, the U.S.A.) found the means to do so almost entirely within their own territories. So, more recently, have Japan and the U.S.S.R. In spite of the large amount of financial aid that has been provided to certain parts of the world since the Second World War it is being appreciated more and more that without efforts and sacrifices in the receiving countries little can be achieved. Nor do royalties from large foreign enterprises such as oil companies established in these countries necessarily go very far. There are certain exceptions, such as Israel and Venezuela, small countries in which the amount of aid or royalties has been very large in *per caput* terms, but Soviet aid to China (all repayable anyway) and Western aid to India have been very small indeed in *per caput* terms though of some importance in certain localities and branches of the economy. In view of what has been said it is worth noting that the massive aid offered by the U.S.A. to Latin America in 1961 (Punta del Este) for the 1960s will be given only if the receiving countries also make efforts themselves to provide capital.

So far, therefore, economic aid in the form of grants and credits has not made a great impact on underdeveloped areas. Indeed, more than half of the non-military aid given by the U.S.A. since the Second World War has gone to West Europe (see Chapter 9) to put this already advanced area on its feet again. Some economists (e.g. G. Myrdal in *Economic Theory and Under-Developed Regions*, London, 1957) have suggested that it might be more helpful to the non-industrial countries of the world to agree on terms of trade more favourable to them and therefore to pay more for the raw materials, sources of energy, and food products that make up the bulk of their exports. It should be noted, too, that a freer trade would be a disadvantage to many of these countries since it would expose their limited but in many cases expanding industrial capacity to severe competition from the more advanced countries. It is better for these countries to have and develop industries even if they are inefficient than for them to have none at all.

Nevertheless the U.S.A. and West Europe still have great hopes of aid to underdeveloped areas and the U.S.A. at present seems concerned with helping these countries into the 'take-off' stage, after which sustained economic growth takes place spontaneously. On this subject the reader is recommended to consult W. W. Rostow's *The Stages of Economic Growth* (Cambridge,

1960). Unfortunately economists tend to overlook the special features and problems of different countries and to imagine that, for example, the same processes should occur in a small country as in a large one. At all events, the combined assistance of government grants and credits and private investment in underdeveloped areas seems likely to increase.

North America and West Europe can also contribute by offering educational facilities in their own countries to persons from poorer countries. In every field the U.S.A. has, of course, so far given most assistance, since its resources are far greater than those of any single West European country but in West Europe itself France has probably made the largest contribution, Britain next; West Germany has lagged behind until recently, while Italy has its own serious internal problem of development in the south. Soviet aid to countries outside the Communist bloc has so far been small in total quantity though often placed where it might be expected to make a large impact.

VII. THE URBAN REVOLUTION

Closely related to questions of population change, mining and manufacturing developments, and differential living standards, is the question of modern urban expansion. A great deal has been written about modern revolutions in agriculture and industry. Less is known by most people about the parallel urban revolution.

Farm workers live principally in small rural communities. Mining, industrial, and most other workers live mainly in urban types of settlement. Not surprisingly, the great development of modern industry, mining, and associated activities has led to the rapid expansion of many existing towns and to the creation of new ones. Advances in agriculture released farm workers from the land and enabled them to take up other activities in towns.

Large-scale migration from rural areas to industrial centres was a feature of England in the later eighteenth and nineteenth centuries. At present it is taking place in almost every part of the world, but varies in intensity from one country to another. Although the whole process of urbanization is closely connected with the changing employment structure[1] of countries, various immediate reasons decide individuals or whole families to move into towns. Among these are the attraction of various amenities and services; the almost universally higher and more reliable wages in manufacturing and other urban activities than in farming; government policy (as in the U.S.S.R. and, more recently, China) forcing people into cities; and, at the other end, overpopulation in rural areas, and the introduction there of agricultural machinery, reducing the number of farm workers needed in a given area. A rapid increase of urban population in a short period is caused by the inflow of people from rural areas rather than by the natural increase of population in the urban areas themselves, though this can contribute as well.

Table 7 shows the broad if not precise relationship between degree of urbanization and proportion of the labour force not engaged in agriculture in selected countries of the world. Re-

TABLE 7

	Percentage of employed population in non-agricultural activities	Percentage of total population classed as urban
U.K.	96	85
U.S.A.	88	70
Australia	85	80
U.S.S.R.	65	50
Italy	65	55
Japan	60	55
Mexico	45	45
Brazil	45	35
India	30	20
China	20	15
West Africa	10	10

cent Statistical and Demographic Yearbooks of the United Nations have been the chief source of material, but it must be stressed that owing to differences in classification of urban

1. The percentage of the total employed population in each branch of the economy.

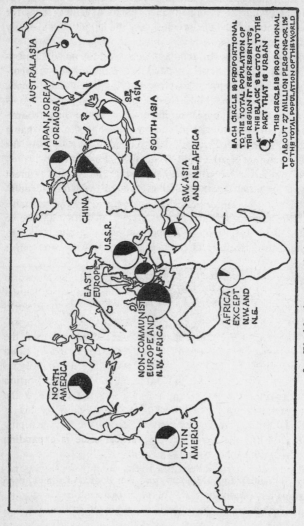

9a. World urban population in the late 1950s.

and rural population in censuses and in definition of different types of employment as well as to lack of recent figures for some countries, the figures, mainly for the later 1950s, are only roughly comparable.

Fig. 9a gives a very generalized picture of the world distribution of urban population in the 1950s. Each circle is proportional in area to the total population of the region it represents. Black sectors in the circles represent the urban percentage of the total. It will be appreciated that on this map urban population is being measured against total population and that it must be shown in relation to some symbol (in this case, the circle) representing population, and not against land area.

Fig. 9b shows the proportion of population living in different sizes of urban centre in different parts of the world. Figures are for the mid-1950s and already there have been appreciable changes in certain areas though these may partly be due to redefinition. Thus the proportion of urban in the U.S.S.R. passed 50 per cent in 1960 and the latest figure for Japan is 55 per cent.

At present about 30 per cent of the population of the world lives in urban settlements. About 8 per cent of the world total is in urban areas with over 1 m. inhabitants. Only in North America, Australia, and parts of West Europe does the proportion of urban dwellers greatly exceed 50 per cent. In the U.S.S.R., most of the rest of Europe, in Japan, and in Latin America it is around 50 per cent, but elsewhere it is mainly no more than 10–20 per cent. Except in the U.K., the proportion is increasing in every main area in the world, while at the same time the total population of the world is increasing as well (i.e. on Figure 9b not only is the urban share creeping along towards the right, but the vertical scale is expanding and the width of the columns increasing).

If present trends continue, then very roughly the total population of the world will have increased four times between 1900 and 2000, from 1,500 m. to 6,000 m., while the urban population will have increased *eight* times, from about 300 m. to 2,400 m., rising from 20 per cent to 40 per cent of the world total. Even this may prove to be an underestimate.

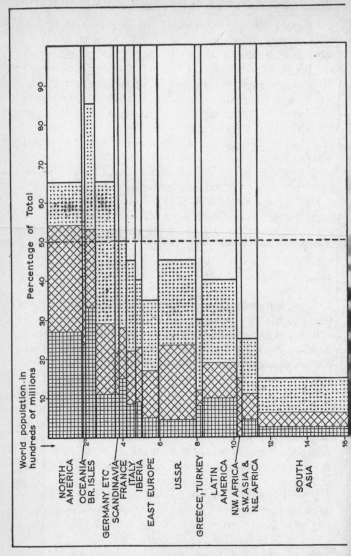

9b. World urban population by size

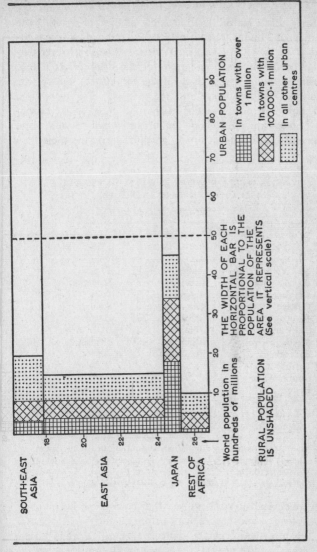

of urban centre in the mid-1950s.

World Population and Production

Table 8 is a list of all urban areas of the world with more than about 2 m. inhabitants in 1960. The principal source is the *United Nations Demographic Yearbook, 1960*. Wherever possible the figure has been given for the agglomeration (e.g. Greater London) rather than for the administrative area (e.g. County of London).

The purpose of this section has been to present some reasonably up-to-date information on urban growth in the world rather than to comment to any great extent on the subject.

TABLE 8

TOWNS OF THE WORLD WITH OVER ABOUT
2 MILLION INHABITANTS IN 1960

Figures in millions

America and Australia		Europe and U.S.S.R.		Africa and Asia	
New York	$14\frac{3}{4}$	London	$8\frac{1}{4}$	Tokyo	$9\frac{1}{2}$
Buenos Aires	$6\frac{3}{4}$	Paris	8	Shanghai	7
Los Angeles	$6\frac{3}{4}$	Moscow	7	Calcutta	6
Chicago	$6\frac{1}{4}$	Ruhr area	5	Bombay	5
Mexico	5	Berlin	$3\frac{1}{4}$	Peking	4
Sao Paulo	5	Leningrad	$3\frac{1}{4}$	Osaka-Kobe	4
Rio de Janeiro	$4\frac{1}{2}$	Manchester	$2\frac{1}{2}$	Tientsin	$3\frac{1}{2}$
Philadelphia	$4\frac{1}{4}$	Birmingham	$2\frac{1}{4}$	Cairo	3
Detroit	$3\frac{3}{4}$			Djakarta	$2\frac{3}{4}$
San Francisco	$2\frac{3}{4}$			Delhi	$2\frac{1}{2}$
Boston	$2\frac{1}{2}$			Shenyang	$2\frac{1}{2}$
Pittsburgh	$2\frac{1}{2}$			Madras	$2\frac{1}{4}$
St Louis	2			Wuhan	$2\frac{1}{4}$
Sydney	2			Chungking	2

Note: Most figures are for the whole built-up area (Greater) or urban agglomeration, not merely the administrative district of the chief centre.
Chief Source: *United Nations Demographic Yearbook, 1960*.

A great deal of work will have to be done by sociologists, psychologists, and geographers before all the implications of the urban revolution can be appreciated. One feature is becoming clear. In some respects urban centres all over the world resemble one another more closely than they resemble adjoining rural areas. Traffic jams and road accidents, bank robberies and organized prostitution, slums and overcrowding, neurosis and lonely people, spivs and teddy boys can be found in some form in any large urban centre, whether it is Communist like Moscow or capitalist like New York, prosperous like Stockholm or poor like Bombay. On the other hand, one would hardly expect to find these, at least in their urban forms, in farming communities in China or Nigeria, Portugal or Mexico. Nor would these rural areas have libraries, theatres, higher educational establishments, well-run hospitals, or elegant department stores.

The great urban centre is detached from the land on which it depends, often precariously placed with regard to food and water supply, strategically a tempting target for a carefully placed guided missile and beset by innumerable other problems. But the urban revolution is in progress, and no more can be done to reverse the process of urbanization than to prevent advances in the technological revolution, which is constantly enlarging the possibilities and dangers before the human race.

Chapter 5

THE REGIONS OF THE OUTER ZONE

I. NORTH AMERICA [1]

WITHIN North America there is great diversity both in relief and in climate. The region stretches almost from the tropics far into the Arctic. In spite of this physical diversity, considerable unity is given to the whole region by the fact that English is spoken almost everywhere (the French-Canadians form the largest non-English-speaking minority). Similarly, most of the inhabitants are of European origin, but the non-whites of the U.S.A. (about 10 per cent of its total population) form a large group. Another striking feature of the region as a whole is the form of its economic development during the last 150 years. The high degree of regional specialization in both the U.S.A. and Canada, and the close economic connexions between the two, mean that every part of the continent makes some particular contribution to the economy of the region as a whole. Finally, since the Second World War strategic considerations have contributed to reinforce the unity of North America. Alaska, north Canada, and Greenland are a forward line of defence for the U.S.A. against possible air attack across the Arctic or North Pacific, but the perfection of inter-continental rockets will no doubt reduce their strategic significance.

North America is separated by sea from all its neighbouring regions except Latin America (see Fig. 10). To the north, across the Arctic Ocean, lies the U.S.S.R. To the west, many thousands of miles across the North Pacific, are Japan and China. Not so far across the North Atlantic is Europe.

North America has about one-sixth of the world's land area but contains only about one-fifteenth of its population. U.S.A. has 179 m. (1960 census) including $\frac{1}{2}$ m. in Hawaii and $\frac{1}{4}$ m. in Alaska, made states in 1959. Canada has 18 m. (1962) and Greenland 25,000. With only about 45 per cent of the area the

1. See also Chapter 9 for a study of the growth of the U.S.A. and its importance as a world power.

U.S.A. nevertheless has 90 per cent of the population. In the U.S.A. itself, about four-fifths of the population lives in the eastern half, while almost two-thirds of Canada's population is concentrated in a very small part of the national territory

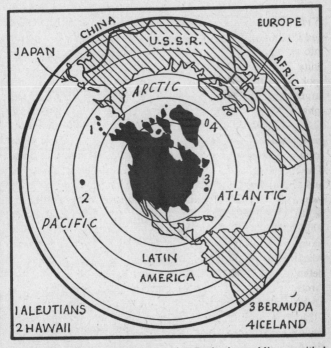

10. The hemisphere of North America. Projection: oblique zenithal equidistant. Centre of projection: Winnipeg, Canada. The circles are at thousand-mile intervals.

– southern Ontario and Quebec. Even in the most intensively used farming regions of North America, however, the density of population is low by European, Indian, or Chinese standards. On the other hand, the U.S.A. has some of the largest urban areas in the world (Greater New York has 15 m. inhabitants, Los Angeles 7 m.) and about 70 per cent of its

Symbols used in regional maps, figs. 11a, 13, 15a-b, 17

LAND USE

Main areas of farming. Here most. if not all, of the land suitable for agriculture is now in use

Areas at present only partly utilized for agriculture. Here there seem to be opportunities for extending cultivation

Dry areas, at present used mainly for grazing but in which cultivation might be extended

AREAS OF VERY LITTLE OR NO USE AT PRESENT

Ice cap

High mountain areas

Coniferous forest

Desert areas

Cold desert (tundra)

Dense tropical forest

O O o Coal and lignite

⊗ Minerals

F Fertilizer minerals

□ □ ▫ Iron ore

A Aluminium ores

G Gold

C Copper ores

L Lead ores

△ △ ▲ Oil and gas

Ch Chrome ores

M Manganese ores

D Diamonds

X Localities of great strategic importance

N Nickel ores
S Silver
T Tin
U Uranium
Z Zinc

Limits of region (land and sea)

Areas outside region concerned

⊙ Towns in areas outside region concerned

Political boundaries within region concerned

 Concentrations of population with more than about one million persons in manufacturing

Concentrations of population with between about 100,000 and one million persons in manufacturing

Other important industrial areas

Large towns (mainly national capitals) with few industries

116

11a. North America. See p. 116 for key.

11b. Industrial North America. In the region shaded on map industry overshadows other activities.

population now lives in urban types of settlement, while even in Canada, which is less highly industrialized, more than 60 per cent is urban.

The population of North America is at present increasing rapidly. This is a result not only of the fairly high natural rate of increase but also of the arrival of hundreds of thousands of immigrants each year from Europe. The number of arrivals in the U.S.A. is much smaller than it was at the beginning of the century (about 250,000 per annum in the 1950s compared with almost 1 m. per annum during 1911–15), and there was very little immigration at all during 1930–45. In contrast, Canada, with only about one-tenth as many inhabitants as the U.S.A. received almost as many as the U.S.A. in the early 1950s, and its future policy appears to be to continue to encourage immigration, though not, perhaps, at the level of the immediate post-war years.

Although agriculture is no longer the largest single employer of labour in North America, as it was in the last century, most of the U.S.A. is used for some kind of farming (see Fig. 11a). In Canada, on the other hand, only a small part of the total area is used for agriculture. The northern half of North America is too cold for farming. Almost all of Greenland is covered by an ice-cap. Northern Canada and much of Alaska are in the zone of tundra (or cold desert), while much of the remainder is occupied by the zone of coniferous forest, in which the soils are generally of little use for cultivation even where climatic conditions are favourable for the growth of certain crops. Much of the western two-fifths of the U.S.A. is too rugged for farming or too dry to be cultivated intensively without irrigation. Even the area of the Great Plains, to the east of the Rocky Mountains, often suffers from droughts and from strong winds which remove unprotected soil.

About three-fifths of the U.S.A. is in farms, but only about one-third of this farmland (or 20 per cent of the total country) is crop-land. Twenty-eight per cent of the total area of the country is forest and woodland. In Canada no more than 2–3 per cent of the total area is crop-land. About 34 per cent is forested. Most of the U.S. crop-land is in the eastern half of the country, where only relatively small areas, such as the higher parts of the Appalachians, are not used for some kind of farming.

In the U.S.A. the number of persons engaged in agriculture is surprisingly small. In 1920 the farm population of the U.S.A. (workers and dependants) was 32 m., or 25 per cent of the total population. In 1954 it was only 22 m., and no more than $13\frac{1}{2}$ per cent of the total population (which had itself increased over that period). In 1950 there were only 8 m. full-time agricultural workers and some 3 m. seasonal workers, in 1960 fewer than 6 m. full-time workers, less than 10 per cent of the labour force. Even so, total farm output has tended to increase, which means that output per worker is far higher than it was some decades ago.

The very high output per worker in agriculture in the U.S.A. (only rivalled in a few countries, including Canada, Australia, and New Zealand) is the result of several developments. In the U.S.A. (with the exception of certain regions) farms tend to specialize in the production of one or a small number of crops or one type of livestock. Generally only a very small proportion of the produce is consumed on the farm itself. When a farm specializes in one particular branch of agriculture (such as grain cultivation or dairying), the farmer can become an expert in that branch and needs only a limited range of equipment. Two other features of U.S. farming are the high degree of mechanization and the large amount of manufactured fertilizer applied per unit of area. Tractors and other machines have been applied widely in the U.S.A. because much of the best farmland is level or gently undulating, and because in most areas fields are large. Obviously, the introduction of mechanization has been much more widespread in the U.S.A. and Canada than in countries such as China or those bordering the Mediterranean, not only because North America is highly industrialized and can therefore mass-produce farm equipment, but also because the farmland has not been divided into minute parcels by generation after generation of peasant farmers.

Yields per unit of area tend to be lower in the U.S.A. and Canada than in countries such as Denmark, the Netherlands, and the U.K., where the amount of land available for agriculture is so much more limited and is therefore used with great care. Nevertheless, North America supplies most of the agricultural commodities it needs and still has a surplus of wheat, meat, cotton, tobacco, and other products for export. Only tropical crops such as coffee and cocoa (which, of course, cannot be grown in North America), and wool, are imported in large quantities. There is, indeed, a superabundance of food in the region, and whereas in most other parts of the world there is a constant struggle to ensure sufficient calories for rapidly increasing populations, in the U.S.A. many citizens are disturbed because they eat too much.

One aspect of U.S. farming is less encouraging. In a land where farmers and government officials are more concerned with surpluses than shortages it is ironical that much of the land at one time farmed in many of the drier areas between the Mississippi and the Rocky Mountains is now of little or no use because the soil has been, and still is being, blown away.

North America is fortunate in having extensive proved reserves of many of the more important economic minerals. Both the U.S.A. and Canada have large deposits of coal and iron ore.

Per caput coal production has always been higher in the U.S.A. than in Canada, but in both countries there has been a tendency during recent decades for total production to decline. In the U.S.A. about 400 m. tons were being produced annually in 1935–9. The total rose almost to 600 m. per year during the later years of the Second World War, but dropped below the pre-war level in 1954 (379 m. tons), and has since fluctuated around 400 m. tons. Oil and natural gas have partly replaced coal in the U.S.A. and Canada while hydro-electric power is also important, especially to the Canadian economy. Even so, oil production has not increased appreciably in either country since 1956, remaining around 25 m. tons per year in Canada and 380 m. in the U.S.A. The U.S. share of the total world output dropped from half to one-third in the 1950s. This is partly on account of the policy of conserving national resources and imports have increased sharply. Proved oil reserves in the U.S.A. are not large enough to last long in many areas but oil shales in Western U.S.A. contain very large quantities and it should be possible to extract these economically soon.

Although the U.S.A. has many other minerals, it now imports part or all of its needs of almost every mineral. It is no longer the world's chief producer of iron ore (the U.S.S.R. overtook it in 1958) but it is by far the largest importer of iron ore. It produces one-quarter of the world's copper, one-sixth of the lead and zinc, but still has to import additional supplies of these metals. It produces at home little or none of its requirements of bauxite, tin, manganese, chrome, tungsten, and nickel. On the other hand it has good deposits of fertilizer minerals – phosphates, potash, and native sulphur (about one-half, one-quarter, and nine-tenths respectively of world output).

Canada produces and exports many of the minerals deficient in the U.S.A. It is the world's leading producer of nickel, platinum, and asbestos, and a large producer of lead, copper, and zinc and recently has become a leading exporter of iron ore (from Labrador). It also has large quantities of nuclear fuels.

The U.S.A. leads the world both in absolute and in *per caput* production in almost every branch of industry. The rapid expansion of industry there during the last hundred years results from the combination of a number of favourable circumstances. It has had abundant supplies of coal, some of the most accessible deposits being in the north-east, where the Industrial Revolution began in the U.S.A. During the present century oil and natural gas, of which it has large reserves, have come to play an important part in industrial development. The U.S.A. has also had many of the mineral and plant raw materials needed for modern industry. From Europe there has been a constant inflow of settlers, among them persons from industrial areas. The U.S.A. itself has formed from the start a large and expanding market. Then there have been few traditions and restrictions to impede the development of industry in such a young nation. Behind everything has been the idea of material progress.

In industry, as in agriculture, there has been a high degree of local specialization in production. This has been possible because a close network of railway lines already covered the more populous part of the U.S.A. by the end of the last century and has been supplemented during the present century by a remarkable system of roads, gas and oil pipelines, and electricity transmission cables. Cheap transport has been called the great key to American progress.

A feature of U.S. development in recent decades has been the concentration of much of the industrial capacity in a small number of large concerns. One of the consequences of this trend has been the standardization of products, facilitating mass-production and resulting in high output per worker. Less than one-third of the employed population of the U.S.A. is engaged in manufacturing – about 15 m. persons – yet almost every branch of modern industry is to be found there, and only Western Europe and the U.S.S.R. can be considered possible rivals with regard to capacity, though no single European country has such a wide range of products.

The earliest centres of modern industry in the U.S.A. were in New England. From there industry spread westwards to the vicinity of the Great Lakes, and south-west along the Atlantic seaboard and into the Appalachians. Even today much of the industrial capacity of the country is concentrated in this north-eastern region, while many of Canada's principal industrial centres lie at no great distance across the boundary. In recent decades there has been a trend towards decentralization, and industry has expanded in the cotton-growing states of the south-east, in the oilfield areas of the south, and in the larger urban centres of the Pacific Coast states where, around Los Angeles, most of the U.S. aircraft factories are located. A feature of great significance to many of the interior industrial centres of north-east U.S.A. and southern Ontario is the new St Lawrence seaway, along which large ocean-going vessels can pass from the Atlantic into the Great Lakes. One of the main functions of the seaway is to enable ore-carrying ships to transport iron ore most of the distance between the Labrador fields and the ports on the Great Lakes.

Although foreign trade has always played an important part

in the economic life of the U.S.A. and Canada since the earliest colonial days, they depend less on it than the U.K. does.

The pattern of U.S. trade has changed fundamentally during the last hundred years. The following figures represent the percentage of the total value of exports taken up by semi-finished and finished manufactures (as opposed to crude materials and crude and manufactured foodstuffs): 1850s, 16 per cent; 1890s, 26 per cent; 1915–20, 55 per cent; 1931–5, 57 per cent; 1941–5, 81 per cent; 1954, 77 per cent; 1959, 75 per cent. During the same period, crude materials and foodstuffs have come to occupy a larger and larger part of the imports. The U.S.A. therefore now exports mainly manufactured goods; motor vehicles and other products of the engineering industry account for one-third of the value of all exports. Even so, U.S. farm products such as grain, cotton, and tobacco are still significant items in international trade. Imports, which are mainly raw materials and foodstuffs, fall into several main groups: tropical foodstuffs and beverages (cocoa, coffee, tea, sugar, and fruits); tropical plant raw materials (rubber); animal raw materials (wool and hides); forest products (wood and paper pulp); non-metallic minerals (oil); and non-ferrous metals (copper, lead, zinc), iron ore and ferro-alloys (manganese), and nuclear fuels (uranium). Although the U.S.A. has important trading connexions with many non-Communist countries in different parts of the world, a large proportion of its foreign trade is with Canada and certain Latin American countries (see Chapter 9).

The *per caput* value of Canada's overseas trade is about twice as high as that of the U.S.A. In contrast to the U.S.A., most of Canada's exports are raw materials (often processed, but not manufactured). Canada is more fortunate than most Latin American countries, which depend on one particular raw material for export, because it has a wide range of products for sale abroad. Forest products (wood, pulp, newsprint, and paper) make up about one-third of the value of exports, minerals (aluminium, nickel, copper, and asbestos) another one-fifth, and wheat and flour about one-twentieth. Canada also exports various manufactures. In recent years, about three-quarters of Canada's imports have been coming from the

U.S.A., and about one-tenth from the U.K. The U.S.A. takes about 60 per cent of Canada's exports. Clearly, then, the two countries have close trading connexions. These connexions are strengthened by the fact that some 35 per cent of all U.S. foreign investments are in Canada, though only 17 per cent of the receipts from investments come from Canada.

Little need be said about living conditions in North America. Undoubtedly the standard of living there is the highest in the world, though there are appreciable differences between different regions. In the U.S.A., in particular, it is not difficult to see from the *Statistical Abstract of the United States* that the average income of Negro and American Indian families is far below that of the whites, but there are also disturbing pockets of depressed whites as well, as in West Virginia.

Although there are no serious problems in North America connected with pressure of population on land or resources, the U.S.A. and Canada are not without other problems. Two problems in the U.S.A. are worth noting, one connected with the inequality of opportunity between the people of European descent and the various groups of non-Europeans (in this group are included the Mexicans, mainly American Indians, who are employed in the U.S.A.), the other connected with the inequality of *per caput* production between the U.S.A. and most other parts of the world.

The position of the non-whites has been discussed briefly in Chapter 2, Section 11. While the original inhabitants of North America, the Indians, have by now either been exterminated or accommodated on reserves, the Negroes live and work in the same areas as the whites, both in the cotton-producing states and in the urban centres of industrial U.S.A. It is ironical that in the stronghold of freedom, equal opportunity, and progress, the Negroes should still remain underprivileged almost 100 years after the Civil War, during which they were freed from slavery. On the other hand, it would be surprising, in view of current prejudices regarding questions of race, if they had been assimilated into the American community in the way that each group of European settlers has.

A second great problem now facing the U.S.A. is the widening gap between living standards and production there and in other parts of the world. The U.S.A. can now hardly trade on equal terms with any part of the world except Canada, Australia, and West Europe. Other countries need its surplus food-stuffs and raw materials such as cotton and wheat just as much as they need its machinery and other manufactures. Many underdeveloped countries simply cannot afford to buy them because they have little to offer that the U.S.A. needs. In the 1950s U.S. exports have in some years been as much as 50 per cent higher than imports. The balance is, of course, made up by U.S. expenditure abroad on such items as tourism, and by both military and non-military aid. As living standards continue to improve and production costs to rise in the U.S.A., it has to give away or sell cheaply what it is unable to sell at current world market prices. For example, it is becoming more and more difficult for the U.S.A. to sell cotton in foreign markets because this commodity can be produced more cheaply in other cotton-growing countries of the world where living standards are lower. In recent years the U.S.A. has had a surplus of cotton in spite of the restriction by the national government on the acreage under this crop. Even the giving away or selling at reduced prices of surplus commodities such as flour and cotton can cause complications by interfering with the foreign trade of other producers. The expansion of U.S. foreign investments in poorer countries in a way tends to aggravate the situation. The production of raw or processed materials is organized by U.S. companies in many different parts of the world, but the materials produced are frequently exported to the U.S.A. and other manufacturing nations, and therefore do not contribute directly, except by providing royalties and employing limited numbers of people, to raise living standards in poorer countries.

Canada, like Australia, is one of the few countries in the world that suffers, or professes to suffer, from under-population. Although Canada has very great forest, fishing, and mineral resources, however, only a very small part of the country – perhaps 5 per cent – has good or reasonable conditions for farming. With present farming techniques Canada could never feed more than a few tens of millions of people. The Canadian environment in many ways resembles that of Siberia (see Chapter 7). In time, of course, some means may be found of utilizing the soils of the coniferous forest zone for agriculture. Not surprisingly, however, most of Canada's capital investment is at present in the development of mineral, forest, and water-power resources. Examples are the oil industry, the projects to increase aluminium output, and the work on large power stations in British Columbia.

Canada's social problems are largely connected with the difficulties of integrating the two main European communities – those of British and French origin. Problems arise from differences in language and religion. About one-half of the total population is of British, and one-third of French, descent.

In the economic and strategic spheres Canada is closely connected with the U.S.A. In many respects Canada's economy is dominated by its more powerful neighbour, although it also has important ties with the U.K. and other parts of the British Commonwealth. In geographical terms it has the doubtful privilege of being located between the U.S.A. and the U.S.S.R., a fact that has not prevented (and may even have encouraged) it from acting independently of the U.S.A. in many post-war political crises.

Although both Alaska and Greenland are thinly populated and relatively unimportant economically they have become vital areas in the defence of the U.S.A. since the Second World War. Alaska's population has increased three times since the 1930s, largely as a result of the establishment there of important U.S. bases, facing the remote north-east extremity of the U.S.S.R., the Chukhotka Peninsula. Many U.S. and West European expeditions have visited Greenland since the war, while the U.S.A. and U.S.S.R. have both given great attention to the exploration of the Arctic Ocean in the last decade.

II. LATIN AMERICA

Latin America consists of twenty-two sovereign states and a number of small colonial territories. After almost 150 years of freedom from European colonial rule, national consciousness has grown strong in most of the republics. The enormous extent over which Latin America stretches (almost 7,000 miles from north-west Mexico to southern Chile), and the great diversity of physical conditions, contributed to the breaking up of the former Spanish American Empire into eighteen modern nations, but in contrast the Portuguese colonies in South America remain united in modern Brazil. Although most of Latin America has therefore been independent from Europe for about 150 years, Iberian influence was so powerful there during the three centuries (sixteenth–eighteenth) of European domination that today a Mexican or a Cuban feels closer in many respects to a distant Brazilian or Argentinian than to a North American living only a few hundred miles away in the U.S.A. A considerable degree of cultural unity is therefore to be found in Latin America in spite of its physical diversity. Spanish is the official language in all the independent nations except Brazil (Portuguese) and Haiti (dialects of French), although in many areas the languages of the original inhabitants, the American Indians, are still used. Roman Catholicism is almost universally professed if not actively practised, even if pre-Christian characteristics have been incorporated in it in some regions. Throughout Latin America many social and economic features of the Iberian colonial period are still preserved. Much of the land remains in the hands of a relatively small number of landowners of European origin. Most of the republics still specialize in the production of raw materials for Europe (and now North America as well) as they did when colonies, though one by one during recent decades they have been breaking away from this economic tradition.

Latin America has about one-fifteenth of the world's population and almost one-sixth of its land area. About three-quarters lies within the tropics. Fig. 12 shows the hemisphere of Latin America. The only land frontier is with the U.S.A., while Africa, with which there is very little contact, and Europe, with which there are significant cultural and commercial ties, are several thousand miles away even from the nearest parts. The other eight regions of the world are located outside the hemisphere of Latin America. It is therefore not surprising that

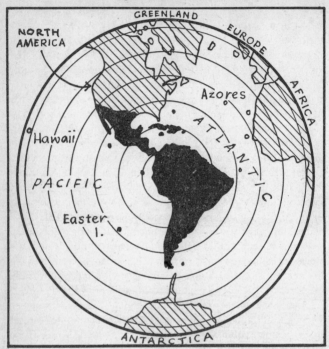

12. The hemisphere of Latin America. Projection: oblique zenithal equidistant. Centre of projection; Iquitos, Peru. The circles are at thousand-mile intervals.

Latin America has generally been little concerned with events in other parts of the world, and was probably less affected by the Second World War than any other extensive land area.

Table 9 contains some basic economic statistics concerning the eleven most populous independent nations. In columns I and II it can be seen that the countries vary greatly both in size and population. The most extensive, Brazil, is larger than the U.S.A., or Australia, while even Uruguay, the smallest in South America, exceeds England in area. Column III shows, again, that density of population varies considerably from one country to another. Many of the smaller islands, not shown in the table,

TABLE 9

	I Area in thousands of sq. mls.	II Population in millions in 1960	III Persons per sq. ml.	IV Crop-land as a percentage of total land	V Production of energy in millions of tons of coal equivalent, 1959	VI Steel output in millions of tons 1960	VII Consumption of energy in kilograms of coal equivalent per inhabitant in 1959	VIII Motor vehicles in circulation per 1,000 inhabitants	IX Percentage of total value of imports coming from U.S.	X Main item of export as percentage of all exports
Mexico	760	34	45	10	29	1	817	22	75–80	Cotton 25–30
Cuba	44	7	159	25	n.	n.	777	30	1958 70 now negl.	Sugar 80
Venezuela	350	7	20	1	199	x	2,512	39	55–60	Oil and prods. 90–95
Colombia	440	14	32	2	12	x	465	11	60	Coffee 80
Ecuador	105	4	38	1½	½	n.	157	6	50	Bananas 50
Peru	480	11	23	1½	4	x	315	12	45–50	non-ferr. Metals 35–40
Bolivia	420	4	10	½	½	n.	142	9	40–45	Tin 70
Chile	290	8	28	4	4	½	787	17	50	Copper 60–65
Argentina	1,080	21	19	10	10	¼	1,033	34	15–20	Pastoral prods. 50
Uruguay	71	3	42	7	n.	n.	800	25	10	Pastoral prods. 85–90
Brazil	3,290	65	20	2	9	1¼	329	13	35–40	Coffee 55
U.K. (for comparison)	94	52	554	20	210	20¼	4,594	123		

n. = negligible quantity   x = small production

have even higher densities than Cuba – some have several hundred inhabitants per square mile. Unfortunately the figures fail to bring out the fact that in every country there are also great differences in density between urban and closely settled farming regions on the one hand and almost uninhabited regions such as the interior of the Amazon basin on the other. In South America, a considerable part of the population lives within about one hundred miles of the coast, partly a result of colonization from overseas, partly because much of the best farmland is located in coastal areas.

The population of Latin America is characterized by the great diversity of its origin. The indigenous inhabitants, the American Indians, were to be found almost everywhere before the arrival of European explorers, but were most numerous in two main areas: Central America (including Mexico) and the Northern Andes. In the sixteenth–eighteenth centuries Spaniards and Portuguese colonized Latin America in relatively small numbers, while larger numbers of African Negroes were imported as slaves. In the nineteenth–twentieth centuries large numbers of Europeans – not only Iberians, but also Italians, Germans, and others – have migrated to South America, mainly to extra-tropical areas (south Brazil, Argentina, and Chile). Smaller numbers of Asians (mainly Japanese, Chinese, and Indians) have also been received in certain countries. There is therefore a great variety of races, with some degree of mixing in almost every part of Latin America. Often, however, one race predominates: African Negroes in Haiti; American Indians in Mexico and the Andes of Ecuador, Peru, and Bolivia; and Europeans in Argentina, Chile, Uruguay, and south Brazil.

In all Latin American countries farming is the occupation of a large proportion of the population. In some areas, including Haiti and parts of Central America and the Andes, it is almost the only activity, and each community or small group of communities is to a large extent self-supporting. In other areas, including most of Argentina and Uruguay, parts of Brazil and Chile, and many of the islands, agriculture is run largely on a commercial basis with specialization in one or more crops or pastoral products for sale to urban areas or for export to

13. Latin America. See p. 116 for key. The inset map shows the main political divisions.

foreign markets. There is a tendency to exaggerate the importance of the special crops such as sugar, coffee, and cotton, and to forget that most of the crop-land in Latin America is used for the cultivation of such food crops as maize, tubers, beans, and rice, which are the main items of diet for most of the inhabitants.

Fig. 13 shows the main areas of rural settlement in Latin America and the areas where conditions are not favourable for farming. The least favourable areas include: the high zone of the Andes, where only limited areas are suitable for cultivation or grazing in the north and the southern part is hardly used at all; the desert areas of north-west Mexico, coastal Peru, northern Chile, and the interior of Argentina; and the dense forests of the Amazon lowlands. Nowhere, except where altitude reduces temperature, are conditions so cold that they prevent some kind of farming.

Considering that these unfavourable regions only account for perhaps half of the total area of Latin America, the figures in column IV in Table 9 show that at least in the larger countries the area under crop-land is remarkably small. Grazing land is not of course shown, and in most of the South American countries pastoral activities are no less important than cultivation. Even so, many large areas are at present little utilized and could be used for some kind of farming. The countries in which possibilities for extending cultivation and grazing appear most promising are those in tropical South America: Brazil, Venezuela, Colombia, Ecuador, Peru, and Bolivia, each of which has a portion of the vast Amazon–Orinoco lowland. In Chile, Argentina, and Uruguay, most of the better-quality farmland is now utilized, although much of it could be used more intensively. The same is true in Central America and the islands, but in Haiti, Puerto Rico, and the smaller islands, the pressure of population is becoming a much more serious problem than it is in Cuba or on the mainland.

Perhaps the most significant feature of mineral production in Latin America is the fact that only one country, Colombia, has extensive proved reserves of coal. The total annual coal output of the continent is merely a few million tons – less than the U.S.A. mines in a week. Only in Chile, Colombia, Brazil (about 2 m. tons each), and Mexico is home-produced coal significant in the national economy, though even here output per inhabitant is very small by U.S. standards. The lack of good coal supplies has been one of the main reasons why modern industrial growth has been so restricted in Latin America.

The region as a whole is in a much better position with regard to oil deposits, though some countries have very small proved reserves and others none at all. In the inter-war period Mexico for a time produced more than one-quarter of the world's oil. The industry was nationalized in 1938 and has only slowly recovered from the difficulties created by this move. It was eclipsed by Venezuela in the 1930s, and this country now accounts for several times as much as all the other producers of Latin America together, though it consumes only a small part of its output, which is produced entirely by foreign companies. Colombia, Peru, Ecuador, and Bolivia are smaller producers consuming most of their output, but Argentinian production only meets part of that country's needs, while at present Brazil produces only a very small proportion of its requirements. In 1960 Venezuela produced 149 m. tons of oil, three-quarters of the Latin American total.

Latin America is a leading world producer of several metallic ores and metals. The following countries produce a significant percentage of the world's total: Netherlands Guiana, British Guiana, and Jamaica together about 50 per cent of the world's bauxite; Venezuela, Brazil, Chile, and Peru, iron ore; Chile, copper; Mexico and Peru, lead and zinc; Bolivia, tin; Cuba and Brazil, manganese.

In many respects the mining industry of Latin America is typical of that in the poorer, little-industrialized areas of the world. Most of the countries have been unable to explore, let alone exploit, their own mineral deposits in the period of modern world industrial expansion. Almost everywhere therefore, mining establishments are owned, financed, and organized by European or U.S. companies. The labour supply is of course local. Most of the metallic ores and metals, and much of Venezuela's oil, are exported to industrial countries outside the region. There has so far been little industrial development based on local minerals, though Latin American countries do benefit from the royalties paid by foreign companies on concessions and production, while Latin Americans employed in foreign companies generally receive higher wages and enjoy better living conditions than their compatriots in agriculture. On the other hand, their standard of living is far below that of mining workers in the U.S.A. or Western Europe. What is more, even the great oil industry in Venezuela directly employs only about 60,000 workers, while the labour force in farming in Venezuela is at least thirty times as large. Consequently only a very small proportion of the national labour force benefits directly. At all events, the attitude of most Latin American governments appears to be that it is a doubtful blessing to have one's minerals in the hands of large foreign companies. The more powerful countries, including Argentina and Brazil, have therefore attempted to control their mining activities.

For many reasons, industrial development on modern lines has been slow and slight in most Latin American countries. The absence of extensive reserves of good coal except in Colombia has almost completely prevented the earlier phases of the Industrial Revolution from spreading into the region. Oil has only begun to play an important part as a source of fuel and power in the last two or three decades, while hydro-electric power has so far been utilized on a large scale only in south Brazil. Another disadvantage is connected with organization and labour supply. With almost no tradition of manufacturing in the colonial period, the supply of labour accustomed to industrial activities has been small. Moreover, the lack of interest in machines and technical matters, which has been typical of the Spaniards and Portuguese, has left the European settlers in Latin America short of technicians. Even now little technical literature is available in Spanish or Portuguese on such subjects as geology and engineering, and a knowledge of English is essential for an expert. Thirdly, again partly a result of the Iberian tradition, the Europeans with capital have often preferred to keep it invested in agricultural establishments or to buy land and build in expanding urban centres rather than to risk investing in industry. The countries are poor, anyway, and lack the capital to build up large industrial enterprises. Finally, many of the republics have too few inhabitants (and the majority of them with little or no purchasing power) to provide big enough markets to make large and therefore economic industrial undertakings possible, while to ensure their survival many existing national industries have to be protected by heavy tariffs on imported manufactures from the U.S.A., Europe, and elsewhere.

Certain branches of light manufacturing, working entirely with imported machinery, and frequently financed and assisted technically by parent establishments in Europe or the U.S.A., do flourish in some of the more populous countries. Cotton spinning and weaving is carried on in almost every republic; most republics satisfy their basic needs in clothing and shoes, various processed foodstuffs and beverages. Some produce items like paper and rubber tyres, while bulky goods such as cement and bricks, which are costly to transport over great distances, are mostly produced locally. In other words, most simple products that can be made with foreign machinery and relatively unskilled labour are manufactured in Latin America. It is the machines themselves, the complicated pieces of equipment – locomotives, motor vehicles, generators – that have to be imported. The engineering industry hardly exists in Latin America, though imported parts of machines are frequently assembled and machines repaired and maintained. Only in Brazil are the beginnings of a large-scale engineering industry to be found.

Until relatively recently Latin America produced almost no steel, the basic raw material in the engineering industry. Even now it turns out little more steel in a year than the U.S.A. does in a fortnight. Several countries now have at least one modern iron and steel works but their capacity is so small in most cases that they lose the advantage of economy from large scale. South Brazil (Volta Redonda) and east Venezuela (Puerto Ordaz) seem the most advantageous places for the industry but even today several hundred thousand tons of Brazilian iron ore are smelted with charcoal – an interesting indication of the state of industrial development in Latin America, for coking coal had almost completely replaced charcoal in Britain 150 years ago and even in Russia 40 years ago.

Developments in all branches of the economy in Latin American countries have been hampered to a considerable extent by poor communications. The great era of railway building with European capital ended about 50 years ago, leaving large areas tens and even hundreds of miles from the nearest line. Moreover, for obvious reasons, many of the lines run from the interior to a coastal port. Only Cuba and parts of Mexico, south Brazil, Argentina, and Chile are adequately served by rail. Almost all existing lines are single track, and few new lines have been built in recent decades. Interest has turned to the construction of roads, generally cheaper than railways to build and maintain and therefore more suitable where traffic is not expected to be heavy. There has recently been some spectacular building in Brazil, while Venezuela and Mexico have reasonably good systems. Air transport has now become the main form of passenger transport in many parts of Latin America, linking the principal towns of each country and the capitals and larger towns of different countries. The rivers Orinoco, Amazon, and Paraná, and their tributaries remain the chief lines of movement in the interior of South America.

With regard to foreign trade, the nations of Latin America have a number of features in common. Column x in Table 9 shows how dependent most of the large countries are on one item of export (and the same is true of the smaller ones and the colonies). In some countries it is a farm product, in some a mineral. The whole economy of Colombia and Brazil, for example, has been greatly affected for several decades now by the fluctuations in the world coffee trade. Almost every country is thus dependent on one or a small number of raw materials for its foreign currency – with which it buys machinery and vehicles as well as various other raw materials, and in some cases considerable quantities of food and fuel as well. The demand for Latin American meat, cereals, and sugar is generally more constant than the demand for semi-luxuries such as coffee or for minerals such as copper and tin, the prices of which often change. In this respect, therefore, Argentina and Uruguay are particularly fortunate, while Venezuela, of course, benefits from the continuing expansion of the world demand for oil.

Another feature of Latin American foreign trade is the growing share taken by the U.S.A. In the colonial period (except the later stages) trade was with Spain or Portugal. In the nineteenth century Britain and other industrial countries of Europe handled a large share. Largely as the result of two wars in Europe and of the industrial expansion of the U.S.A., that country now supplies about half of all the imports of Latin America and takes about two-fifths of the exports. Broadly speaking, the closer the country to the U.S.A., the larger is the proportion of its trade with it. In contrast, there is relatively little trade among Latin American countries themselves, largely because in so many respects their economies are similar. Most striking of all, perhaps, is the decline during the present century of Britain's trade with many Latin American countries, the result of growing competition from the U.S.A., from other West European countries, and even from Japan.

Although living standards in Latin American countries are far below those in the U.S.A. and the more prosperous countries of Europe, there are very great differences within the region itself between one country and another and between different regions within individual countries. This is brought out in Table 9, especially in Column VII (*per caput* consumption of energy). In other words, there is a very wide range between the poorest areas (e.g. Haiti, north-east Brazil) and the most prosperous (e.g. Buenos Aires province, Sao Paulo state), not to be found in most other major regions of the world, and the varying levels of underdevelopment make Latin America of particular interest in a study of development problems.

The more prosperous countries of Latin America are those situated south of the tropics – Argentina, Uruguay, and Chile, and the southern part of Brazil. Paraguay, Bolivia, and Ecuador, the islands except Cuba, and the smaller Central American republics, are the poorest. The contrast within countries is generally between the capital city and some other large towns on the one hand and the rest of the country on the other. Most of the wealthier citizens reside either permanently or periodically in the larger towns and most of the industrial establishments are located there. Towns such as Havana, Caracas, Lima, and Rio de Janeiro are the showpieces of their countries. Their luxurious commercial and residential buildings and superficial air of prosperity hide from the brief visitor the general poverty to be found in the rest of the country and even in the poorest quarters of many of the towns themselves.

Lack of space prevents a description of each country, so Table 10 is provided to show briefly the distribution of various branches of production among five main groups of country in Latin America, the amount of each item being expressed as a percentage of the total for Latin America as a whole.

TABLE 10

	Mexico and C. America	Andean*	Islands	Brazil	South†
Population	22½	19	10	32	16¼
Arable land	21	12	5	21	41
Livestock units	14	15	3	37	31
Mining	15	68	7	3	7
Manufacturing	21	16	9	22	32
Grain	22	7	2	31	38
Sugar	11	8	56	19	6
Coffee	13	18	5	64	0
Cotton	37	16	0	39	8
Cattle	15	15	3	38	29
Energy	11	78	3	3	5
Metals	32	40	15	5	8

* Venezuela, Colombia, Ecuador, Peru, and Bolivia.
† Argentina, Chile, Uruguay, and Paraguay.

In conclusion, two important developments of the late 1950s cannot be overlooked: the Latin American Free Trade Association and Cuba. The Cuban revolution, resulting in the overthrow of the regime of Batista by Castro in 1959 proved, like the revolution of Mexico fifty years ago, to be something far more serious than the traditional skirmish in the Latin American political scene. A Communist regime supported by both the U.S.S.R. and China is at present (1964) in power and Castro's efforts in defying the U.S.A. have won enormous admiration throughout Latin America, even if his methods and achievements at home are now regarded with less enthusiasm than at first. At first sight the establishment of Castro's Communist regime seems an unexpected but welcome step (from the Communist point of view) towards domination of Latin America by the Communist bloc. But it is possible that by causing counter-measures in other Latin American countries and by inducing the U.S.A. to offer massive financial aid to the continent as a whole it may prove a setback to Communist penetration elsewhere in the region. Cuba is a poor consolation if it means the end of the spread of Communism into Latin America.

Of more fundamental importance to Latin America and to world affairs in the future may be the creation of L.A.F.T.A., an economic union already joined by the big three (Brazil, Mexico, and Argentina) and several other influential countries in the continent. L.A.F.T.A., which came into being in 1962, is aimed at increasing trade among Latin American countries, providing a large single market in place of many small ones, and stimulating regional specialization to cater for this. U.S. aid offered at the Punta del Este Conference (Uruguay) in 1961 should help, but an effort is required from the member countries themselves as well.

III. AFRICA EXCEPT THE NORTH [1]

For the purposes of this book, the most northerly countries of Africa facing the Mediterranean and cut off from the rest of the continent by the Sahara desert are treated with South-west Asia, with which they have more in common both physically and culturally. By separating Egypt from the Sudan, the Nile valley is unfortunately divided, and it should be appreciated that the north-eastern part of Africa has much in common with

1. The reader wishing to find out more about Africa than space allows in this chapter is strongly recommended to consult A. Boyd and P. van Rensburg's *An Atlas of African Affairs* (London, 1962).

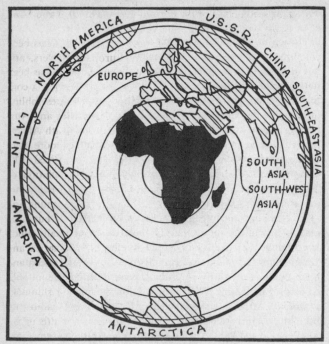

14. The hemisphere of Africa. Projection: oblique zenithal equidistant. Centre of projection: Leopoldville, Congo. The circles are at thousand-mile intervals.

Arabia. Without the northern countries (Morocco, Algeria, Tunisia, Libya, and Egypt), Africa still has over one-sixth of the world's land area but only about one-fifteenth of the population.

Until about one hundred years ago Africa was hardly penetrated by European colonial powers. There were many footholds along the coasts, points where European ships took on supplies and, in many localities, captured or purchased slaves. Only in the southern part of Africa did Europeans (Dutch settlers) colonize the continent in considerable numbers. The systematic exploration of Africa by Europeans only began during the second half of the last century, yet by 1914 almost all of the continent had been annexed.

The region has a number of distinctive features. It has been colonized only relatively recently by European powers, and this is one main reason why so far European influence has been felt much less strongly in Africa than in Latin America, a continent not without certain features and problems resembling those of Africa. What is more, unlike Latin America and Australasia, the population is, with the exception of South Africa, almost entirely indigenous. Even in South Africa more than three-quarters of the inhabitants are Africans or mixed. The primitive subsistence economy of most of the population of Africa has only been modified superficially by European penetration. Railways have been built between interior farming and mining areas and coastal ports to carry raw materials, but large plantations specializing in particular crops are generally much less important in Africa than in parts of Latin America and South-east Asia. Many export commodities, such as cocoa and palm kernels, are grown in small quantities by a large number of communities and collected at certain centres for shipment overseas. Outside South Africa there has so far been almost no development of manufacturing on modern lines and little urban development. Educational and medical facilities in Africa are poor or non-existent outside a small number of towns. In view of the fact that all countries except South Africa are at a very low level of development and of the changes that are taking place politically as colonies gain independence, Table 11 shows only the population of the main political units in the early 1960s.

Many of the new countries of Africa are quite small in area by world standards and very small in population. Apart from two in the north, only five, Nigeria, Ethiopia, South Africa, the Congo, and the Sudan have more than 10 m. people. Given the very low *per caput* income outside South Africa the total purchasing power of the market in these new countries is minute, and together it is no larger than that of say Belgium or the Netherlands, in an area several hundred times larger. The level of development is to some extent modified by the presence of

European settlers in certain areas. In Kenya and Mozambique they are about 1 per cent, in Angola 2 per cent, in Northern Rhodesia $3\frac{1}{2}$ per cent, in Southern Rhodesia $7\frac{1}{2}$ per cent, and in South Africa nearly 20 per cent. There are also appreciable numbers of Asians, mainly Indians, in some areas, notably in Uganda and Tanganyika (about 1 per cent), and in Kenya and South Africa (3 per cent). In other parts of Africa there are, of course, limited numbers of European residents but usually these are not permanent settlers and they rarely own land as they do in the remaining British and Portuguese colonial areas.

Lack of reliable demographic figures for most parts of Africa makes it impossible to assess accurately the rate of growth of population but it has been estimated (*United Nations Demographic Yearbook, 1960,* Table 1) that in many areas the annual increase is between 1 and 2 per cent and that in some countries, especially in West Africa, it is more rapid than this. Little has been done so far, however, to introduce modern medical services, and the number of doctors is still very low. In many areas there is an average of only one doctor to about 20,000–30,000 people (contrast about 1 to 1,000 in West Europe); in reality it is mainly the urban areas that enjoy modern medical facilities, while in rural areas they may be entirely lacking. As improvements are made the rate of increase of population may be expected to rise.

With regard to the distribution of population, Africa resembles Latin America more closely than India or China. There is no single very large concentration but rather a number of areas with a relatively high density (suggested roughly in Fig. 15a) including the coastal belt in West Africa and favourable valleys and plateaux in East Africa. South Africa has around Johannesburg the only mining and industrial concentration of any size in Africa. On the other hand, except in the north, in the Sahara Desert, no large area is virtually uninhabited like the Amazon basin of South America. In their tropical environment the Africans reached a higher level of technology and a greater density of population before the Europeans came than the American Indians did in the tropical lowlands of South America, although both societies were based largely on the apparently wasteful agricultural system of shifting cultivation, in which a piece of land is cleared by a farming community and used until yields decrease to a certain level, then abandoned. In time, of course, the same area is used again and again but the system implies that far more land is out of use than under cultivation at any given time.[1]

Africa is still essentially a farming continent and the practices used before the coming of the Europeans still predominate. Most rural communities are concerned almost entirely with producing food for their own needs. The food crop may be millet or sorghum (mainly in the drier parts), maize (in many of the more humid parts), rice, bananas, or various roots and tubers (manioc, sweet potatoes, and yams). Livestock is generally of poor quality, relatively unimportant as a source of food, and often merely a symbol of wealth and prestige.

In addition to the many diseases that affect plants, animals, and human beings in Africa and make the development of agriculture difficult, there are many areas where physical conditions are unsuitable for intensive farming (see Fig. 15a). Northwards the climate becomes increasingly arid towards the centre of the Sahara as the rainy season grows progressively shorter. There is also a smaller area where conditions are too dry to support more than a poor cover of vegetation, the Kalahari desert of South-west Africa. Parts of East Africa, on the other hand, are too rugged to be of much use for farming. Owing to its proximity to the equator, nowhere in Africa is too cold for agriculture, except the highest parts of the mountainous east and south. Within a limited area in west and central Africa, the rainfall is very heavy and a dry season almost non-existent, and as in the Amazon region of Latin America, clearance of the forest vegetation is difficult without suitable equipment. When all these unfavourable conditions have been taken into consideration, a large part of the continent remains suitable for farming. It is the primitive and frequently wasteful methods of cultivation that have kept the density of population low in

1. For an appreciation of agricultural problems in the tropics, an understanding of the advantages and disadvantages of this system is essential. See P. Gourou's *The Tropical World*, London, 1954.

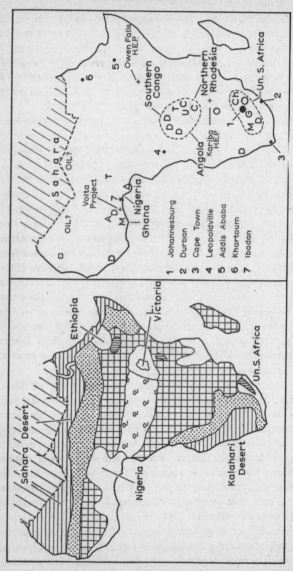

15a–b. Africa except North. a Physical background. b Minerals and towns. See p. 116 for key.

1 Johannesburg
2 Durban
3 Cape Town
4 Leopoldville
5 Addis Ababa
6 Khartoum
7 Ibadan

these parts of Africa. With the elimination of plant and animal diseases, the introduction of new types of plant and livestock, and the wider use of fertilizers, the more favourable parts of Africa could undoubtedly be made to produce far more than they do at present. Production could be increased both by obtaining higher yields in existing areas of farmland and by the utilization of new lands.

For the industrial nations of Europe and North America, which lie outside the tropics, Africa is an important source of a number of tropical plant commodities. While far less important than Latin America for the production of coffee, Africa accounts for much of the world's cocoa. Ghana is the world's leading producer, while Nigeria rivals Brazil for second place and former French colonies in West Africa also produce a large quantity. Palm kernels and groundnuts are important items of export from Nigeria and other parts of West Africa. On the other hand, little of the world's rubber comes from Africa, although there are large areas where climatic conditions are suitable for its cultivation. In South Africa, which lies outside the tropics, agriculture is generally more specialized than in the rest of Africa. The country is able to support a number of large urban centres and to export several farm products, including wool and sub-tropical fruits. Central Africa has extensive areas of forest, the Congo having the largest reserves, but at present little timber is exported.

The large-scale modern mining industry of Africa is organized entirely by non-Africans. The equipment and technicians come from outside the continent and the production is almost all exported for consumption in the leading industrial countries of Europe and North America. The main mineral-producing zone in Africa extends north–south for a distance of about 1,500 miles between Kabinda in the Congo and Kimberley in South Africa, the central part being in the Rhodesias. There are other mineral-producing areas of some importance in Nigeria and Ghana.

Proved reserves of coal, oil, and natural gas are at present limited, considering the size of Africa, but most parts have not yet been explored in any detail. Conditions are favourable for

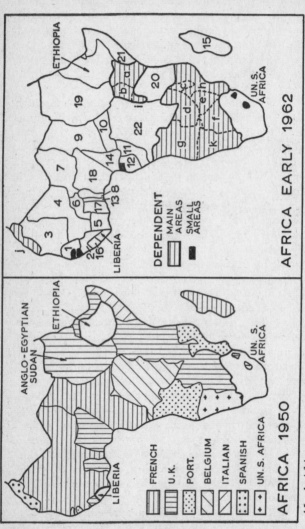

15c-d. Africa except North. c Political divisions in 1950. d Political divisions early in 1962 (see Table 11). Note: The former Union of South Africa is now the Republic of South Africa. By early 1964, Rwanda, Burundi, Kenya, Uganda and Zanzibar were independent.

TABLE 11

PRINCIPAL POLITICAL UNITS OF AFRICA WITHOUT NORTH AT THE END OF 1961

Independent	Population in Millions		Dependent	Population in Millions
1–15 Ex-French			*a–f British*	
1–8 Former Fr. West Afr.		a	Kenya	7
1 Senegal	3	b	Uganda	7
2 Guinea	3	c–e	Fed. of Rhodesia and	9
3 Mauritania	1		Nyasaland	
4 Mali	4	f	Bechuanaland	¼
5 Ivory Coast	3	*g–h*	*Portuguese*	
6 Upper Volta	4	g	Angola	5
7 Niger	3	h	Mozambique	6
8 Dahomey	2	i	Ruanda Urundi	5
9–12 Former Fr. Equatorial Afr.			(Belg. trust)	
9 Chad	3	j	Spanish Sahara	1
10 Cen. Afr. Rep.	1	k	S.W. Africa	¼
11 Congo	1		(under Un. S. Afr.)	
12 Gabon	½			
13 Togo	1			
14 Cameroun	3			
15 Madagascar	6			
16–20 Ex-British				
16 Sierra Leone	2			
17 Ghana	5			
18 Nigeria	34			
19 Sudan	12			
20 Tanganyika	9			
21 Somalia	2			
22 Congo (ex-Belgian)	14			
Liberia	1			
Ethiopia	22			
Un. S. Afr.	15			

By the end of 1961 the 25 independent states were all represented in the United Nations

147

oil both in parts of the Sahara and in West Africa. There is also a large potential of hydro-electric energy, especially in the Congo and Nile basins. South Africa (36 m. tons) and Southern Rhodesia (4 m. tons) are the only countries with more than a negligible production of coal, while Algeria and Libya, in the north, are the leading oil producers. A limited amount of oil comes from Nigeria and former French colonies. Outside southern Africa the consumption of energy (see Table 6, pp. 101–2) is lower in Africa than in any other part of the world except South-east Asia.

There are extensive deposits of high-grade iron ore in several parts of Africa, but only in South Africa is this used locally for the production of pig iron. Sierra Leone and Liberia have in recent years become exporters of iron ore. Africa is an important source of certain other metals : manganese from Ghana and South Africa; chrome from Southern Rhodesia and South Africa; copper from Northern Rhodesia (one-quarter of world's smelter production) and the Belgian Congo; zinc from the Congo; and tin from Nigeria and the Congo. Outside South Africa, however, mining gives direct employment to only a very small part of the total population.

For the production of three other minerals, Africa is of particular importance. South Africa accounts for about one-third of the world's gold, while the former Belgian Congo has in recent decades produced a large part of the world's industrial diamonds and since the war has also been a leading producer of uranium. The recent troubles in the Congo can be more readily understood when this is appreciated.

There are several reasons why there has so far been very little industrial development on modern lines in Africa, outside South Africa. The most important reason, perhaps, is that European penetration began relatively late, and even when most of the continent was held by European powers it was regarded as a source of raw materials and a market for European manufactures. But the current view of many Africans that their continent would be more advanced industrially if it had not been for European colonization is not supported by facts. The least advanced parts are Ethiopia and Liberia, the areas least affected by Europeans, and the most advanced are those in which Europeans are most numerous, particularly South Africa, Southern Rhodesia, and Algeria. The Europeans might have done more to industrialize Africa than they did, and this, together with the lack of educational facilities and of communications allowing the economic integration of regions, has undoubtedly been more of a hindrance than lack of sources of energy and raw materials. A new organizational problem has been created by the small size of most of the new political units of Africa.

South Africa is by far the most important industrial country in Africa. Industrial expansion has no doubt partly been a consequence of mining development and the concentration of an appreciable part of the population in urban areas. The output of iron and steel per inhabitant is higher in South Africa than in any Latin American country, though not so high as in the leading industrial countries of the world. *Per caput* production of cement and fertilizers (particularly superphosphates) is again high by Latin American and, of course, African standards. Heavy industry is relatively more important than light industry in South Africa, an unusual feature for a young industrial country outside Europe and North America. Usually such branches of industry as the manufacture of textiles are established before metallurgical and chemicals industries.

In the Rhodesias and the Congo there has also been some recent industrial expansion, and here again the influence of the older mining activities has been significant. Elsewhere only the beginnings of modern industrial expansion are to be found. Since the war, for example, some large modern cotton mills have been opened in Nigeria.

In general, Africa is very poorly provided with communications. Railways are few and modern motor roads almost nonexistent outside South Africa. The number of motor vehicles in circulation is extremely low in proportion to the population in most countries. Again, the *per caput* value of overseas trade is very low, and most countries export only one or a small number of agricultural or mining products.

From what has so far been said here about Africa the reader

will appreciate that living standards are very low. Indeed, in most rural communities conditions hardly differ from those prevailing perhaps for several thousand years. The shortage of statistical data does not hide the fact that medical services are few and educational facilities non-existent in many areas. Almost everywhere, however, some form of European influence has already been felt, and the old economic and social structure has been modified, if only slightly. What is most important and also surprising is that the political units created by the Europeans during the period of colonization appear to have come to stay in spite of the fact that many of the boundaries were decided without serious consideration either of cultural or of physical conditions. There are numerous instances of a modern boundary cutting across a cultural group (language area) or a unit of political and economic organization (tribe). In particular some of the smaller new independent countries of West Africa seem particularly to lack compactness and viability. The grouping of the smaller political units and the emergence of a limited number of economic units would reduce this problem, especially if boundary adjustment could be made. It is worth pointing out, of course, that what is referred to as African nationalism often means consciousness of belonging to Africa (or at least Negro Africa) as a whole, rather than to a particular country in it. Naturally the question is greatly complicated in those areas in which there are permanent European settlers. What their fate will be is difficult to foresee, but in time it seems inevitable that they will have to lose the dominating position they hold, since they are everywhere a minority and it is only a matter of time before the Africans become sufficiently advanced economically and socially either to drive them out or to accept them and live with them on an equal footing. France and Belgium now no longer have any colonies in Africa, and whether voluntarily or from pressure both inside and outside, Britain and Portugal will surely have to leave their remaining colonies soon. Even so, South Africa and the Rhodesias could remain European-dominated for some time and, were it not for the racial question, this area could undoubtedly make a considerable contribution towards the economic development of the rest of Africa.

Africa is more fortunate than most of South and East Asia in that it is not overpopulated. There is no doubt that the continent could produce much more food than it does, though even approximately how much more, it is impossible to say. Non-African help in the form of experts, farm equipment, and fertilizers is essential if progress is to be made, yet the failure of a large, highly planned enterprise like the groundnut scheme suggests that improvements can more confidently be expected if gradual changes are brought about in existing methods of farming than if attempts are made to reorganize African agriculture completely. A large amount of financial aid must be given to Africa before substantial improvements can be expected. In recent years the U.S.A. has invested large sums in African mining enterprises, but the amount of money given or lent in the form of grants and credits has so far been negligible except to Libya, Morocco, and Tunisia in North Africa. French aid, on the other hand, has been large since the war and continues to those former colonies that have chosen to stay within the French Community. All the former British colonies apart from South Africa remain in the British Commonwealth but, on account of its more numerous commitments elsewhere, Britain has done less to help its African territories than France has. Now Africa is for the most part open to any country in the world that likes to offer it assistance and it remains to be seen how soon the U.S.A. will give Africa Marshall Plan treatment.

IV. AUSTRALASIA

In addition to Australia, which is nearly as large as Europe and has come to be thought of as a continent, Australasia consists of numerous islands, of which New Guinea and the two parts of New Zealand are the largest. Many of the smaller islands are far out in the south-west Pacific.

Australia and New Zealand have mostly been colonized by settlers of British origin, and many of the smaller islands are also in the British Commonwealth. This fact gives some unity to the region. The eastern part of New Guinea is also in the British Commonwealth, but west New Guinea is to be part of Indonesia. The whole of New Guinea and the smaller neighbouring islands are generally considered as part of Aus-

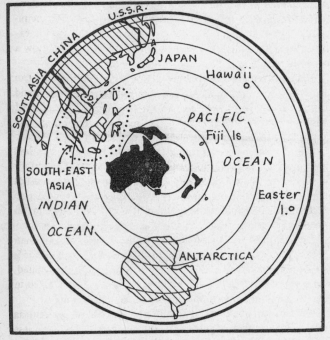

16. The hemisphere of Australasia. Projection: oblique zenithal equidistant. Centre of projection: Brisbane, Australia. The circles are at thousand-mile intervals.

tralasia, though in their climate, vegetation, indigenous population, and economic life they resemble the neighbouring islands of South-east Asia more closely than they do Australia or New Zealand.

Australasia has about one-fifteenth of the world's land area, but only about one-two-hundredth of its population. Fig. 16

shows the hemisphere of Australasia. The closest region is
South-east Asia (hence the importance attached by Australia
to its relations with Indonesia, formerly the Netherlands East
Indies) and at no more than a few thousand miles are South
Asia, China, Japan, and the U.S.S.R. The regions with which
Australasia has the closest cultural and commercial connexions
– Western Europe and North America – are in the other hemi-
sphere, although the U.S. sphere of interest in the Pacific ex-
tends into the hemisphere of Australasia and Hawaii is now a
state of the U.S.A.

Australasia has only relatively recently attracted European
settlers – Australia for little more than 150 years, New Zealand
for not much more than 100. The European settlers, most of
them of British origin, number about 10 m. in Australia and
about 2 m. in New Zealand. In these countries the indigenous
population has been exterminated (as in Tasmania), has had
lands confiscated (as during the Maori Wars in the last century
in the North Island, New Zealand), or, in places, has been left
almost undisturbed (as in northern Australia). In contrast to
Australia and New Zealand, there are very few Europeans in
New Guinea and the other islands of the south-west Pacific.

The density of population in Australia, not much more than
3 persons per square mile, is exceedingly low (cf. U.K. 555,
U.S.A. 49) and in reality much of the country is uninhabited,
while more than half of the total population is concentrated in
the five most populous urban areas.

We tend to think of both Australia and New Zealand as
essentially farming countries. Although each is more or less
self-supporting in food and each has a large surplus of farm
produce for export, only about 15 per cent of the employed
population is engaged in agriculture in Australia and about
20 per cent in New Zealand. So great is the degree of mechanization in the various activities connected with farming that
although agricultural output has increased enormously during
the last decades, the number of persons employed in agriculture
has hardly changed. In both countries only a surprisingly small
proportion of the total area (not much more than 1 per cent in
Australia and about 2 per cent in New Zealand) is crop-land

(excluding sown pastures), but much of the remainder is used for grazing. In Australia the greatest obstacle to agriculture in most areas is shortage of water. About one-third of the interior is desert, not used at all for farming, while another third is poor-quality grazing land. The most humid part of Australia, the south-east, includes, ironically, the most rugged part of the country. New Zealand is nowhere too dry for some kind of farming, but there are extensive rugged, high mountain areas, especially in the South Island. In both countries agricultural production has been increased in recent years less by extending farming into new lands than by improving pastures with the introduction of the most suitable fodder plants and fertilizers. The optimistic forecasts made in the inter-war years about possibilities of settlement in Australia have been revised, and a recent booklet for prospective immigrants (*Australia in Brief*, 1956) suggests that the 600,000 square miles of 'temperate' country, including most of the best farmland, might eventually support a total of 25 m. people enjoying present living standards. One reason for this 'downgrading' of the Australian environment may be to support the White Australia Policy.

It was gold that attracted many settlers to Australia and New Zealand in the last century. Mineral production is no longer of great importance in the New Zealand economy, while in Australia gold is no more important now than several other minerals, of which lead and zinc are exported, coal and iron mainly used locally. Australia is fortunate in having good reserves of coal, including coking coal for the smelting of iron ore, but coal output has stayed around 20 m. tons per year in the 1950s (cf. 210–30 m. in Britain) while oil imports have increased fast. No commercial oil is produced in Australia itself.

In addition to coking coal, Australia has extensive reserves of iron ore. These are located at a considerable distance from its main coalfield. Finally, important deposits of uranium ore have been found in several localities and uranium oxide is mined.

It is somewhat surprising to learn that in Australia there are now approximately twice as many persons employed in various branches of industry as in farming. Most of Australia's industrial development has taken place in the last forty years, having been stimulated by the two world wars, during which the supply of manufactured goods from Europe was reduced. The emphasis has not only been on the production of consumer goods, as in Latin America, but also on the establishment of heavy industry, as in South Africa. In spite of the modest number of inhabitants of its home market (which for many purposes can be said to include New Zealand), Australia now has an engineering industry of considerable capacity. New Zealand is not so highly industrialized as Australia and produces mainly light manufactures. Even so, it now has more persons employed in industry than in farming, though here, as in Australia, much of the industry is not manufacturing but the processing of farm products. The strength of the Australian economy can be measured by the great scale of the Snowy River scheme in the south-east, producing hydro-electric energy and diverting water for irrigation.

Both countries are well served by railways, but road transport and, in Australia, coastal shipping services, have taken much of the former traffic of the railways. Air transport is important for the movement of passengers and mail and, in remoter parts of Australia, even for the transport of livestock.

In both countries there is a high degree of specialization in farm production and various commodities are exported in large quantities – wool, wheat, beef, and fruits, from Australia; wool, dairy produce, mutton, and lamb from New Zealand. In addition, minerals and, in recent years, manufactures, have figured among the exports of Australia. Neither country therefore depends on a single item of export to the extent that most Latin American countries do. New Zealand is now the third producer of wool in the world after Australia and the U.S.S.R.

Australians and New Zealanders enjoy a high standard of living. The best idea of the high level of production is perhaps given by the following comparison between Latin America and Australia: Latin America has twenty times as many inhabitants as Australia, but produces less than half as much coal and about the same amount of steel; it has in circulation approximately the same number of motor vehicles. In total farm output Australia rivals Argentina, which has twice as many people.

Australia and New Zealand play a more important part in world affairs than their small total population alone would merit. There are several reasons for this. Australia itself is very **large** territorially, if not in population, and an even larger

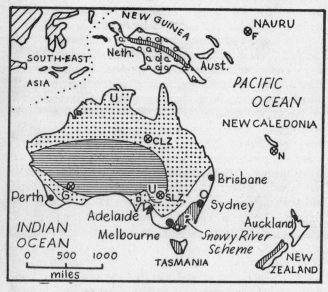

17. Australasia. See p. 116 for key.

part of the earth's surface is occupied by Australasia (or Oceania) with its numerous British islands and island groups scattered over the south-west quarter of the Pacific Ocean. Then there is the fact that Australia and New Zealand could both hold at least two or three times as many inhabitants as they do at present – hence their potential importance in the future. In addition, there is the high level of productivity and in particular the great export trade in high-grade wool, which reaches all the important industrial countries in the world. Australia produces 30 per cent of the world's wool and 60 per cent of its merino wool. New Zealand accounts for 10 per cent of the world's total (thereby producing considerably more per inhabitant than its more populous neighbour).

Australia and New Zealand are not without their problems. They are as far away as they could be from Britain, with which they have such important cultural and commercial links. They are underpopulated, yet are unwilling to receive immigrants that are not 'white'. The interior and northern parts of Australia are empty. It is doubtful, however, if even with the most elaborate and costly works of irrigation the empty northern part could support more than a few million people (most conservative estimates put the figure rather in the region of a few hundred thousand) – at present there are only a few tens of thousands of inhabitants, many engaged not in farming but in mining. In other words, northern Australia, might, over a long period, absorb the surplus population *of a few months or a few weeks* from India or China – a drop in the ocean.

Another matter of some concern is the tendency for immigrants who arrive in Australia to settle in the larger urban areas rather than in small centres or rural areas. Greater Sydney and Greater Melbourne each have about 2 m. inhabitants and together account for 40 per cent of Australia's total population. In New Zealand, again, the same trend is evident, and the four largest urban areas now have about 40 per cent of the country's population.

When thinking of Australia as a wool power, we should therefore remember how small its population is. We should not forget that both Australia and New Zealand have been developed almost entirely by British settlers and only since the beginning of the Industrial Revolution. They have been important sources of food and raw materials for the industrial population and industries of the mother country. Their economies are complementary to that of the U.K., though they rely much less on British manufactures and send a much smaller proportion of their exports there than they did a century, or even fifty years ago. Understandably, therefore, they are particularly concerned about Britain's proposed entry into the European Common Market, but they are also beginning to appreciate not only the need but also the advantages of trading more with neighbouring Asia.

New Guinea and the other islands of the south-west Pacific contrast in almost every way with New Zealand and Australia. They mostly lie within the tropics, and their natural vegetation is mostly dense forest. The Japanese invasion of the area in 1942 and the search for oil there during the last few decades have at last begun to open it up. Apart from their obvious strategic significance, some of the other islands of the south-west Pacific are important sources of minerals (Nauru, phosphate rock; New Caledonia, chrome ore and nickel) and of tropical crops for Australia and New Zealand.

Chapter 6

THE REGIONS OF THE INNER ZONE

I. WEST EUROPE

FOR the purposes of this book the countries of Europe without a Communist regime in power are grouped together to form one region. Although there are differences among them, the fact that they are all opposed to Communism gives them a common interest, while it may not be long before they are almost all in an economic union, if not a political one. Turkey and Yugoslavia are not included in the region.

West Europe is small in area (only 2 per cent of the world's land surface) but it has a population of about 305 m., more than 10 per cent of the world's total, produces about 15 per cent of the world's energy (but consumes nearly 20 per cent) and produces more steel than either North America or Comecon, 30 per cent of the world's total (see Fig. 8, pp. 92–3).

Fig. 18 shows that the hemisphere of West Europe contains a large amount of land (contrast Figs. 10, 12, 16). This has often been given as a reason why the area has long held an influential position in world affairs, but an equally strong case could be made out for some other parts of the world.

Small though it is, West Europe is characterized by considerable physical diversity: fertile lowlands, high mountain regions, forests both coniferous and deciduous, and seas penetrating far into the continent, leaving nowhere more than a few hundred miles from the coast. Cultural diversity is marked, too, on account of the presence of many different languages, religious groups, and strongly developed nation states. But the languages and religions have the same general origins, and national consciousness has been greatly reduced since the war, thanks to increasing travel and trade among countries as well as a common interest in defence.

Fig. 19a shows the broad features of the distribution of agricultural land in West Europe and Fig. 19b the countries. In Table 12, Column II the approximate area of arable land in each country is indicated but quality of the land is not indicated. For example Spain has a large area of arable land, the Netherlands only a small area, but in the Netherlands the quality of the land is generally superior and farming practices are more

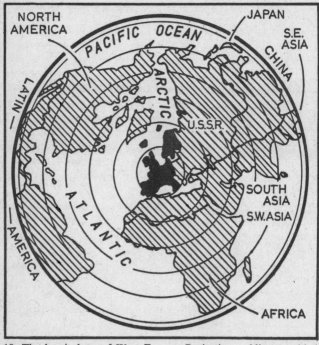

18. The hemisphere of West Europe. Projection: oblique zenithal equidistant. Centre of projection: Brussels, Belgium. The circles are at thousand-mile intervals.

advanced. The northern half of West Europe is one of the most efficiently farmed areas in the world, whereas in the southern half more rugged and dry conditions combine with complicated systems of land tenure, small fields, and a large labour force without alternative employment, to make yields relatively low both per worker and per unit of area except in especially favoured districts. For centuries now there has been little ex-

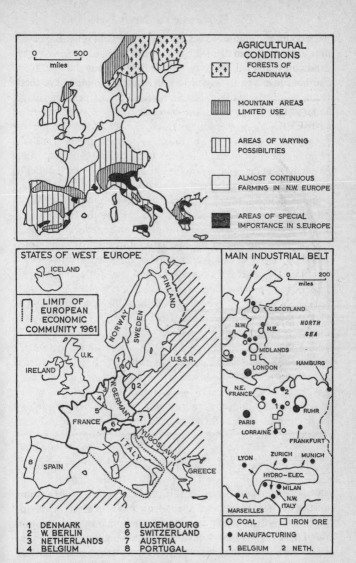

19a–c. West Europe. a Agricultural conditions. b States of West Europe. c Main industrial belt.

pansion of the cultivated area in West Europe but the limit of production per unit of area has not been reached and, given the present relatively slow rate of increase of population, West Europe can expect to become less dependent on imports of food from other regions than it has been in recent decades. Most countries do however import more than they export, but part of this consists of tropical products that could not be grown in the region anyway. One of the main items of import is wheat, because the U.K., the Benelux, Switzerland, Germany, and parts of Scandinavia are deficient in this product although France, Italy, and Spain satisfy their own needs.

Forestry and fishing are important activities in parts of West Europe. Much of Scandinavia is forested and the higher parts and areas of poorer soil are often forest-covered in the rest of Europe. With increasing aridity southwards the conditions become unsuitable for forest growth and the Mediterranean woodland is generally of poor quality and little commercial use. Fish is a significant source of protein food in several European countries. The main fishing grounds are in the northern seas and the countries such as the U.K. and Norway with long coasts facing these are among the world's leading fishing nations, although in the 1950s the share of the world catch landed in West Europe has declined sharply with the rise of the U.S.S.R., South Africa, Peru, China, and other areas.

Although West Europe is deficient in foodstuffs, the value of imports of sources of energy and of raw materials for industry (both mineral and vegetable) into most countries there greatly exceeds the value of their imports of food. This is because, apart from its large deposits of coal and more limited reserves of high-grade iron ore, its forests and hydro-electric power, the region is poorly provided with the ingredients of modern industry. Even the coal is confined mainly to one principal zone (see Fig. 19c) extending from central Scotland through England, north-east France, and the Benelux to the Ruhr. Sweden and Spain have reserves of high-grade iron ore, while the coal-producing countries have abundant low-grade iron ore. Some non-ferrous metals are available in small to moderate quantities in the southern part of the region but do

TABLE 12

	I Population in millions, 1960 or nearest year	II Arable land in thousands of sq. kms., 1950s	III Production of energy in millions of tons of coal equivalent in 1959*	IV Consumption of energy in millions of tons of coal equivalent in 1959	V Output of steel in millions of tons in 1960	VI Per caput consumption of all sources of energy in kilograms of coal equivalent, 1959	VII Private cars in circulation per 1,000 inhabitants in 1959
France	45	210	70	107	17	2,370	112
Belgium-Lux.	9½	10	23	36	10	3,850	74
Netherlands	11½	10	15	30	1½	2,680	39
W. Germany	55	90	165	176	33	3,270	70
Italy	50	150	20	50	8	990	33
E.E.C. total	171	470	293	399	69½		
U.K.	52	70	210	240	24	4,590	96
Sweden	7½	40	4	22	3	3,000	147
Norway	3½	10	4	9	½	2,480	54
Denmark	4½	25	1	11	½	2,390	78
Switzerland	5	5	2	9		1,690	86
Austria	7	15	10	14	2½	1,960	46
Portugal	9	40	1	3		360	16
E.F.T.A. total	88½	205	232	308	30½		
Spain	30	190	17	25	2	830	7
Ireland	3	15	n.	4		1,340	53
Finland	4½	25	1	6		1,400	36
Greece	8½	35	1	3		400	5
Others total	46	265	19	38	2		
W. Europe total	305½	940	544	745	102		

Malta (350,000 inhabitants), Iceland (170,000), and some very small units are not included. W. Germany includes W. Berlin.

Columns III–VII show some aspects of industrial development and living standards in West Europe. For convenience the countries are arranged in three groups: the Common Market countries (E.E.C.), the European Free Trade Association (E.F.T.A.) and others. Of the others, Greece is associated with E.E.C.

* Note that the conversion for hydro-electricity understates the importance of this item.

not go far towards satisfying the needs of industry. The most serious deficiency is oil. In spite of progress since the war, West Europe still produces no more than 1–2 per cent of the world's oil, while deposits of natural gas, although important in some areas, are not comparable with those of North America, the U.S.S.R., or northern Africa.

In spite of the lack of many raw materials, manufacturing employs a considerable part of the labour force in most European countries – nearly half in the U.K. and Belgium, and not much less in West Germany, Sweden, and Switzerland. In the Mediterranean countries, however, agriculture employs considerably more people than manufacturing. The great increase in industrial output in most countries in the 1950s has been achieved mainly by increased productivity per worker, and employment in industry has not usually increased much.

Coal, used for producing steam power, and coke for smelting iron ore, formed the basis of industrial expansion in the earlier period of the Industrial Revolution. The U.K., Belgium, France, and Germany, with good coalfields, were the earliest to apply the techniques of the Industrial Revolution on a large scale. Towards the end of the last century it became possible to utilize hydro-electric power, and certain parts of Europe, which produced little or no coal, were able to expand manufacturing without depending too heavily on imported coal. They include Sweden and Norway, Switzerland, North Italy, and Catalonia (Spain). Until very recently oil has been of little importance as a source of power in European industry, most of it being used for transportation. But this situation is now rapidly changing and the importation of oil has doubled in a matter of a few years. Large new oil refineries, importing crude oil mainly from South-west Asia and northern Africa, are springing up both in the Mediterranean ports and in north-east Europe. Nuclear fuels are not produced in large quantities in Europe and their utilization, like that of oil, will have to be based on imported materials; and so far the contribution of this source of energy has been negligible. In addition to oil, most raw materials for industry are now imported.

From the earliest years of the Industrial Revolution, Europe has had to import cotton. Since then the list of imported materials has constantly been growing. Other fibres such as wool and jute, timber, and most of the metals needed are among the items imported for industry.

West Europe has a long tradition of industry, and several hundred years ago a number of areas were already specializing in manufacturing. Among them were parts of Spain, northern Italy, Germany, and Flanders. There was also an important trade between different parts of Europe. The Hanseatic towns in the north and Genoa and Venice in the Mediterranean handled much of the maritime traffic. In many respects England was less developed industrially and commercially than some parts of the Continent. It was in Britain in the eighteenth century, however, that many techniques were applied for the first time in industry and agriculture and large modern factories run by steam-driven machinery were first built. Iron ore was smelted with coke instead of charcoal, complicated machinery was used in textile and later in other establishments, and railways and steamships revolutionized transportation. These new techniques subsequently spread to other parts of Europe where coal was available, and to other parts of the world, such as the U.S.A.

West Europe now has a very wide range of manufacturing, and some industrialization is to be found even in the most backward countries, Portugal and Greece. The main concentration of industry is still broadly related to the main coalfields, however, and stretches from Britain through Belgium and northeast France to north central Germany (see Fig. 19c). Away from this area there are some small but locally important coalfields in south central France and north Spain. The older metallurgical and heavy engineering industries are closely connected with the coalfields, and the older textile districts are here, too. As coal was moved more freely by rail and sea after the middle of the nineteenth century industry also grew up away from the coalfields. The utilization of hydro-electric energy, and progress in the transmission of electricity, have further attracted industries away from the traditional districts. Imported oil is now encouraging development, especially of the chemicals industry, in many ports. Large new iron and steel works have also been built or are planned in several ports: Port Talbot in Wales, Europort near Rotterdam, Taranto in south Italy. A further attraction to industry is a very large concentration of urban population; outstanding examples are London and Paris.

Until the post-war period, industry was developed and located in each country according to the needs of the particular national economy. Now, with the forming of economic groupings, firms are beginning to think in terms of producing for a larger 'home' market, and location of their plant in relation to the main concentration of consumers in West Europe could be an important consideration. A belt between London and the Ruhr has the largest number of people within a small area. Away from this 'core', the number of people within a given distance of any place is much smaller. In this respect, therefore, the future prospects of Scandinavia, Spain, peninsular Italy, and Greece do not seem bright. In view of the shifting emphasis from coal to oil, the coalfield areas in which production costs are high and which are somewhat marginal in relation to the 'core' area suggested (e.g. South Wales, north-east England) do not seem to have a hopeful future either.

In 1953, the value of mining and manufacturing production was distributed among the leading industrial countries of West Europe as follows (*United Nations Statistical Yearbook, 1960*, Table 11, and *1961*, Table 11).

Percentage of West European total

	Total	Mining	Manufacturing Heavy	Light
U.K.	31	36	33	27
W. Germany	22	26	24	18
France	12	11	12	12
Italy	9	4	9	10

Sweden, Belgium, the Netherlands, and Spain each had 3–4 per cent of the total.

Since 1953 the rate of expansion of industrial production has been faster in some countries than in others, as the following figures show for the period 1953–60. 1953=100.

West Europe

Over 160		140–60		Under 140	
Italy	180	Netherlands	157	Sweden	130
W. Germany	179	Finland	155	Belgium	129
Greece	172	Norway	144	U.K.	126
Austria	169	Denmark	142	Spain	125
France	161			Ireland	122

As a result the share of Britain has declined since the early 1950s, mainly on account of more rapid growth in the three other largest countries, West Germany, Italy, and France. How long this trend will continue and to what extent it has been due to growing cooperation among the E.E.C. countries will not be clear for some time.

In 1953 the industrial production of West Europe was only two-thirds as great as that of North America, although the population of West Europe was more than 50 per cent greater. Owing to slower expansion in North America than in West Europe the gap has now narrowed appreciably. On the other hand, of course, it widened in the decade before 1953, when the North American economy expanded enormously. With roughly the same population as Comecon, West Europe still has a larger heavy industrial production and is far ahead in light industry. In the long run, however, the prospects of expansion in West Europe do not seem so good as in North America or Comecon, on account of lack of oil and natural gas and of many key raw materials. The region will continue to depend heavily on other parts of the world, and its economy will therefore be more susceptible to fluctuations in world trade and to the economic policy of other countries.

The future of industry and prosperity in West Europe and the role of the region in world affairs both depend to a considerable extent on the success of economic union (see Chapter 10). To conclude this section, therefore, it seems appropriate to discuss briefly economic cooperation among countries since the war. Fig. 19d shows groupings in 1961.

Cooperation in West Europe has arisen partly at least out of the Second World War. O.E.E.C. (Organization of European Economic Cooperation – now O.E.C.D., Organization for Economic Cooperation and Development) was set up to coordinate the recovery of West Europe after the war, while N.A.T.O. (North Atlantic Treaty Organization) was founded in 1949 to coordinate defence. Each of these involves nearly all the countries of West Europe. Closer cooperation has sub-

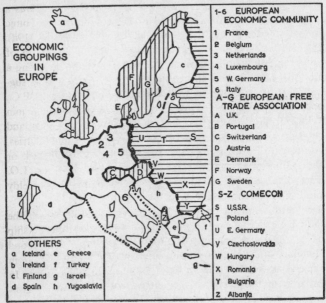

ECONOMIC GROUPINGS IN EUROPE

1–6 EUROPEAN ECONOMIC COMMUNITY
1 France
2 Belgium
3 Netherlands
4 Luxembourg
5 W. Germany
6 Italy

A–G EUROPEAN FREE TRADE ASSOCIATION
A U.K.
B Portugal
C Switzerland
D Austria
E Denmark
F Norway
G Sweden

S–Z COMECON
S U.S.S.R.
T Poland
U E. Germany
V Czechoslovakia
W Hungary
X Romania
Y Bulgaria
Z Albania

OTHERS
a Iceland
b Ireland
c Finland
d Spain
e Greece
f Turkey
g Israel
h Yugoslavia

19d. Economic groupings in Europe, 1961–2. By early 1964 Greece and Turkey were associated with E.E.C. while Albania's position in Comecon was in doubt.

sequently arisen among more limited groups of countries. Apart from Comecon (see Chapter 7), which is the U.S.S.R. and East Europe, there were in 1961 two main groups of countries and a number of countries in neither group (see Fig. 19d).

The European Economic Community (E.E.C.) or the 'Six' is commonly referred to as the Common Market. This, however, is only one of several aspects of cooperation, the two other main ones being the European Coal and Steel Community (E.C.S.C.) set up in 1952 and the European Atomic Energy Community (Euratom), formed in 1957. The Common Market agreement was signed and ratified by the Six in 1957 (Treaty of Rome) and there have since been large reductions in tariffs between the countries and moves to establish a uniform tariff round the bloc. It should be noted that Benelux, formed in 1947 by the three smaller members of the present Six, was a similar idea. Since the formation of E.E.C. another economic union has been formed between seven countries (see Fig. 19d), the European Free Trade Association, with the purpose of reducing tariffs among member countries, but not providing a uniform tariff around the bloc. Nor has there been any suggestion of political union in E.F.T.A., as there has in E.E.C., and consequently several countries unwilling or unable to join E.E.C. have joined E.F.T.A., notably Switzerland, Sweden, and Austria, while Finland is also interested. These four countries, through their own policy (the first two) or by treaty with or obligations to the U.S.S.R., have remained outside N.A.T.O. Fig. 19d shows that the E.E.C. is a more compact and wieldy piece of territory than E.F.T.A.

Several members of E.F.T.A., together with most of the non-aligned countries, have recently been seeking membership or associate membership of E.E.C. They include Britain and Denmark in E.F.T.A., Greece, Spain, and Ireland, also in West Europe, and Turkey and Israel in South-west Asia. In addition many former French colonial areas are to be associated. It is not surprising, therefore, that with this snowball effect the E.E.C. countries are reluctant to admit the British Commonwealth. The original Six would be swamped, the unit would lose its compactness and the whole complicated organization thrashed out between the members would have to be abandoned to make way for a still more elaborate set-up. Moreover, in addition to the advantage of having a larger market, comfortably achieved for present purposes with the population of around 170 m., each member of E.E.C. has 'personal' reasons for entering, and these might be upset by the entry of too many other countries. For example, West Germany is interested in gaining support and strength to achieve unification, France in drawing on capital from the other members for its associates in Africa, and Italy in reducing the strength of its Communist Party by diluting it in a larger economic and, presumably, eventually political, unit. The position of Britain in Europe is discussed in a special section in Chapter 10 (Section v).

II. NORTH AFRICA AND SOUTH-WEST ASIA

North Africa and South-west Asia together cover nearly 8 per cent of the world's land surface (divided almost exactly equally between them) but have only 5 per cent of the population, 150 m., of which nearly two-thirds are in South-west Asia. Physically the region has much in common throughout, since it is mainly sub-tropical and falls within the great Afro-Asian arid belt. Culturally, too, almost the whole area has considerable unity on account of the predominance of Moslems in the population, but the Arab cultural (language) area excludes more than a third of the population (notably Turkey, Iran, and Afghanistan). There are, too, intrusions of European settlers, particularly in Algeria, while in Israel the Israelis are largely of European origin recently, if of Asian origin initially. Further unity is given to the region on account of its economic life, which depends partly on agriculture in an extremely difficult setting of deserts, rugged mountain areas, and occasional irrigated valleys and reasonably humid coastlands, partly on oil, which brings in little but appreciable royalties to certain countries.

European influence in North Africa and South-west Asia has not generally been so widespread and profound as in America or even India, nor did it come suddenly over a short period as it did in the rest of Africa. North-west Africa succumbed to slow but thorough French conquest in the last century, but most of the rest of the area remained under the control of the Ottoman Empire, centred in Turkey, until the present century. After the downfall of this empire, which was completed in the First World War, Turkish interest diminished as the country embarked on its own programme of westernization, leaving the rest open to European penetration. British interests were strong, especially on account of the Suez canal (opened

1869) and the direct route to India. Germany, Russia, France, and Italy were also interested in the region before the First World War, and Italy controlled Libya from 1912. As a result of the First World War, however, Britain and France came to exert the strongest influence in the area in the inter-war period, acquired mandates (e.g. Syria), protectorates (along the Persian Gulf), and various other forms of loose political control; they also developed the oil reserves of the Persian Gulf area.

Since the Second World War, political independence has come to almost every part of North Africa and South-west Asia, and as well as Turkey, Iran, Afghanistan, Saudi Arabia, and the Yemen, which were already independent, nine new countries had emerged to have a seat in the United Nations by early 1962 (Iraq, Egypt, Syria, Lebanon, all 1945, Israel 1949, Libya 1955, Morocco 1956, Tunisia 1956, Cyprus 1960). Algerian independence in 1962 marks the end of European political influence apart from some small British spheres of influence in Arabia. In view of the small size of many of the countries it is understandable that unity, both political and economic, should have been considered among the Arab countries, and the unwanted presence of Israel has further stimulated resentment and cooperation among certain of these. Even so, the modest attempt to unite Egypt and Syria politically (the united Arab republic, 1958–1961) was a failure.[1] Some form of union has also been seriously considered by the so-called Maghreb peoples of North-west Africa, especially those of Morocco, Algeria, and Tunisia. Culturally they differ appreciably from the Arabs further east, while economically they are more closely associated with West Europe than with South-west Asia.

Table 13 shows some features of the different countries. In column I and Fig. 20a it can be seen that they vary greatly in area. Israel, Cyprus, and the Lebanon are each roughly the size of Yorkshire, while Algeria, Libya, Saudi Arabia, and Iran are each several times as large as France. Turkey has about 30 m. people, whereas Cyprus and several of the small

1. Egypt is still officially known as the United Arab Republic but is referred to throughout this book simply as Egypt.

TABLE 13

	I Area in thousands of sq. mls.	II Arable as percentage of total area	III Population in 1960	IV Moslems as percentage of total population	V Production of oil in millions of tons in 1960	VI Consumption of all sources of energy in kilograms of coal equivalent per inhabitant in 1959	VII Consumption of steel in kilograms per inhabitant in 1959	VIII Newspapers in circulation per thousand inhabitants per day in late 1950s
Morocco	172	18	11	95	n.	135	13	23
Algeria	920	3	11	90	9	235	41	29
Tunisia	48	30	4	90	n.	163	19	22
Egypt	386	3	26	90	n.	235	9	25
Libya	680	n.	1	95	n.	292	n.a.	7
Syria	71	19	5	80	n.	286	27	19
Saudi Arabia	620	n.	6	100	61	191	20	2
Yemen	75	n.	4	100	n.	n.a.	n.a.	n.a.
Iraq	172	5	7	95	47	336	38	10
Kuwait	6	n.	¼	100	82	2,160	n.a.	n.a.
Jordan	37	5	1½	95	n.	156	n.a.	20
Lebanon	4	29	1½	40	n.	567	116	100
Israel	8	19	2	5	x	1,122	145	210
Cyprus	4	43	½	20	n.	785	n.a.	112
Turkey	302	20	27	100	x	246	14	32
Iran	636	10	21	100	52	334	21	5
Afghanistan	251	8	13	100	n.	20	n.a.	1
U.K.	96	30	52		n.	4,594	332	573

n. = none or negligible   x = small production   n.a. = not available

NOTE: Bahrain, Kuwait, Qatar, Muscat and Oman, Trucial Oman, and Aden (P.) are not shown in the table.

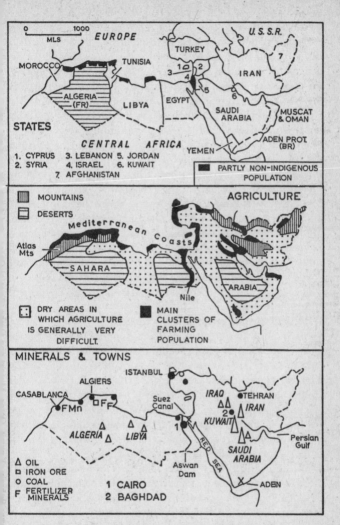

20a–c. North Africa and South-west Asia. a Political units. b Physical background and agriculture. c Minerals and towns.

political units along the Persian Gulf have fewer than 1 m. each. Population is of course distributed very unevenly in most of the countries. The black areas in Fig. 20b show where the density of population is highest. In North-west Africa most of the population is near the Mediterranean coast. In Egypt nearly the whole population is squeezed into the area irrigated by the Nile, only about one-thirtieth of the national area. In Arabia most people live around the margins. Although the density of population in the region is below the average for the world as a whole, in reality density is very high in the areas of any use for farming. At the same time urban growth is proceeding rapidly, even if the degree of urbanization is not yet high compared with West Europe. Several towns have over 1 m. inhabitants: Cairo (3 m.), Alexandria, Istanbul, and Tehran. Many smaller but fast-growing centres owe their existence and expansion to mining activities. Not only is there a shift from rural areas to urban centres but the total population of most countries is now growing very fast. In Iraq, Jordan, and Syria it exceeds 3 per cent per year; in Iran, Turkey, Egypt, and Algeria it is about 2·5 per cent.

Lack of figures make it impossible to say precisely what proportion of the population depends on agriculture but in most countries it is still probably more than half. Exceptions include Israel and the small oil units of the Persian Gulf. As already stressed, reasonably good agricultural land is very limited in extent, depending either on sufficient precipitation or on irrigation (see Fig. 20b). Away from these districts yields are low per unit of area, whether from the extensive cultivation of cereals or from the grazing of sheep, goats, and camels. Cattle raising and dairying are very restricted.

The agricultural life of each country is devoted almost entirely to supplying the national market with food. Only certain areas have a surplus product of any importance for export: wine from Algeria, cotton from Egypt, fruits from the eastern Mediterranean coastlands, and some wool. The prospects of increasing agricultural output appreciably are not great in the immediate future. Irrigation could be extended in some countries, especially Egypt and Iraq, but new works, such as the

Aswan dam in Egypt, require more capital than the area can provide. Higher yields might be achieved in many of the areas already under cultivation but outside Egypt there is virtually no manufacture of fertilizers. The introduction of mechanization in some areas, especially Turkey, has enabled greater use to be made of areas of limited rainfall but even this creates a problem by causing a drift of population to the towns. If the position of agriculture is generally unsatisfactory, the contribution of forestry and fishing to the economy of North Africa and South-west Asia is negligible.

At first sight mining and industry might seem to offer alternative employment and prospects of expansion. Apart from oil and natural gas, however, mineral deposits are not generally large and production is confined to a few areas; but exploration is far from complete. North-west Africa has been a source of certain minerals for the French for some decades: high-grade iron ore, phosphates, and manganese ore in particular. Egypt produces some phosphates and Turkey is a leading producer of chrome ore. Only Turkey (4 m. tons) produces more than 1 m. tons of coal per year and even this amount is slight. The hydro-electric potential is small apart from the spectacular possibilities offered by the Nile.

With few plant and animal raw materials for industry, and limited deposits of most minerals, oil would seem to offer the greatest hope for the region, but in reality at present very little is consumed in South-west Asia and North Africa, although in 1960 almost exactly one-quarter of the world total came from here. This is the result of a number of circumstances, among them the fact that the oil is extracted almost entirely by West European and U.S. companies for consumption elsewhere. But if the countries were able to use more of the oil there would be no great difficulty in their reaching some arrangement with the foreign companies. The root of the matter is the backwardness of the producing countries and the fact that three of the four outstanding producers also have small populations. To transform the economy overnight, and benefit from the oil is impossible, as has been indicated already in Venezuela.

In Table 13, column v shows the main producing countries.

In addition to the five shown Qatar (8 m. tons) and the Kuwait Neutral Zone (7 m. tons) are important producers. Altogether in 1960, 272 m. tons were produced out of a world total of 1,090 tons. In 1950 the same region produced only 88 m. out of the world total of 438 m. In spite of the supposedly unstable nature of South-west Asia its oil production has increased three times in the last decade. It has the largest reserves in the world and the lowest production costs. Each producing well gives several times as much oil as in Venezuela (this is partly due to the type of oil) and many times more than in the U.S.A. Algeria and Libya are newer areas of development. France has been concerned particularly with oil and gas in the Saharan region of Algeria, while enormous areas of Libya have now been granted to foreign companies as concessions for exploration. French Saharan oil production has risen from $3\frac{1}{2}$ m. tons in 1959 to nearly 19 m. in 1961.

Production throughout the region is mainly in the hands of a limited number of large companies. British and Netherlands interests account for the production of about half the oil in Kuwait, Iran, and Iraq. The U.S.A. is strongly represented in Saudi Arabia. Until a few years ago profits were usually shared on a fifty-fifty basis between the company and the host country. Recently Italy and Japan have offered terms more favourable to the producing countries and bargaining continues between other companies and the particular countries in which they operate. The continuing expansion (contrast Venezuela) suggests that it is still profitable to extract oil in South-west Asia. For what it is worth, the income receipts from U.S. direct investments in petroleum in the Middle East in 1958 were $U.S. 645 m. from a total investment of 1,218 m. From Venezuela receipts from investment in petroleum were only 375 m. from 2,300 m. invested.[1]

In spite of the great publicity given to the oil industry of South-west Asia and its enormous contribution to the economy of industrial West Europe, the impact on the producing countries has not been very great. Firstly, the industry only employs a small percentage of the total labour force in Iran, Iraq, and

1. *Statistical Abstract of the United States, 1960*, p. 869.

176

Saudi Arabia; Kuwait is a different matter. Only a limited part of the population therefore actually benefits from the relatively high wages and various services provided. Secondly, the policy since the war has mainly been for the oil to be shipped crude from the producing areas along the Persian Gulf. Refining capacity is only about one-third that of production and the employment possibility of refining has therefore been reduced. Thirdly, the royalties from the companies have not always been invested usefully.

From the point of view of the companies, money is invested to produce oil as cheaply as possible. Roads, towns, and various amenities are provided by them but obviously these are built primarily to serve the oilfields, and whether or not they will have any other future use can hardly be expected to concern the companies. As in all branches of mining, there invariably remains the question of finding employment for the workers if and when reserves are exhausted. At present this does not preoccupy the oil countries, for the industry is still expanding. A further question which is also of little concern to the oil companies, is the use made of the oil royalties. These may find their way into the pockets of a limited number of individuals or they may be spent on grandiose public buildings. They could more usefully be spent on works of construction to create alternative employment and a source of income for the government once the oil royalties begin to diminish or, like Venezuela, the countries might themselves invest in oil production.

In spite of the very large production of oil in South-west Asia and the growing producton in North Africa, consumption of energy per inhabitant is low in every country (Table 13, column VI) once allowance has been made for energy consumed directly in the production, transportation, and refining of oil. It is not surprising to find, therefore, that modern manufacturing industry is not developed to any great extent in the region. Only Turkey has a small iron and steel works ($\frac{1}{4}$ m. tons per year), but a larger one is planned for Algeria. The engineering industry hardly exists anywhere. Cement is produced in moderate quantities in several countries, fertilizers

177

in small amounts, while the manufacture of textiles has been developed in Egypt and Turkey. Of the larger countries, Algeria, Egypt, and Turkey have made most progress in industrialization, while Israel and the Lebanon also have some capacity and experience. In Arabia, Iran, and Afghanistan, apart from the oil concerns, modern industry is virtually non-existent.

From what has been said, therefore, it can be seen that although the whole of North Africa and South-west Asia is underdeveloped there are considerable differences in level of development between member countries. Those with oil obviously have the great advantage of the royalties. On the other hand those with European settlers have superior organization. With neither of these advantages, however, Turkey and Egypt have advanced above the general level of Asian and African countries. In Table 13, column VIII, the number of newspapers in circulation per 1,000 people gives a rough idea of the level of cultural as well as economic development. Israel, the Lebanon, and Cyprus are well ahead of any others and those countries could certainly contribute technicians and skilled workers to South-west Asia as a whole. North-west Africa, Turkey, and Egypt are nearer the average for the region, while Arabia, Iran, and Afghanistan are among the poorest areas in the world.

As modern economic units, most of the countries of North Africa and South-west Asia are too small in total national income on account of their limited population *and* low *per caput* national income. Some form of economic (and political) union seems desirable but the region lacks a large concentration of population on which an economic union could be based. Moreover, trade between the member countries is at present slight (as in Latin America); and as the same sort of products come from most countries it would be absurd to encourage exchange of products in the future. Moreover, even if union were an economic advantage, and national and cultural prejudices allowed it, communications are at present so poor that only shipping services could be developed in the near future to cater for increased inter-regional trade. The Suez Canal, of course, would be a vital link.

The way things are going, it seems that the prospects of economic union are slight. Turkey and Israel are seeking association with the European Common Market while Turkey is a key N.A.T.O. country as well. Algeria may well prefer to keep strong economic links with France. Egypt is as interested in Africa as in South-west Asia, while the U.S.S.R. is interested in Afghanistan, which is located reasonably near the growing industrial areas of Soviet Central Asia. The Persian Gulf area is economically heavily dependent on West Europe and North America. At present, therefore, centrifugal forces seem very strong and it does not seem likely that a single strong force in world affairs will emerge from any combination of existing political units.

III. SOUTH ASIA

In this book South Asia is taken to be the Indian sub-continent, an area only about half the size of Europe but with more inhabitants than North and Latin America together. For more than 150 years the region was under British control, but this was superimposed on a great variety of languages, religions, and customs. Even so, as a result of British influence in unifying the area there emerged only four sovereign states when independence was achieved after the Second World War: India, Pakistan, Ceylon, and Burma (included in the region of South-east Asia). Nepal and Bhutan on the south side of the Himalayas remain independent units, while the fate of Kashmir, in the extreme north, is undecided.

South Asia occupies little more than 3 per cent of the world's land area but has nearly 20 per cent of the world's population. It has land frontiers with South-west Asia, China, and South-east Asia, but is almost completely cut off from these neighbouring regions by high mountain ranges, plateaux, and deserts, and to this day has no rail connexions with them and only long and difficult roads which, for the most part, can be used only by pack animals. Indeed, the region is more easily reached by sea than by land, and between about 1500 and the middle of the eighteenth century Portugal, Holland, England,

and France all at various times established trading stations and forts in coastal areas.

Table 14 provides figures concerning India, Pakistan, and Ceylon (for Nepal and Bhutan almost no figures are available) as well as South-east and East Asia, which are dealt with in the next two sections of this chapter. In South Asia, India is the largest country both in area and in population. Within each country the density varies greatly from one part to another. The Thar Desert and the high mountain areas are almost uninhabited, while the Ganges valley has a very high density of rural population over a large area. Although there are several large urban areas in India (Calcutta and Bombay each have more than 5 m. inhabitants, and Madras, Delhi, and Hyderabad 1–2 m.), only 20 per cent of the total population is classified as urban. The remaining 80 per cent is distributed over the surface of India in more than 550,000 villages (about 40 times as many as there are in Britain). The other countries of South Asia also have only a small proportion of urban dwellers.

South Asia is characterized by its predominantly agricultural economy, high density of population in farming areas, and generally very low level of economic development. Agriculture employs about 70 per cent of the population in the region. Most rural communities are chiefly concerned with growing their basic needs of food, but in some areas there is specialization in certain crops. This dates from the British period when India was an important source of plant raw materials and certain foodstuffs and beverages. Now the cotton and sugar are consumed within the region but tea and jute continue to be exported. Rice is the leading cereal in most of India and in East Pakistan but wheat is more widely grown in the northwest and in West Pakistan. In the Indus valley irrigation is essential for agriculture but elsewhere land is irrigated by rivers or wells to supplement rainfall, which is irregular in occurrence. Only in the highest parts of the Himalayas are conditions too cold for agriculture. About half of South Asia lies within the tropics, and the high ranges to the north help to prevent the cold conditions of the interior of Asia from being felt even in the more northerly lowland areas. Many areas are rugged and too difficult for cultivation. In spite of the drawbacks of aridity, unreliable rainfall, and steepness of slope, about 40 per cent of the total area of India is under crops, 20–25 per cent in Pakistan and Ceylon.

Much of the farmland of South Asia has been cultivated for centuries and even millennia, though, of course, by simple means. It is therefore to be expected that much of the best land is now settled and little remains to be brought under cultivation. In the arid parts of the region, as also in neighbouring South-west Asia, there are still opportunities for irrigating new lands. In general, however, farm production will have to be raised by obtaining higher yields in existing areas of cultivation, and there are various reasons why it is difficult to make more efficient use of the land. There is the problem of obtaining mineral fertilizers. The *per caput* production and consumption of these is at present insignificant in most parts of the region. The religious attitude to livestock in many areas makes it difficult to develop an efficient kind of mixed farming making the maximum use of available land and animals. There are nearly half as many cattle and buffaloes as humans, but their function is merely to serve as draught animals. Then there are questions of organization and land tenure. Finally, it is difficult for different regions to specialize in the crops (or livestock) they are best suited to produce (as happens in the U.S.A.) because the transport system would be unable to provide adequate facilities for the necessary inter-regional movement of goods.

In India attention has been given to improving agriculture in the 1950s, with widespread programmes aimed at educating the peasantry in new techniques. Model settlements were organized and cooperation widely encouraged. In the early 1950s appreciable progress was made. On account of greater emphasis on industrial growth in the later 1950s (roughly the Second Five Year Plan, 1956–60) progress has recently not been so favourable. India has had to import more and more grain and has been saved from famine by an assured supply from the U.S.A. In Pakistan there is a sharp contrast between East and West. In East Pakistan conditions are worse than in most parts of India, whereas in West Pakistan the extension of irrigated

TABLE 14

	I Area in thousands of sq. mls.	II Arable land as percentage of total	III Population in millions in 1960	IV Moslems as percentage of total population	V Consumption of all sources of energy in kilograms of coal equivalent per inhabitant in 1959	VI Consumption of steel in kilograms per inhabitant in 1959	VII Newspapers in circulation per thousand inhabitants per day in late 1950s
India*	1,265	40	420	5	145	9	9
Pakistan	365	22	90	85	55	3	9
Ceylon	25	23	10	5	100	7	20
Burma	262	13	21	4	50	n.a.	8
Thailand	198	12	22	3	65	10	4
S. Vietnam	66	n.a.	14	n.	55	n.a.	28
Malaya	50	16	7	50	240	33	21
Indonesia	575	7	91	90	135	3	11
Philippines	115	22	25	5	150	15	19
Formosa	14	25	10	n.	500	20	43
S. Korea	38	21	24	n.	215	n.a.	57
Japan	143	14	93	n.	965	163	398
U.K. (for comparison)	94	30	52		4,594	332	573

n. = none or negligible   n.a. = not available

Other units (population in millions): Nepal (9), Bhutan (1), Cambodia (5) Laos (2), Singapore (1½), Br. Borneo (1½), Hong Kong (3), Macau (¼) Portuguese Timor (½), Ryuku Islands (1).

* For convenience includes Kashmir-Jammu, the status of which is still disputed.

land offers possibilities for greater production. Ceylon is one of the most favoured parts of South Asia.

With regard to mineral production, South Asia is fortunate in having both coal and iron ore deposits (in India), but neither of these are in very large reserves. Until recently oil and natural gas were not produced, but as a result of exploration reserves have been found both in India and in Pakistan. Production is still small.

The region is poorly provided with most other minerals, but India accounts for about one-sixth of the world's production of manganese ore, most of which it exports. Coal production in India is about 50 m. tons per annum. This comes to about one-tenth of a ton per inhabitant, compared with more than 4 tons per inhabitant in the U.K. About 8 m. tons of iron ore are produced each year.

Coal has formed the basis for heavy industry only in one main area of India, a district some 150 miles to the west of Calcutta. Elsewhere in South Asia the amount of power consumed in manufacturing is very small and modern industrial development is largely confined to a few large towns, including Calcutta, Bombay, and Hyderabad. Further modern industrial expansion based on hydro-electric power may be expected in parts of South Asia, but the importance of the traditional domestic industries in rural communities should not be underestimated and at least some of the future industrial expansion in the region may be expected in these.

The first modern industry in South Asia grew up from the processing of raw materials for export. The next stage was the manufacture of certain agricultural raw materials, mainly jute and cotton, not surprisingly in Calcutta (jute), Bombay, Ahmadabad, and Karachi (Pakistan), ports already handling these commodities. The Bombay and Calcutta areas are to this day the main concentrations of industrial population, and in addition to textile manufacturing have much of India's engineering and chemical industries. With the new emphasis on iron and steel, and engineering, a new industrial region is emerging. This lies west of Calcutta around Jamshedpur, where there was a large iron and steel works even before the war. Fig. 21c shows the approximate location of India's large new integrated works and the country mainly concerned in each case with the construction. Bokaro is still only projected. Assets of this area include coking coal, iron ore, manganese, and hydro-electric power.

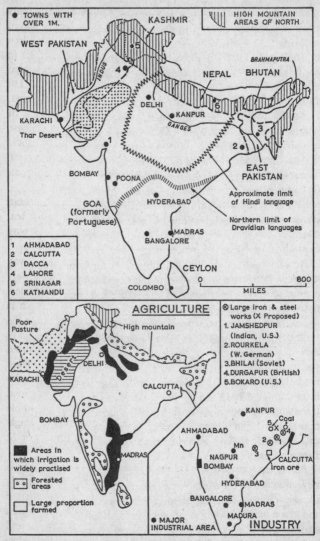

21a–c. South Asia. a General map and political divisions. b Physical background and agriculture. c Industry.

In spite of progress made in industrialization in India, only a few million persons, or 2–3 per cent of the total employed population, are engaged in large or moderate-sized modern factories and, in comparison with China, progress in India in the 1950s has not been very impressive. *Per caput* consumption of energy was roughly equal in India and China in 1952: 110 kilograms. In 1959 it was only 145 in India but 510 in China. Likewise in 1952 both countries produced about 2 m. tons of steel but in 1959 the Indian figure was only 3 m., the Chinese figure 20 m. The period of comparison is of course too short to judge long-term trends and it should also be appreciated that China is putting more emphasis than India on heavy industry. Even so the contrast is striking, to say the least.

Modern industrial development is slight both in Pakistan and in Ceylon and is concerned largely with processing (tea, jute) or light manufacturing (textiles). West Pakistan is hoping for industrial expansion based on its natural gas.

Although the countries of South Asia inherited a railway system from the British period, the region is comparatively poorly provided with a network of communications, considering its size and population. The main defect of the system is the almost complete absence of motor roads to supplement the railway network. Emphasis is still on improving the railways rather than on providing roads, for the high price of imported motor vehicles and motor fuel make it impossible to develop road transport at a time when so many other projects require large capital outlays. Some idea of the insignificant role of road transport in South Asia is given by the fact that the whole region has fewer motor vehicles in circulation than a single metropolitan area in the U.S.A. the size of Baltimore or St Louis.

Per caput foreign trade is low in India, but overseas trade is nevertheless vital to economic progress. Exports consist mainly of agricultural raw materials, but no less than one-quarter of the value of India's exports is now made up of jute and cotton manufactures. The largest group of imports is metals and machinery, including the machinery needed to equip the industrial establishments of the region; but in recent years oil and wheat have been imported in large quantities. Trade with the U.S.A. has grown impressively in the late 1950s and is now roughly equal to that with the U.K. U.S. aid is also increasing, but during the whole period 1945–59 it amounted only to about $U.S. 650 m., or about 10 shillings per inhabitant of India. Pakistan's foreign trade is even more dependent than India's on the export of raw cotton and raw jute, while Ceylon exports mainly tea and rubber.

In conclusion a few of the main problems of the countries of South Asia may be noted. India has one great advantage : it is compact territorially and not large and yet has a very large population and in sheer numbers is therefore a large national market, though the total national income is less than that of Britain or France. But the territorial compactness is not matched by cultural uniformity. The religious problem was to some extent overcome by the partition into India and Pakistan, but India has fourteen major languages, four of which belong to a completely different language family from the others, Dravidian (see Fig. 21a). Hindi, spoken widely in north central India (see Fig. 21a), is to be the official language of the whole of the Indian Union but at present English is the official language since it is understood throughout India at least by persons involved in administration and organization. Not only does the enormous problem of illiteracy have to be overcome; over half the population will have to take up Hindi. The states of India are based largely on languages and at present there is considerable regional consciousness within these. Representatives of the Dravidian language states have even demanded secession of this southern group from the rest of the Union on the grounds of different cultural background and of neglect of their economic interests by the central government.

The main preoccupation of Pakistan is the fact that it is divided into two parts separated by about 1,000 miles of Indian territory. The two parts are very different in every way except that they are both predominantly Moslem. West Pakistan resembles South-west Asia in many respects, East Pakistan is more like South-east Asia. In Ceylon serious trouble has arisen in the 1950s through the presence of nearly 1 m. Tamil-speaking Indians, but apart from this drawback Ceylon should be able to progress in view of its position and promising conditions for agriculture. Nepal and Bhutan lie almost entirely in the mountainous north and are isolated from India by difficult approaches. The Chinese are exploiting this fact by building roads south from Tibet. The fate of Kashmir (and Jammu), with a population of about 5 m., has not yet been decided; at present it is occupied partly by India, partly by Pakistan. Its population is predominantly Moslem and for this reason should belong to Pakistan, but its rulers have been Hindu. Pakistan irrigation interests are involved in the region.

IV. SOUTH-EAST ASIA

South-east Asia is a region of peninsulas, islands, and seas. Like West Europe and South-west Asia, no part of it is more than a few hundred miles from the nearest coast. In the generally small size of its political units, lack of a large concentration of population to form a starting point for economic integration, and very low level of development in most places, it resembles South-west Asia. Instead of being arid, however, it is largely covered with dense forest except where this has been cleared for cultivation, while it produces very little oil and has twice as many people. Movement across islands and from one mainland river basin to another is made difficult by the presence of high mountain ranges.

South-east Asia is on the sea route between South and East Asia and has been influenced by these regions for thousands of years, and by European powers for several hundred. Buddhism spread into parts of the region by land from the north, while the Moslem religion reached it by sea from South-west Asia. The first European navigators and traders arrived early in the sixteenth century, attracted by the region's tropical products, which could not be cultivated in temperate Europe.

In the sixteenth century Spain annexed the Philippines, and Portugal established footholds in various other islands, but during the following century the Dutch largely replaced the Portuguese in the East Indies and built up an important colony which subsequently became known as the Dutch East Indies and is now Indonesia. Only during the nineteenth century did European powers begin to annex large territories on the mainland of South-east Asia. The British took the Malay Peninsula and Burma as well as the northern part of Borneo, where Dutch control had not been established. Towards the end of the century France moved into Indo-China, while in 1898 the U.S.A. acquired the Philippines, which had by then been a Spanish colony for some four centuries. In the whole of South-east Asia, therefore, only Siam (now Thailand) and Formosa remained free from European domination. The Japanese invasion of South-east Asia in 1941–2 took the whole region out of European or U.S. control, and post-war attempts by France and the Netherlands to re-establish themselves met with little success. The U.S.A., on the other hand, granted independence to the Philippines without attempting to re-annex it. In 1957 Malaya was given its independence, and in 1963 Singapore and the British territories in Borneo were added to it to form Malaysia. In 1963 the Netherlands ceded West New Guinea to Indonesia. Hong Kong and Portuguese Macau and Timor are the only remaining European colonies in the area.

Table 14 (p. 182) provides some basic figures regarding the more important countries of South-east Asia. Indonesia has almost half of the total population of the region, but its inhabitants are very unevenly distributed among its many islands, Java alone having nearly two-thirds of the Indonesian total. Throughout South-east Asia the high density of population in the lowlands and on terraced hill slopes suitable for cultivation contrasts with the very low density in the rugged areas and in some lowland forest areas that have so far hardly been settled.

Agriculture is the principal activity of South-east Asia, and everywhere the population is predominantly rural. Specialized commercial farming has acquired great importance in certain areas, especially in parts of Malaya and Java. Over most of the region, however, subsistence agriculture is practised, and each community provides most of its own food and other requirements. Rice is the principal food crop of the region, but manioc is an important food in Indonesia and bananas are widely cultivated. Of the specialized crops produced mainly for export to industrial countries outside South-east Asia, natural rubber (Indonesia, Malaya, and Thailand account for about 90 per cent of the world's total) and copra (about 90 per cent of the world's total comes from the Philippines and Indonesia) are the most important, although it was the spices of the region that first attracted European traders.

Unlike India, China, and Japan, South-east Asia still has large areas into which cultivation could be extended. The relatively small island of Java (about the size of England) has almost two-thirds of the population of Indonesia, yet accounts for less than one-tenth of its total area. Conditions on the larger neighbouring islands of Sumatra and Borneo do not differ greatly from those in Java, yet while Java has about 60 m. inhabitants, they only have 15 m. and 7 m. respectively, yet are much larger. In other countries of South-east Asia there also appear to be opportunities for extending the farming area. In addition, of course, yields could be greatly increased throughout the region, as in many other predominantly rural parts of the world.

Although a large part of South-east Asia is forested, timber is not widely exploited for export or consumption in industry. Fishing is not run on efficient lines, but even so, in some districts this activity provides one of the main sources of protein food.

South-east Asia has a number of important mineral deposits, the exploitation of which has only been undertaken by European colonial powers. All but a small part of the output is exported. The region has no important coalfields. Oil, on the other hand, is produced in two main areas, Indonesia (Sumatra) 20 m. tons in 1960, and British Borneo 6 m. tons. Burma is a small producer. There may be oil deposits in other parts of the region, but in the dense forest and the rugged mountain areas the search for oil is more difficult and costly than in South-west Asia and other parts of the world where there is little or no cover of vegetation. Of the metallic minerals, tin is by far the most important in the region, and Malaya (one-third) and Indonesia (one-sixth) together account for about half of the world's output. Other minerals produced in South-east Asia include iron ore in the Philippines and Malaya, chrome in the Philippines, and bauxite in Indonesia. Japan is a large importer of these items.

Apart from essential processing industries connected with the production of commercial crops such as rubber and of minerals such as tin, there are almost no modern industries at all in South-east Asia. Lack of coal has no doubt contributed to retard the development of manufacturing in the region. Equally serious obstacles have been the almost complete lack of facilities for advanced education, the absence of a tradition of manufacturing (except of village crafts), and the reluctance of former colonial powers to introduce industries into areas regarded by them as markets for their own home industries. In the whole of South-east Asia, with more than 200 m. inhabitants, no steel is produced except in small quantities in Formosa, the engineering industry is non-existent, almost no cement or fertilizers are produced, and except in Hong Kong, Formosa, and some towns in Java even light industry is almost unknown. The large urban areas owe their growth to the expansion of administrative and commercial functions rather than industries.

The whole region, with the exception of Java and a few other small areas, is very poorly provided with railways and is almost without good motor roads. The movement of goods and passengers between the various islands and peninsulas and between South-east Asia and other parts of the world is handled almost entirely by shipping services.

Foreign trade is largely limited to the export of a few agricultural and mineral raw materials (rubber, tin, and copra being the main items) and of rice (in quantities which vary greatly from year to year, depending on the surplus available). Most of the imports are manufactured goods. Except in Malaya, Hong Kong, and Formosa, *per caput* value of foreign trade is everywhere very low.

Living standards in South-east Asia are among the lowest in the world. The main areas of agricultural settlement are already densely populated and many organizational problems confront governments wishing to resettle people in new areas. With almost no industries, even the few large and rapidly growing urban centres are a burden, depending as they do on a surplus of food from already overpopulated rural areas. Greater Djakarta (Indonesia) is estimated to have more than 3 m. inhabitants, and Manila, Saigon, Bangkok, and Singapore each 1–2 m. The territory of Hong Kong grows virtually no food but holds 3 m. people.

The value of exports is relatively small, and the amount of equipment that can be imported for agricultural and industrial projects is consequently not large. U.S. foreign aid has been of great importance to the economy of the Philippines and Formosa, while large British investments in Malaya and Hong Kong have transformed these two areas, though in different ways, just as the Dutch transformed Java. Elsewhere investment and aid have only been slight.

Of the countries of South-east Asia, only Indonesia looks like a major world power. It is fifth in the world in population (over 90 m.), is large territorially, and extends over a vast archipelago in what since the war has proved to be a very explosive area in world affairs. Its size and population are not however matched by economic strength and its only really large non-agricultural enterprise, the oil industry, employing about 50,000, is in the hands of foreign companies. Moreover there has been considerable difficulty in maintaining cohesion among the islands, of which about 2,000 are inhabited. No doubt the constant propaganda against the Netherlands has been maintained to keep attention from internal problems; and the claim to West New Guinea, with which Indonesia will not be in a position to do anything useful at present now it is to have the area, is no doubt a continuation of the policy which has led in the past few years to the expulsion of almost all the Dutch, and the Chinese settlers as well. Up to a point the Philippines are a smaller version of Indonesia but relations with the former colonizing power, the U.S.A., are better than those between Indonesia and the Netherlands.

On the mainland, Burma and Thailand have very much in common. Pressure on land is not so serious as in India or

China and there has been little incentive to industrialize. With growing population the traditional rice surplus of these countries is diminishing and they have little else to offer for export. Former French Indo-China has been less fortunate since the war, on account of the struggle between Communists and non-Communists in Vietnam. It is now divided into four political units of which Laos and Cambodia are absurdly small and depressingly backward. Vietnam was partitioned in 1954 when open warfare ended, but a struggle continues, affecting particularly Laos and S. Vietnam.

Smaller but more advanced economically than the rest of South-east Asia are Malaya (independent) with Singapore (a British colony), Hong Kong and Macau, and Formosa. Malaya has been developed by Britain to grow rubber and to produce tin, and contrasts with the British possessions on Borneo, which, apart from the oil they produce, have not been developed far. Hong Kong and Macau are minute territorially and have no resources, but have exploited their coastal position first as trading centres and more recently for manufacturing. There is a move to unite Malaya, Singapore, and the British possessions in Borneo to form a new political unit, Malaysia.

Formosa's current importance in world affairs is far greater than its size, population, or production merit. The island is only about twice the size of Wales, though it has nearly 10 m. inhabitants. About half of the population is rural, but some industries have been established with U.S. aid. The island has been settled by Chinese during the last three centuries, the original inhabitants having been relegated by these to the mountainous parts. It was occupied by Japan in 1895. It is claimed by Communist China but held by Chinese nationalist forces backed by the U.S.A., and remains one of the major problem areas in world affairs today, as well as being a U.S. showpiece for China and South-east Asia.

In summary, a number of problems of South-east Asia may be suggested. One is peculiar to this part of Asia: the ease with which insurgents of one kind or another can operate within the forested environment without coming under the control of a central authority. Uprisings have lasted long in

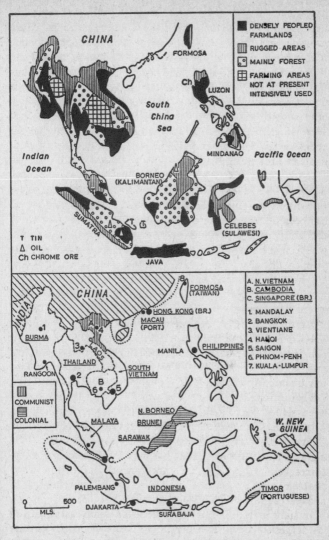

22a–b. South-east Asia. a Physical background and agriculture. b Political divisions. Malaya, Singapore and British Borneo territories now make up Malaysia.

Burma, the Philippines, Malaya, Indonesia, and of course former French Indo-China. Another problem is the extremely low level of cultural and economic development in all but a few areas, and the almost complete absence of modern industry. This situation is perpetuated and aggravated by the way in which population is dispersed among a large number of islands and of lowlands on the mainland (see Fig. 22a, the areas in black). To weld these together into one economic unit an efficient system of coastal shipping services would be essential, but, as in South-west Asia, the countries of South-east Asia have little to exchange with one another anyway, since their products are either similar or else of no use within the region (tin, rubber). Trade among countries is slight and the usefulness of economic union without the participation of an industrial country (Japan seems the most likely) is very limited. The same centrifugal forces are at work as in South-west Asia. The future of North Vietnam, Hong Kong, and Formosa seems ultimately to be absorption by China. Indonesia and the Philippines trade extensively with Japan and Australia, while Malaya still has strong economic links with West Europe and the U.S.A. The presence of considerable numbers of Chinese settlers in some areas adds strength to the argument that the whole area may come under Chinese influence (but their recent expulsion from Indonesia was a setback), and the U.S.A., U.S.S.R., India, and Australia all seem concerned that this should not happen. The Western powers have only had limited success in organizing the region militarily against Communism, the S.E.A.T.O. countries (Thailand and the Philippines) only having one-quarter of the total population.

V. JAPAN AND SOUTH KOREA

North of the area described in the last section Japan, South Korea, and the Ryuku Islands (under U.S. military control) are the only places remaining free from Communist control. They differ from South-east Asia in lying outside the tropics, having a different historical background and a more advanced level of economic development (see Table 14, p. 182). To the

U.S.A. they are of enormous importance as military footholds in East Asia against Communism and, like Formosa and the Philippines, have received large quantities of military and economic aid.

After faltering during the decade following the war and depending heavily on the U.S.A. for aid, Japan has not only recovered from the loss of its empire and the damage at home but has made remarkable advances in the last few years in the expansion of heavy industry. In the early 1930s its overseas territories had as many inhabitants as Japan itself and were several times as large. Manchuria was an important source of coal, iron, and steel, and, like Korea and Formosa, also supplied Japan with food. As a result of the Second World War, Japan lost not only its conquests in China, made in the late 1930s, and its vast new empire in South-east Asia won during the war, but also its older possessions. Post-war Japan differs little in area from the Japan which started to industrialize itself on modern European and U.S. lines in the 1870s. On the other hand it now has about three times as many inhabitants as it had then.

There are now about 95 m. people, living in an area about two-thirds of the size of France. What makes matters more difficult is the fact that only about one-sixth of Japan's surface is cultivated and, indeed, cultivable, for most of the country is mountainous and the land too steep to farm or without any soil cover at all. In other words, the home-produced part of Japan's food supply comes from an area about half the size of England. The arable land in Japan, scattered throughout the country in numerous small coastal lowlands and interior valleys, is intensively cultivated. Rice, the cereal with the highest yield per unit of area, occupies more than half of the area. To achieve the highest possible yields, large quantities of chemical fertilizer are used. As a result of the need to utilize so much of the farmland for rice, there is little room for pastures or for crops producing raw materials for industry. The fact that much of the non-agricultural surface of Japan is forest-covered is some compensation. The impossibility of producing more than small quantities of protein foods from livestock has forced the

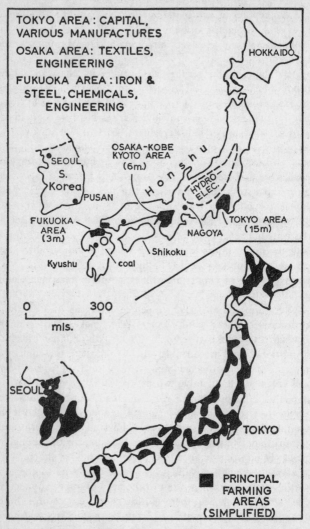

23a–b. Japan and South Korea. a (*above*) Towns and industry.
b (*below*) Principal farming areas.

196

Japanese to obtain much of their protein from the sea. The fishing industry is efficiently run and its activities extend not only into the seas between Japan and mainland Asia, one of the best fishing areas in the world, but also far out into the Pacific. The Soviet Union has deprived Japan of some of its best fishing grounds, however, by making the Okhotsk Sea into territorial waters, and the Japanese catch of 6 m. tons is no larger than in the 1930s, although the country is still the leading fishing nation in the world.

Japan has important, though not large, deposits of several minerals. It produces some 50 m. tons of coal per annum (about half a ton *per caput* compared with more than 4 *per caput* in the U.K.). On the other hand, its oil deposits and production are insignificant. In addition to coal, Japan produces iron ore, manganese, copper, zinc, and sulphur.

Since the 1870s Japan has grown into an industrial nation of considerable importance. Coal and hydro-electric power form the basis of fuel and energy supplies, but the country has few home-produced raw materials apart from its timber and the above-mentioned minerals. *Per caput* consumption of energy is much lower in Japan than in the leading industrial countries of the world and the percentage of the total employed population engaged in manufacturing is much smaller than in the U.K. or Germany. Agriculture still employs about three times as many people as industry – an interesting contrast with Australia, where industry employs twice as many as agriculture.

At first Japanese industry was based largely on the manufacture of textiles and other light industrial products. Even in the 1930s the iron and steel industry was modest compared with that in the U.S.A., U.S.S.R., Germany, or Britain, and engineering was directed towards preparing for the war. Since the war the steel industry has made a remarkable recovery, output rising from $1\frac{1}{2}$ m. tons in 1948 to $12\frac{1}{2}$ m. in 1958 and no less than 28 m. in 1961. Progress in the chemicals industry and in some branches of engineering has been equally astounding. Metal goods, ships, and iron and steel have passed the traditional cotton, silk, and rayon textiles in value in the exports of the country, almost all of which, of course, are processed or manufactured goods. Japan leads the world in shipbuilding.

Economic progress in Japan, as in West Europe, depends on increased trade and on finding, for exported manufactured goods, markets able to supply raw materials, fuel, and food in return. Oil and oil products, raw cotton and wool, and iron ore are among the major items of import, while wheat, rice, and sugar have to be obtained abroad to supplement home-grown food. So far Japan has made little use of oil in its economy (contrast West Europe) and it is fortunate in having hydro-electric energy in addition to home-produced coal; these two sources nearly satisfy all the energy requirements.

Although the economy of Japan resembles fairly closely that of Britain, West Germany, and Italy, the standard of living is much lower, and conditions for most of the population much more austere than in the affluent countries of West Europe. Increasing population has prevented the benefits of industrialization from making such a great impact as in West Europe. Now, however, the birthrate is falling sharply and the rate of increase slowing down in a spectacular fashion. With its already large industrial capacity and its technically advanced and able population, the future prospects are brighter than they seemed a decade ago, especially now that Japan has almost managed to balance its trade with the U.S.A. But greatly increased trade is essential. South-east Asia seems the most convenient source of many of Japan's requirements, and trade with Formosa, the Philippines, and Thailand is appreciable. It is much greater however with the U.S.A., Canada, and Australia. In addition, there are growing links with Latin America and India. Communist China, however, obviously offers by far the greatest potential market, though at present trade between the two countries is negligible.

Korea, like Germany and Vietnam, is one of the countries unfortunate enough to remain divided as a result of the Second World War and subsequent conflicts. The Communist-controlled northern half, with about 10 m. inhabitants, or one-third of the total population, has most of Korea's mineral and forest reserves and some hydro-electric power stations. South

Korea, with about 20 m. inhabitants, depends almost entirely on agriculture, although there, as in North Korea, much of the land is too rugged for cultivation. Living standards are lower in South Korea than in Japan and the prospects for industrial expansion limited.

Chapter 7

THE COMMUNIST STATES

I. THE SOVIET UNION

THE U.S.S.R. is the oldest, most extensive, and, at present, economically the most powerful member of the Communist bloc or, as it is called in Soviet publications, the *socialist camp* – the member states of which are run by Communist Parties.

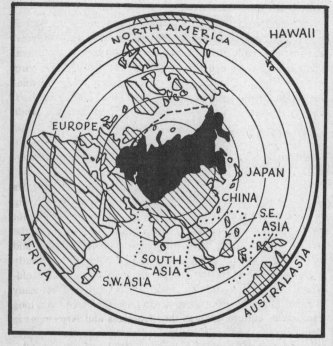

24. The hemisphere of the U.S.S.R. Projections: oblique zenithal equidistant. Centre of projection: Novosibirsk, Western Siberia. The circles are at thousand-mile intervals.

The Soviet Union

It is the largest single sovereign state in the world in area, covering nearly one-sixth of the land surface, but its population of 220 m. (1962) is only one-fourteenth of the world's total. The U.S.S.R. occupies the eastern half of Europe and the northern two-fifths of Asia.

Although both physical and cultural conditions vary greatly from one part of this vast country to another, a high degree of political and economic unity is provided by the presence in power of the Soviet Communist Party since 1917. In the inter-war years it was the only 'Communist' country, and an important aim of the regime was to make it as self-sufficient as possible, an easier task in such a large unit than in a small one.

The population of the U.S.S.R., 209 m. in the 1959 census, is increasing by between $3\frac{1}{2}$ and 4 m. per year. In 1961 the total was shared equally among urban and rural types of settlement, whereas fifty years ago only one-sixth was urban. Some parts (e.g. the Western Ukraine) are still deeply rural, while the mining and industrial areas (e.g. Ural region) are highly urbanized. There are many towns with around 1 m. inhabitants, while Greater Moscow has 7 m. and Leningrad 3 m. As a result of war losses, which affected men more than women, there are nearly five women to every three men among people over about 35 years of age in 1962.

About four-fifths of the population of the U.S.S.R. consists of Europeans and of peoples of European descent now living in the Asiatic part. Some two-thirds of the Europeans (or not much more than one-half of the total population of the U.S.S.R.) are actually Russians; the rest are Ukrainians and Belorussians (speaking languages that do not differ greatly from Russian) and smaller groups, such as Latvians and Moldavians. The Asian citizens of the U.S.S.R. belong to many different linguistic groups and range from peoples with a long tradition of culture, such as the Georgians and Armenians in Transcaucasia and the Uzbeks in Central Asia, to primitive tribes of pastoral nomads such as the Nentsy and Chukchi in Siberia. Strictly speaking, therefore, it is as inaccurate to refer to the U.S.S.R. and to Soviet citizens as Russia and Russians, as it is to call the British Commonwealth England and all its members English.

The U.S.S.R. is divided into fifteen Soviet Socialist Republics. The largest and most populous, the Russian Soviet Federal Socialist Republic (R.S.F.S.R.), is inhabited mainly by Russians, while the other republics, such as the Ukrainian S.S.R. and the Uzbek S.S.R., are formed round the more important of the various national groups after which they are named. In all the republics, however there is an appreciable percentage of Russians, while many Ukrainians have also settled outside the Ukraine itself, particularly in Asiatic parts of the U.S.S.R. (see Table 1, p. 53).

For the purposes of economic planning the U.S.S.R. has been divided into planning regions. There were about fifteen (the number frequently changed) until 1957, when 104 new *sovnarkhoz* regions were created. The planning regions, which are really convenient groups of administrative divisions, have played an important part in determining the distribution of new investment in the Soviet period.

The population of the U.S.S.R. is very unevenly distributed over the national territory. About three-quarters of the total lives in the European part, which occupies less than one-quarter of the total area. In the Asiatic part there are two main concentrations of population: a long but relatively narrow zone between the coniferous forest and semi-desert zones, served by the Trans-Siberian Railway, stretching between the Urals and Lake Baykal, and settled mainly by Russians and Ukrainians; and a discontinuous zone of irrigated land in Central Asia, between the desert and the high mountain ranges stretching between the Caspian Sea and the boundary of China, and settled mainly by Asians.

Before the Revolution of 1917 agriculture was by far the largest single employer of labour in Russia. Even now it accounts for about 35 per cent of the employed population (contrast 10 per cent in the U.S.A., 4 per cent in England). In spite of the large labour force and the apparently good opportunities for agriculture in parts of the country this branch of the economy has not been developed so successfully as heavy

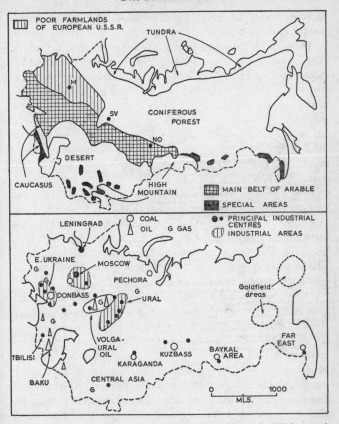

25a–b. The U.S.S.R. a Agricultural possibilities. b Mining and industry.

industry. This is due partly to the conditions of the environment, partly to Soviet organization.

Severe limits are set by environmental conditions to the expansion of the cultivated area and to the types of crop that can be grown (see Fig. 25a). About 17 per cent of the U.S.S.R. is tundra (cold desert) and nearly 50 per cent is coniferous forest, with soils generally unsuitable for cultivation and the growing season too short for most farm crops to mature. In both these zones there are many areas where the subsoil is permanently frozen (permafrost). Another 10 per cent of the U.S.S.R. is desert or semi-desert. A small part consists of rugged high mountain areas. Even in the remaining 20 per cent,

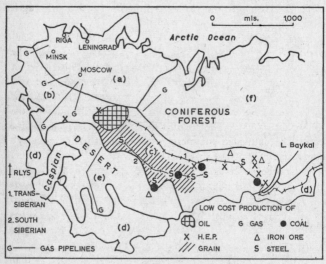

25c. Development regions in the U.S.S.R.

which is mostly steppe or cleared broadleaf forest, rainfall is not everywhere reliable, and dry seasons not infrequently reduce harvests. At present about 10 per cent of the total area of the U.S.S.R. is sown land, another 10 per cent grazing land, though not much of the latter is of high quality.

Farming can only be extended into the colder two-thirds of the U.S.S.R. (as into the coniferous forest zone of Canada) when some means has been found to make the forest soils suitable for cultivation. Small areas are already utilized, but their economic significance is slight, though magnified by Soviet propaganda. To make use of the arid 10 per cent of the country, costly works of irrigation must be constructed. Here, however, the area that can ultimately be irrigated is limited to the amount of water entering the deserts by river from better-watered mountain regions. During the mid-1950s, the sown area was greatly increased by bringing in steppe and semi-desert lands only partly used, east of the Volga; but harvests from here have varied greatly from year to year. Now, therefore, it seems that farm output can be increased more by obtaining higher yields in existing farming areas than by further extending agriculture into marginal lands.

Considerable importance has been attached by Soviet planners to the production of industrial raw materials, and the U.S.S.R. is more or less self-sufficient in the production of cotton and flax. Since no part of the country lies in or even close to the tropics, the range of crops that can be cultivated is limited, and the rubber tree (*Hevea brasiliensis*) is among the important tropical plants that cannot be grown. Sugar cane cannot be cultivated commercially, and most of the country's sugar requirements are produced from beet.

The timber reserves of the U.S.S.R. are more extensive than those of any other country in the world. So far, only the forests of European U.S.S.R. have been widely exploited. With coastlines on several different seas and oceans the country also has access to a number of important fishing areas. At present the Okhotsk and Caspian Seas are the most productive.

The U.S.S.R. is probably better provided with minerals than any other single country in the world. Its proved reserves of coal are the largest in the world. It also has abundant high-grade iron ore deposits and, apparently, large oil reserves. The exploration of resources is claimed to have shown that no mineral vital to the country's economic expansion is lacking. There are deposits of uranium in various localities, and in 1956 diamonds were discovered in eastern Siberia. Although gold is supposed to have no place in the Soviet economic system it is also produced in Siberia and is used in foreign trade.

The main producing coalfields are those of the Donbass (eastern Ukraine), Kuzbass, Karaganda, and Vorkuta (Pechora), which produce high-grade coal, including coking coal for the smelting of iron ore, and those of Tula and the Urals where lignite or low-grade coals are mined. The main sources of high- and medium-grade iron ore are at present Krivoy Rog and Kerch, about 200 miles from the Donbass, and in the Ural region, some 1,200 miles from the coking coal of the Kuzbass and 600 miles from that of Karaganda. The Caspian–Caucasus area was the main source of oil until the 1950s, but for some time output has been increasing rapidly in the Volga–Ural region, and this now accounts for at least 80 per cent of the total Soviet production. Important producing areas of other minerals include the Ural range and Kazakhstan.

Although the Soviet Communist Party claims the credit for the great progress that has been made in certain branches of industry during the last thirty years, nothing comparable could have been achieved without the many plant and mineral resources available in various parts of the country. The U.S.S.R. has abundant sources of fuel and power and many sites suitable for the construction of large hydro-electric power stations. Among the home-produced raw materials for industry are cotton, flax, and timber; non-ferrous metals such as copper, lead, zinc, aluminium ores; ferro-alloys such as manganese; and raw materials for the manufacture of chemicals, including fertilizers – apatite (for phosphate fertilizers), potash, and sulphur.

On the organizational side, heavy industry has benefited (even if Soviet citizens have suffered great hardships) from the drastic measures taken to develop mineral production and heavy manufacturing by investing in these a large part of the capital available for investment. But the reader should not overlook the fact that important industries were inherited from pre-Revolutionary times, so that in the early days of the Communist period the U.S.S.R. was not without industrial plant and skilled workers (see Chapter 8, Section 11).

During the Soviet period new branches of manufacturing have been developed. The most important, perhaps, are the engineering and chemicals industries, built up from almost nothing. Notwithstanding these great achievements, many branches of industry have been neglected. In particular, the U.S.S.R. is still far behind the U.S.A. and West Europe in the production of consumer goods, both in quality and in output per inhabitant.

In spite of attempts by Soviet planners to decentralize industry, much of the capacity is still concentrated in three main areas: the central part of European U.S.S.R. (around Moscow); the Donbass coalfield and associated centres on the Lower Dnieper and neighbouring areas; and the Ural region (see Fig. 25b). Most of the Soviet pig iron and steel is produced in the Donbass area (one-half of the pig iron and one-third of the steel) and Urals (one-third of each), while the Moscow area is of outstanding importance for textiles and for engineering products requiring skilled labour. Outside these three main regions there are, of course, other important concentrations of manufacturing – mostly individual centres, such as the Baltic and Black Sea ports, with shipbuilding yards, and the Volga towns, with various branches of engineering. The Kuzbass coalfield area is something of an exception, for it has the best coal reserves in the U.S.S.R., a large iron and steel works, and a concentration of several large mining and manufacturing towns. Industries of regional rather than national importance have also been established in the parts of the U.S.S.R. that are most distant from the main areas of manufacturing – for example, in Soviet Central Asia and the Soviet Far East, but Soviet propaganda has tended to exaggerate their significance.

In a country the size of the U.S.S.R., with great distances between the various concentrations of population and the various areas of production, economic expansion has depended very heavily on the provision of an efficient system of transport. In some respects progress has been held up through the inadequacy of the system. The railways carry about 80 per cent of tonnage of all goods moved in the U.S.S.R., while the Volga (with associated rivers, canals, lakes, and seas) is at present the only important system of inland waterways, accounting for two-thirds of the traffic handled by these. Roads are largely feeders to the railways. To handle the constantly increasing volume of goods traffic the railway system of pre-1917 Russia (with about 40,000 miles of route in use after the First World War) has been used more and more heavily, its efficiency being improved by such means as double-tracking and electrification. New lines have also been built, and bring the present total route mileage to about 75,000 (cf. U.S.A. 220,000). Although the route mileage is less than double what it was four decades ago, the railway system is being used much more heavily now, for the volume of goods traffic (measured in ton kilometres) was more than 20 times as great in 1961 as in 1913. It appears, however, that many key railways are working to full capacity, and economic progress will therefore be held up unless new lines are constructed or the inter-regional movement of goods is cut down by the more rational use of local raw materials. At all events, even if the Soviet rail system is the most heavily used in the world, it should be remembered that it is cheaper to avoid carrying goods over long distances altogether, if possible. Even now, in spite of the great inter-regional movement of goods, there does not appear to be the degree of regional specialization that is to be found in North America. In particular, the U.S.S.R. lacks the extensive highway system of the U.S.A., and is only now beginning to make much use of long-distance gas and oil pipelines. A start has now been made on the provision of a national electricity grid.

Foreign trade is much less important to the economic life of the U.S.S.R. than to most countries of West Europe, to North America, and to Japan. About three-quarters of the total value is with other members of the Communist bloc, much more of it with East Europe than with China. In general, the U.S.S.R. exports raw materials (oil, iron ore, timber, cotton) and food (wheat) to East Europe and receives manufactured goods (equipment for factories, rolling stock, light manufactures); while it sends China machinery of various kinds in return for an enormous variety of items obviously collected where possible to pay for essential imports. The U.S.S.R. trades widely with other parts of the world but the amount involved is not usually great. It goes to countries like New Zealand, South Africa, and Argentina for food and wool, buys various tropical products from many areas and a certain amount of machinery from West Europe. In the present century manufactured goods and metals have been replacing the traditional exports of the Russian Empire, grain, timber, and meat.

In the early 1960s Soviet trade with China has been diminishing. On the other hand there is increasing interdependence among the U.S.S.R. and the Communist countries of East Europe except Yugoslavia and Albania. To what extent Soviet foreign trade is governed by political rather than economic considerations is discussed in Chapter 8.

In conclusion, two outstanding problems of the Soviet economy at present must be noted. Firstly, there is a striking discrepancy between distribution of population and distribution of the best resources (or areas in which production costs are low); and secondly, development of different branches of the economy has not been at all even.

In Fig. 25c the U.S.S.R. has been divided into six main areas. One third of the population is in region (a), but this has very few resources, being deficient in energy, steel, food, and many other important items. Region (b) has good conditions for agriculture, and heavy industry is well represented in the Donbass area though production costs of coal and steel are higher here than in region (c). Region (b) more or less pays its way. Region (c) has only a small part of the total population but the best oilfield, the cheapest steel and grain, the best coalfield and many non-ferrous metals, and the best sites for large hydro-electric power stations. This is the area in which a large amount of investment is being placed during the current 7-Year Plan (1959–65), but labour is short. Region (d) is deficient in many items but from different parts makes special contributions (tea, cotton). Regions (e) and (f) make little contribution at present. In a capitalist economy the inhabitants of region (c), producing more per person than anywhere else, would (presumably) enjoy higher living standards than those anywhere else. In the U.S.S.R. the same trend may be occurring, but this region seems destined to subsidize the other regions of the country unless many more people can be moved into it.

Table 15 shows clearly the second problem mentioned, the unharmonious growth of different branches of the economy. Agriculture, road transport, light industry, and housing have been neglected because an excessive amount of capital has been invested in heavy industry in order to make the U.S.S.R. a powerful country militarily and to establish the foundations

TABLE 15

	1913	1926	1940	1956	1961
Population (millions)	159	147	192	200	216
Rural	131	121	131	113	108
Urban	28	26	61	87	108
		1928		1955	
Coal (m. metric tons)	28	32	140	276	360
Lignite ,, ,,	1	3	26	115	150
Oil ,, ,,	10	12	31	71	166
Pig iron ,, ,,	4	3	15	33	51
Steel ,, ,,	4	4	18	45	71
Cement ,, ,,	2	2	6	22	51
Fertilizers ,, ,,	0·1	0·1	3	10	15
Cotton fabric (m. metr.)	2,672	2,678	3,954	5,904	4,900
Motor vehicles (thous.)	—	7	145	445	555
Cattle (millions)	52	60	48	61	82

necessary for future general industrial development. That this policy saved the U.S.S.R. from defeat by Germany in 1941–2 surely justifies it, for the Germans quickly occupied the Donbass and would subsequently have overcome the Russians if they had not been provided with other heavy industrial areas built up in the 1930s in the Urals and Kuzbass, beyond the reach of the enemy.

II. EAST EUROPE

In this book Communist East Europe is treated as a major world region because at present it is clearly isolated economically and distinct politically from West Europe, yet differs in important ways from the U.S.S.R., which dominates six of the eight member countries with varying degrees of intensity. Yugoslavia broke away from the Soviet bloc in 1948 but still has a centrally planned economy. Poland and Hungary were able to achieve some degree of independence in running their internal affairs after 1956. Albania now looks to China rather than the U.S.S.R. for leadership and aid. East Germany is very obviously occupied by the U.S.S.R. Czechoslovakia, latest to enter the bloc (1948), seems, like Bulgaria, to be favourably disposed towards the U.S.S.R., possibly on account of economic advantages it has derived from being the most advanced industrial country in the whole of Comecon. The way things are going at present it seems that the U.S.S.R. is more concerned with making the East European countries dependent on it *economically* than it was some years ago. On the other hand there has been a gradual relaxation of the political hold. This trend coincides with a gradual shift from emphasis on each country having a complete range of industry, whether suited or not (e.g. the absurd iron and steel works near Frankfurt-on-Oder, East Germany), to emphasis on what each particular country is best suited to produce (e.g. Czechoslovakia high-quality consumer goods, Poland coal). In this way each country would serve the whole of Comecon in some special way and gradually become no more than another economic region in the bloc.

Having said this it is sufficient to point out that in each country (except Albania which is too small and Yugoslavia which has gone its own way) in the post-war period economic development has taken place roughly on the lines of that in the Soviet Union in the inter-war period, with 5-Year Plans, emphasis on sources of energy, iron and steel, engineering, chemicals, electrification, and on collectivization in agriculture. Even when allowance has been made for exaggerations in the representation of data showing increases in production, the growth of some branches of industry has been impressive. Thus, for example, *per caput* consumption of energy is now higher in Czechoslovakia than in any country of West Europe.

A glance at Table 16 shows, however, that there are great differences among countries in area, population, and level of development (see Columns v–vii). As in West Europe, differences in level of development are due partly to varying historical and cultural backgrounds, partly to different physical conditions and resources. Poland, for example, has long been influenced strongly both by Prussia (subsequently Germany) and Russia, Bulgaria by the Ottoman Empire.

In all the countries of Communist East Europe except Albania an appreciable proportion of the total area is used for cultivation and all but a small part of the remainder is grazing land or forest. Conditions, therefore, are good for farming over large areas, and generally the tracts of poorer soil in both low-land and mountain areas are forested. Apart from Czechoslovakia all the countries are more or less self-supporting in basic foodstuffs and, unlike the more highly industrialized nations of West Europe (such as Belgium and the U.K.), do not import much food. On the other hand, of course, both luxury foods from tropical and sub-tropical areas, and many animal and vegetable raw materials, must be imported. Cotton, for example, is one of the principal imports of Czechoslovakia.

East Europe is well endowed with certain minerals, but many important ones are not produced in more than small quantities. Only Poland and Czechoslovakia produce an appreciable amount of hard coal. Poland, producing about 100 m. tons per annum, is not far behind the U.K. in *per caput* production. All the countries produce lignite – East Germany by far the most (about 200 m. tons). Compared with ordinary coal, lignite is low in heating value, while its uses are more restricted and, in particular, it is not used for making pig iron. Oil is only produced in large quantities in Romania (but the $11\frac{1}{2}$ m. tons in 1960 was not much more than 1 per cent of the world's total). There are several deposits of iron ore in East Europe, though none is large, and East Germany, Poland, Czechoslovakia, and Hungary, therefore, have to import part of their requirements of this mineral. Several other minerals are produced in large quantities: potash in East Germany (about 25 per cent of world total); manganese ore in Romania and Hungary; bauxite in Yugoslavia and Hungary; and zinc in Yugoslavia and Poland.

The degree of industrialization varies greatly between the countries of East Europe. Albania has almost no industries, while Bulgaria, Romania, and Yugoslavia are still predominantly agricultural, although attempts have been made in the post-war period to set up large modern industrial establishments. Hungary is intermediate. The most highly industrialized areas are to be found in Czechoslovakia, southern Poland, and the southern part of East Germany. Most of the combined total of 13 m. tons of steel in Poland and Czechoslovakia came from the vicinity of the Upper Silesian Coalfield (see Katowice

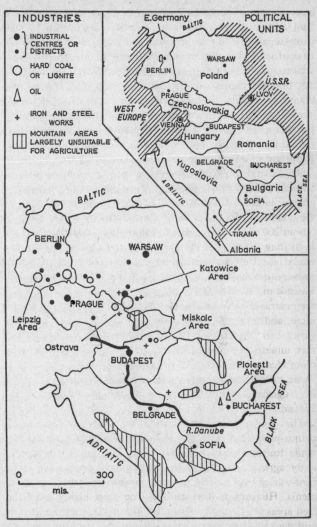

26a–b East Europe. a (*inset*) Political divisions. b Industrial areas.

and Ostrava, Fig 26b). The leading industrial countries of East Europe also have important engineering industries, while East Germany and Czechoslovakia in particular have a surplus of consumer goods for export, mostly to their less highly industrialized Communist neighbours, to the U.S.S.R. and to China. As their economies expand and their population grows these countries will undoubtedly trade more. The U.S.S.R. cannot provide all the raw materials they need, while for products of tropical agriculture and for high-quality manufactured goods they must obviously look outside the bloc since basically their problems are like those of the countries of West Europe: limited resources, small area, and a comparatively large population which is growing quite fast in some of the countries.

The position of East Europe in world affairs is at present far from clear. From the point of view of the West, the chance of 'liberating' the area from Soviet domination by force was lost in 1956 at the time of the uprising in Hungary, if indeed there really was a chance even then. Now hope rests on changes in the regimes within the countries and growing contact with West Europe and North America through trade and even financial aid (e.g. U.S. aid to Poland). The emergence of a large economic union in West Europe and of Comecon in East Europe and the U.S.S.R. do not seem at first sight to encourage this. But in the eyes of the West the various regimes apart from that of East Germany do appear to be growing more 'respectable', while the U.S.S.R. is less opposed to the regime in Yugoslavia than it was. The greatest danger now lies in the Berlin problem, the inability of East Germany to advance under Communism in the way that the other countries appear to be doing, and the claim by many West Germans not only that East Germany is merely temporarily separated from West Germany but also that the lands of inter-war Germany lying farther east and now in Poland and the U.S.S.R. must be recovered and resettled by Germans. A further complication is the claim by Sudeten German refugees in West Germany to be resettled in their former homeland of north-west Czechoslovakia, without however making an actual territorial claim.

From the point of view of the Soviet Union, East Europe is

TABLE 16

	I *Area in thousands of sq. mls.*	II *Population in millions, 1960*	III *Arable land as percentage of total area*	IV *Output of crude steel in 1960 in millions of tons*	V *Consumption of steel in 1959, kilograms per inhabitant*	VI *Consumption of all sources of energy in 1959, kilograms of coal equivalent per inhabitant*	VII *Newspapers in circulation per thousand inhabitants per day in late 1950s*
East Germany	42	17	48	3	314	4,390	118
Poland	121	30	55	6½	195	3,000	142
Czechoslovakia	49	14	44	6½	438	4,590	189
Hungary	36	10	63	1¾	174	2,180	124
Romania	92	18	40	1½	124	1,250	132
Bulgaria	43	8	40	¼	72	1,180	195
Albania	11	1½	13	n.	n.a.	260	45
Yugoslavia	100	19	31	1¼	78	790	59
U.S.S.R.	8,650	214	10	63	276	2,940	151
China	3,700	700	12	18	20	510	9
U.K. (for comparison)	96	52	30	24	332	4,590	575

n. = none or negligible   n.a. = not available

less obviously vital militarily than it was in the immediate post-war period when it was occupied by the Soviet army. It was then considered to be a massive buffer zone to hinder a new land attack on the U.S.S.R. from West Europe. In the post-war period, too, the U.S.S.R. was able to exploit the area economically; equipment was taken to the U.S.S.R. from East Germany, coal was obtained from Poland at unrealistically low prices. Now the situation is changing and the U.S.S.R. has in recent years given aid to East Germany, Hungary, and Albania.

III. CHINA AND ITS COMMUNIST NEIGHBOURS [1]

The emergence during the last decade of modern Communist-controlled China as a major world power is perhaps one of the most significant events in world affairs in the present century. China has remained the most extensive and most populous region of the world never to be annexed by European empire-building nations during the last five centuries. As the Russians strengthened their hold on Siberia and Central Asia they did challenge the Chinese claim to certain thinly populated outer provinces, while Portuguese Macau and British Hong Kong are the last relics of attempts by the maritime powers of Europe to establish trading stations in the coastal provinces. Japan, the first Asian power to adopt modern European industrial techniques, was the only country to go far towards overcoming China when it annexed Manchuria in the early 1930s and later in that decade embarked on the conquest of the rest of China.

During the last decade, Communist China has gone a long way towards establishing control over what in the nineteenth century was loosely called the Chinese Empire. Its sphere of influence also includes North Korea, in which Chinese forces operated during 1950–3, North Vietnam, and the Mongolian People's Republic, a buffer state between the U.S.S.R. and China. It has gone further by challenging the boundaries of a number of non-Communist states, particularly India and Burma, while it considers nationalist Chinese Formosa (like the Mongolian People's Republic) to be part of mainland China, the Chinese People's Republic. The control of more remote parts of this empire, particularly Tibet and Sinkiang, has been strengthened by the construction of roads and railways into these areas and by the settlement of Chinese there, among the inhabitants who are non-Chinese (see Fig. 28e).

China covers about one-thirteenth of the world's land area (excluding Antarctica) but has almost one-quarter of the world's population. Neighbouring regions with which it shares long land boundaries are the U.S.S.R., South Asia, South-east

1 In this region are included the Communist-controlled Mongolian People's Republic, North Korea, and North Vietnam.

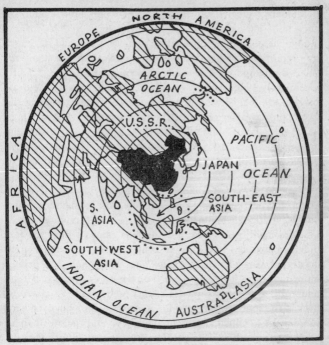

27. The hemisphere of China. Projection: oblique zenithal equidistant. Centre of projection: Wuhan. The circles are at thousand-mile intervals.

Asia, and Korea. It also has a short common boundary with Afghanistan (South-west Asia) in the mountainous Pamir area. Japan and Formosa are at no great distance from China by sea. In addition, all the other regions of the world, except Latin America, fall wholly or partly within the hemisphere of China (see Fig. 27).

Since the Chinese Communist Party has in many ways modelled itself on the Soviet Communist Party and has copied many features of Soviet economic development, the reader should constantly bear in mind the resemblances and differences between the two countries when studying the problems of modern China. If only temporarily, Communist China has chosen to europeanize itself on Soviet lines. It has, for example, introduced collectivization in agriculture, and it stresses the importance of heavy industrial development. In many respects contemporary China can be compared with the U.S.S.R. in the early 1930s, yet it would be a mistake to carry the comparison too far, because in area, population, and resources the two countries differ greatly. In some respects, moreover, China has even taken Communism further, as, for example, in the establishment of communes in rural areas. The comparative development of the two countries is further discussed in Chapter 8.

The population of China is now about 700 m., of which about 95 per cent are Han Chinese, the remainder being various national minorities of which the Mongolians and Uighurs have been given 'autonomous' status within the Republic. Between 15 and 20 per cent of the population is now urbanized; Shanghai has at least 7 m. inhabitants and Peking more than 5 m. (see Fig. 28d). Population is distributed very unevenly over the national territory and about 95 per cent lives in the south-eastern two-fifths (see Fig. 28c), but even here the density is much higher in the plains and valleys than in adjoining mountain districts. The total population is thought to be increasing by about 20 m. (2·8 per cent) per year, twice the population of Belgium.

Though roughly comparable with Europe in area and population, China is a land of greater physical extremes (see Figs. 28 a and b). It lies nearer the tropics but, on account of its location on the eastern side of a great land mass, has an enormous annual range of temperature, with severe winters except in the far south. Rain comes mainly in the summer with the monsoon but varies very much from year to year. Rivers are liable to flood after the rains. Moreover a very large part of China consists of rugged mountain ranges and cold, high plateaux. In much of the northern half, shut off from the monsoon rains, rainfall is insufficient for cultivation without irrigation, and Sinkiang and the Mongolian People's Republic together form one of the world's largest desert areas. Not sur-

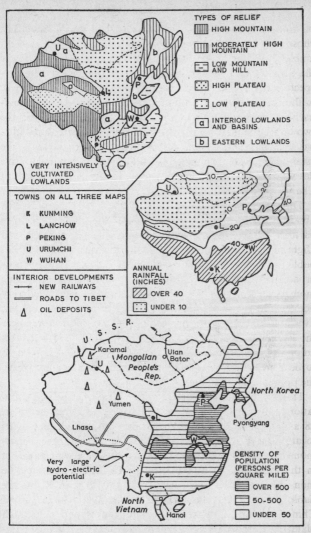

28a–c. China, the Mongolian People's Republic, N. Korea, and N. Vietnam. a Relief. b Rainfall. c Density of population and interior developments.

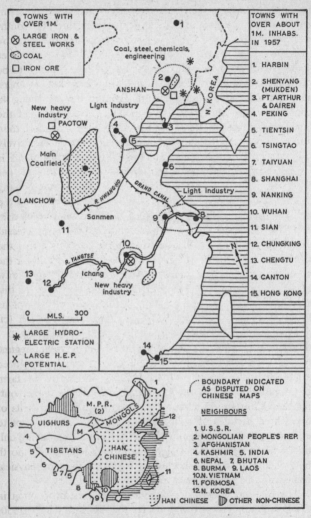

28d-e. China. d Towns and industries. e Peoples.

prisingly, then, most of China is of little or no use for farming. About 20 per cent of the country's area, mainly the south-western part, is too high, cold, and rugged to support more than very poor pastures except in a few small areas. Another 40 per cent, mainly the north-west and north, is too arid to be of much use for cultivation, and, like the high mountain areas, supports only poor-quality pasture. Even in the remaining 40 per cent, where almost all the population lives, much of the land is too rugged to be of use for cultivation. Not more than about 10 per cent of the total surface of China is intensively utilized for farming. Most of this better-quality farmland is occupied by the food crops that ensure the highest yields per unit area – rice in the south, soya beans, wheat, and kaoliang in the north. Livestock is a luxury, and meat and dairy produce hardly enter the diet of most Chinese families, while even fish, such an important source of protein in Japan, is at present caught in relatively small quantities in China, considering the size of the population. Moreover, little land is available for the cultivation of industrial crops. Cotton, the principal textile raw material, occupies much of the land devoted to crops of this kind. Yet another disadvantage of China is the poverty of its forest reserves. Only about 5 per cent is forest-covered (cf. almost 50 per cent in the U.S.S.R.).

Great importance has been attached by the present regime to increasing farm production. Collectivization was introduced almost everywhere in the early 1950s. This form of farm organization does not itself automatically ensure higher output, and Chinese leaders must have learnt from the results of over three decades of collectivization in the U.S.S.R. not to expect great benefits from it. There was talk of extending cultivation into new areas of steppe and semi-desert in the north but, whether through a shortage of tractors or adverse physical conditions, little seems to have been done.

The best single measure of growth of farm production in China is grain. The output has risen steadily through the 1950s from 108 m. tons in 1949 to 154 m. in 1952 and 185 m. in 1957, jumping to 254 m. in 1958 and reaching 275 m. in 1959. Totals for 1960 and 1961, years in which very bad droughts affected the Yangtze and Hwang-Ho valleys, were much lower, thus proving that in agriculture, as opposed to industry, nature does not allow continued expansion even under a Communist regime. With population growing fast, pressure on agricultural land is increasing; yields could be raised greatly, assuming that, by the fullest use of high-yielding strains of rice and other plants, and of mineral fertilizers, Chinese production per unit of area could be made to reach the Japanese level. But the output of fertilizers was negligible in the early 1950s and, apparently because of a lack of the minerals needed for their manufacture, little progress seems to have been made in this branch of industry.

With regard to mineral deposits, China is not so well endowed as the U.S.S.R., though it is claimed that many new deposits have been discovered during the Communist period. Most important of all, perhaps, is the fact that China has extensive deposits of high-grade coal. Among recently discovered minerals are large supplies of iron ore and oil. Iron ore is found in close proximity to coking coal in several localities. The oilfields, on the other hand, are in the interior of China, and the field at Yuming, where most of China's very limited output is at present produced, has only recently been linked by rail with the main centres of population to the east, while another oilfield at Tsaidam is not yet served by rail at all. China also has important deposits of certain other minerals, including tin, antimony, and tungsten. Other metals, including copper, lead, and zinc appear to be lacking.

In the U.S.S.R. the Soviets inherited important mines and industrial establishments (though damaged) from tsarist days. In the same way the Chinese Communists have come into possession of the former Japanese-run iron and steel industry of Manchuria as well as the large textile factories of Shanghai and elsewhere, established by various foreign countries. Communist China, therefore, has not been without a base on which to build up its industries. Another advantage of China, not shared by the U.S.S.R. or India, is the presence of abundant reserves of coal in the vicinity of many of the existing large urban centres. In contrast, the oil deposits and many of the suitable sites for large hydro-electric power stations are located in inaccessible areas far from the principal concentrations of population and industry.

Home-produced raw materials for industry are not plentiful. Considering the large population of the country there is little timber, and there are few important minerals other than coal, iron ore, and oil. The amount of land available for the production of plant and animal raw materials is strictly limited owing to the need to use almost all of the better farmland for food production. The difficulty of transporting bulky goods between the different regions of the country is another obstacle to industrial expansion. China only has about 16,000 miles of railway – less than the U.K. or France. It has almost no modern motor roads, while the Yangtse is the only inland waterway. In many respects, therefore, China is not in such a good position to embark on rapid industrial expansion as the U.S.S.R. was when it began thirty years ago. As in the U.S.S.R., the emphasis has been on the expansion of various branches of heavy industry – iron and steel, engineering, chemicals (particularly fertilizers), and cement, and some of the coal mines and iron and steel works are reported to be among the most efficient and modern in the world. But in an attempt to boost industrial output further, rural areas were encouraged from 1958 to contribute various manufactured items as well, including iron and steel. Here success was limited. Moreover the bad condition of agriculture has made it necessary to shift labour back to the land from industrial projects since 1959. Table 17 gives a rough idea of production in some main branches of mining and manufacturing. 1962 is the last year of the Second 5-Year Plan.

The production of consumer goods has also been increased in the 1950s, and the output of such manufacturers as cotton cloth, paper, bicycles, and rubber footwear increased 2–3 times during the First 5-Year Plan (1953–7). Most impressive of all, perhaps, has been the creation during the last few years of China's engineering industry. The large iron and steel industry built up by the Japanese in Manchuria in the 1930s was regarded mainly as a source of pig iron and steel for Japan itself.

TABLE 17

	Early 1940s Peak Year	1952	1957	1959	1961	1962 Target
Coal (m. tons)	62	64	117	350	n.a.	200
Oil (m. tons)	$\frac{1}{3}$	$\frac{1}{2}$	$1\frac{1}{2}$	n.a.	n.a.	$5\frac{1}{2}$
Electricity (thous. m. kwh.)	6	7	19	n.a.	n.a.	42
Steel (m. tons)	$\frac{1}{10}$	$1\frac{1}{3}$	5	13	15	$11\frac{1}{4}$
Chemical fertilizers (m. tons)	$\frac{1}{8}$	$\frac{3}{8}$	$\frac{3}{8}$	n.a.	n.a.	3
Cement (m. tons)	$2\frac{1}{4}$	3	7	12	n.a.	13
Cotton yarn (m. bales)	$2\frac{1}{2}$	$3\frac{1}{2}$	5	n.a.	n.a.	$8\frac{1}{2}$

n.a. = not available

Consequently, China has had to build up its engineering industry almost from nothing, and Soviet equipment and technical aid have therefore been vital. Soviet assistance was given in more than 150 of the largest 700 industrial undertakings (not all, of course, engineering) of the First 5-Year Plan. The list of engineering products now turned out in China is impressive, and includes lorries, steam locomotives, rolling stock, various machine tools, scientific precision instruments and apparatus, and farm and textile machinery.

An important feature of Communist planning in China has been the move to decentralize industry. Even now most of the steel is produced in South Manchuria, and many of the consumer goods are made in the Shanghai and Peking areas, while the Shansi-Shensi field accounts for most of the coal. At least two large new iron and steel works have, however, been built in the interior of the country, at Paotow and Wuhan (see Fig. 28d).

This development is not unlike the establishment of iron and steel centres in the Ural region and Kuzbass in the U.S.S.R. during the 1930s. Likewise, new cotton manufacturing establishments are being opened in the cotton-growing regions of the middle Hwang-Ho and Yangtse valleys, as they were in the cotton-growing lands of the Soviet Union (Soviet Central Asia and Transcaucasia).

There are many obstacles to industrial growth in China and

it is appreciated that the output from most branches is at present modest even in absolute terms, let alone *per caput* terms. At present, for example, China only produces about half as much steel as West Germany, yet it has 12 times as many people. The population of China is so large and is growing so rapidly that *per caput* industrial production, which is extremely low at present, can hardly be expected to approach the *present* level in the U.S.S.R. until some decades have passed, and, indeed, may not do so at all.

China's foreign trade is growing fast and the number of partners has been increasing during and since the late 1950s, while the proportion of the total with the U.S.S.R. and East Europe has been diminishing. Traditional products such as silk and tea still figure among China's exports, but various new light manufactures are also being exported, even though they must be needed at home. China has to import many raw materials for industry and at the same time it requires industrial equipment and various machines. Failures in agriculture have also compelled it to import large quantities of grain recently.

If living standards are to be raised in China many obstacles have to be overcome. Two questions which lie behind all matters of economic progress not only in China but also in all the poorer countries of the world, have to be solved. Farm output must be raised and the rate of increase of population slowed down. Nowhere in the world is the problem more acute than in China. Only when measures are taken to solve these problems can the benefits of industrialization be felt by the whole community and improvements in education and living conditions be universally introduced. The Chinese Communist government is concerned with both the problems mentioned, but in a country in which most of the inhabitants are poor, illiterate peasants, the task of introducing birth control is not an easy one. Nor does the regime appear to have had a clear-cut policy towards limiting the size of families.

Finally, the three other countries included in this section must be mentioned. The Mongolian People's Republic is mainly desert, with only about 1 m. inhabitants, and is used mainly for grazing. It is crossed by a railway between the U.S.S.R. and China. North Korea and North Vietnam are smaller but have much larger populations. Each is separated from its non-Communist southern part. North Korea has some industries but North Vietnam is almost entirely agricultural.

Chapter 8

THE SOVIET UNION

I. TERRITORIAL EXPANSION OF RUSSIA [1]

THE state of Kiev, known as Rus, was in existence more than
a thousand years ago. It was located in the lands between the
Baltic and Black Seas, inhabited by East Slav peoples. By 1223,
when the first Tatar invasion of European Russia took place,
Rus had broken up into a number of principalities. Most of
these were overrun and subjugated by Mongol and Tatar invaders in the thirteenth century. Only in the north-west, in the
lands of Novgorod, did the Russians remain largely independent of their Asian conquerors. By about 1450, however,
Asian influence was weakening and the principality of Moscow
had already gained control over a considerable part of central
European Russia. Between that date and 1533, when Ivan IV
became Tsar, the Russian state in Europe expanded rapidly,
absorbing the lands of Novgorod to the north-west, north, and
north-east and recovering territory to the south from the Asian
invaders. At this period Russia was emerging as a nation and
becoming powerful enough to begin large-scale empire building in lands not inhabited by Europeans (see Chapter 2).

Soon after the accession of Ivan IV in 1533, the Russians
penetrated east and south-east to established footholds on the
Volga, capturing Kazan and Astrakhan on the middle and
lower Volga in the 1550s. Eastward penetration into the coniferous forests of Siberia followed, and by the 1640s Russian
explorers had reached the shores of the Pacific Ocean at points
several thousand miles to the east of Moscow. By 1689, when
the Treaty of Nerchinsk was signed between Russia and China,
limiting further southward expansion by the Russians into
Asia, several million square miles of territory had already been
annexed by Russia.

Siberia, which was several times as large as the Russia of

1. The reader is advised to refer to Fig. 29 while reading this
section.

1533, was inhabited only by small scattered tribes, the members of which lived (and still do) by hunting, fishing, and reindeer herding. Climatic conditions in Siberia were even more harsh than those in European Russia, with long severe winters and spring flooding. The Russian invaders moved mainly along

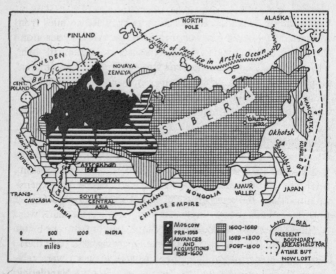

29. The growth of the Russian Empire, 1533 to the present. For a more detailed map of boundary changes in European Russia, see Fig. 30.

the rivers. There was almost no cultivable land in the areas acquired in the seventeenth century. Few Russian colonists followed the soldiers, administrators, men of religion, and traders, largely because there were more favourable lands to settle nearer home and because movement was so slow and difficult anyway. There was abundant timber, but this commodity was not lacking in European Russia itself. There were also gold and furs, and these attracted some settlers, although the Russians did not colonize Siberia in large numbers until the present century, after the construction of the Trans-Siberian Railway.

Territorial Expansion of Russia

After 1689 the eastward thrust of the Russians continued across the Bering Strait into North America. Alaska was annexed and a line of forts was established along the Pacific coast. The most southerly, Fort Ross, established by the Russians in 1812, was only sixty miles north-west of San Francisco, in what was then a Spanish colony and is now the state of California, U.S.A. Fort Ross was more than 9,000 miles from Moscow by overland route across Siberia and then by sea along the Pacific coast. In this way the Russians and Spaniards, who had set out from opposite ends of Europe, and in different directions, met, after almost three centuries, on the other side of the world.

After the accession of Peter in 1682, interest in territorial expansion shifted to European Russia, and in spite of the drive into North America in the eighteenth century, efforts were largely concentrated on regaining lands inhabited by Russians and Ukrainians from foreign domination and on establishing footholds on the Baltic [1] and Black Seas, partly at the expense of the Ottoman Empire (Odessa and the Crimea were taken towards the end of the century). In Europe, the Russians were fighting the Swedes, Turks, and other peoples who were better equipped to resist Russian penetration than the tribes of Siberia had been in the previous century. Territorial gains were relatively small, though important. During and after the Napoleonic Wars, Finland and Poland were added to the Russian Empire, but at this time Russian interest in Asia was reviving, and three great advances were made there during the nineteenth century. Transcaucasia was overrun early in the century, Central Asia was gradually annexed between about 1840 and 1900, and the Amur valley and Sakhalin Island in East Asia were also taken during this period.

The Russian Empire in Europe and Asia reached its greatest extent by about 1900, though in 1867 Alaska had been sold to the U.S.A. for $U.S. 7,200,000, and Russia had thus lost its foothold in North America. Territory was lost in the war with

1. Work began on the construction of the settlement of St Petersburg (now Leningrad) in 1703. The city was the capital of Russia between 1714 and 1918.

Japan (1904–5) and during the First World War and the subsequent period of foreign intervention in Russia. The U.S.S.R. regained some of these lands, together with some relatively small areas, only after the Second World War. The present territory of the U.S.S.R. is still slightly smaller than the Russian Empire was in 1900 (see Fig. 30 for boundary changes in Europe), and it is obviously inaccurate, therefore, to talk of Soviet territorial expansion during the present century, though Soviet influence has, of course, been extended, without the actual annexation of territory, into East Europe and, to a lesser extent, into China. During the inter-war period the U.S.S.R. claimed as Soviet territorial waters all of the Arctic Ocean lying between its northern coast and the North Pole, while possession of the Kurile Islands since 1945 has given it virtual control over the Okhotsk Sea.

During the last four hundred years, therefore, Russia has developed from a European state of modest dimensions into the largest state in the world, covering not much less than one-sixth of the total land area of the earth's surface excluding Antarctica. The strength of the U.S.S.R. lies in the fact that it is continuous and compact (and in this respect it may be compared with the U.S.A.) whereas the sea empires built up by other European powers during the same period have been scattered over the world and held together only by long, vulnerable sea routes.

II. INDUSTRIAL DEVELOPMENT IN RUSSIA

Although the expansion of certain branches of industry has been spectacular in the U.S.S.R. during the Soviet period, it is a mistake to assume that there were no industries in Russia before this. Before 1700 there were numerous ironworks in the area between Moscow and Tula and many small industrial establishments elsewhere in European Russia. During and after the reign of Peter the Great (1682–1725) Russians were sent to Western Europe for technical education, and foreign technicians were brought into the country. Shipbuilding industries were established in St Petersburg and Archangel, and

30. Changes in the European boundary of Russia during the twentieth century.

what in the eighteenth century became one of the largest iron industries in Europe was developed in the Urals. Most of the iron produced was used in the manufacture of armaments and agricultural implements. Towards the end of the eighteenth century Russia was the world's largest producer of iron and was even exporting some to England.

In the nineteenth century a textile industry, protected by tariffs, was built up in the area around Ivanovo, to the northeast of Moscow, and foreign capital, machinery, technicians, and, until late in the century, cotton, were imported. The construction of railways in the 1860s and 1870s in the Ukraine made it possible to transport the iron ore of Krivoy Rog to the coking coal of the Donbass (Donets basin), where a large iron and steel industry grew up, also with the help of foreign capital and technicians. In the 1890s, once again with foreign capital, large-scale oil production began in the Baku area, and in 1900 Russia was producing about half of the world's oil. On the eve of the First World War, therefore, Russia was already an industrial country of some importance, although in capacity and efficiency its industries were far behind those in the U.S.A. and the leading industrial nations of Western Europe. The following industrial areas could be distinguished (see Fig. 31):

1. The Moscow (or central) region, with light industries (mainly cotton textiles). 2. The Donbass and associated centres of mining and manufacture, producing five-sixths of Russia's coal (about 25 m. tons per year) and most of its iron and steel goods. 3. The moribund iron industry of the Urals, which was still run on charcoal and therefore unable to compete with the Donbass (in 1913, about 20 per cent of Russia's iron came from the Urals, 70 per cent from the Donbass). 4. Individual centres, mostly ports, with special industries: Baku and Batum (oil refining), Odessa, Archangel, and St Petersburg. 5. Poland, with textile and other industries (this part of the Russian Empire was lost during the First World War).

Industrial development during the Soviet period may be summarized thus:

1. Pre-1928: the rehabilitation of war-damaged industries in the areas already mentioned and the inauguration of a plan

(GOELRO) to electrify European Russia. Lenin attached great importance to electricity, and is often quoted as saying: 'Communism is Soviet rule plus the electrification of the whole country.'

2. 1928–41, the first three 5-Year Plans. During this period Soviet industrial capacity was greatly expanded, new branches

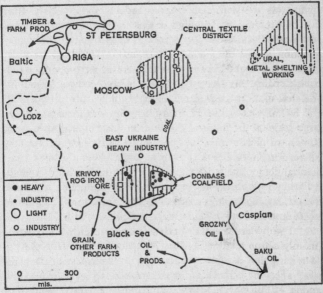

31. Industrial areas and centres in Russia before the First World War.

of industry introduced (engineering and chemicals, in particular), fresh sources of minerals exploited, and factories constructed in parts of the U.S.S.R. where previously there had been little or no industrial development. The most spectacular achievement of this period was, perhaps, the Urals–Kuzbass *kombinat* (see Chapter 7) using Urals iron ore and Kuzbass (and later Karaganda) coking coal to build up an iron and steel industry which in capacity now rivals the Donbass industry (itself greatly expanded since 1928).

3. 1941–50, the war and the post-war rehabilitation of industry. Much of the Soviet industrial capacity in European U.S.S.R. was destroyed during the war, but the Volga towns, Urals, and Kuzbass developed rapidly. The Fourth (post-war) 5-Year Plan (1946–50) was devoted largely to reconstructing war-damaged areas. During the war and post-war period, however, attempts were also made to introduce some degree of industrial self-sufficiency in the regions most distant from European U.S.S.R., including Transcaucasia, Central Asia, and the Soviet Far East.

4. Post 1950, the Fifth 5-Year Plan (1951–55) and the Sixth, until it was abandoned as too ambitious in 1957, continued the emphasis on heavy industry, but the serious state of agriculture was admitted and new lands brought under cultivation (1953–5). In 1959 a Seven-Year Plan (1959–65) was introduced. One very important feature of this was the shift of emphasis in the supply of new energy from coal to oil and gas (a process long under way in the U.S.A.).

Features of the 1950s have been the training of large numbers of technicians, the first commercial production of atomic power, the beginnings of automation, and rapid advances in certain branches of industry, particularly engineering (no doubt with the help of scientists from East Europe), to bring the U.S.S.R. up to the level of West Europe and the U.S.A. at least in some aspects of industry. Spectacular achievements have been the completion of the world's largest hydro-electric power station on the Volga near Kuybyshev, the expansion of oil production in the Volga–Ural field from about 15 m. tons in 1950 to about 120 m. tons in 1960, and the *fourfold* increase in steel production between 1948 (18 m. tons) and 1961 (71 m. tons). Important long-term undertakings are the establishment of a third heavy industrial base to rival the Donbass and Urals (see Chapter 7) in the area between Karaganda and Lake Baykal and the creation of a system of oil pipelines from the Volga–Ural oilfields into Siberia and into East Europe.

What has so far been achieved is dwarfed by the programme for the period 1960–80. This envisages a sixfold increase in industrial production, a fourfold increase in productivity per industrial worker, a tenfold increase in electricity production, a fourfold increase in the output of steel and sources of energy, and so on. Even agricultural production is to be increased three to four times, and the railways are to handle three times as much traffic. The plan presupposes a further advance of cultivation into marginal lands and therefore an increasing element of luck in farm output, which already fluctuates greatly and has lagged behind expectation. It also envisages a level of consumption of non-renewable sources of energy (coal, oil, natural gas) at a rate hitherto unknown even in North America. It is ironical that, to prove its worth, the Communist Party of the U.S.S.R. feels it necessary to risk ruining marginal agricultural land and to encroach so lavishly on the world's reserves of energy (of which it is fortunate enough to have about half) in an even more drastic way than the U.S.A. has done.

III. AIMS, METHODS, AND ACHIEVEMENTS OF THE SOVIET COMMUNIST PARTY

The Communist Party of the U.S.S.R. has been in power without interruption since 1917. Over most of this period, much of the power and many of the decisions appear to have come from a single individual – Lenin before his death in 1924, Stalin for nearly thirty years until 1953, and for several years now, Khrushchev. Behind these men, however, has been the massive strength of the Party with its membership since the war of 7–8 m. full members.[1] Apparent discord at certain periods and particularly since 1953 has not shaken the control of the Party in the country as a whole, and the continuity of the presence and influence of this self-elected and self-perpetuating minority, a privileged but devoted *élite*, should be stressed. The strength of the Communist Party rests on the way it has penetrated every aspect of the life of the country, compelled most influential persons of the community to join it, recruited members from all the nationalities, not only from the Russians, and maintained its limited numbers – one citizen in

1. The membership of the Communist Party of China is about twice as large, while the total world strength is about 40 m.

about thirty – while making it customary for everyone to spend a period as a Young Communist. Political opposition is not tolerated; a strong police force, armed forces with party members well represented, control of the Press and broadcasting, restrictions on the movement into and out of the country of people, literature, and goods, these are still essential features of the U.S.S.R. even if there has been some relaxation since Stalin's death.

In very broad terms the Soviet Communist Party has always had and still has two principal aims, firstly to raise living standards through economic expansion and a transformation of the economic and social life from capitalism through socialism to communism, and secondly to encourage, where expedient, the 'inevitable' spread of the socialist (in the Soviet sense) system and ultimately of Communism to the rest of the world. The first aim, which concerns mainly internal matters, is discussed in this section; the second, which is connected principally with external relations, is dealt with in Sections IV (other countries in the Communist bloc) and V (non-Communist countries).

Internal policy has been dominated by the transformation of a mainly privately-owned, privately-run economy into a state-owned, state-organized, centrally planned, one. Industry, mining, and transport were taken over first, the re-organization of agriculture into either state-owned farms (*sovkhoz*) or collective farms (*kolkhoz*) took place later (mainly 1929–33). Having virtual control of all productive and commercial activities by the early 1930s, the state, through various planning bodies, has subsequently been able to decide what emphasis should be given to different branches of the economy and which regions should be developed fastest. During and after collectivization the standard of living of the peasants was drastically reduced, and by high taxes, compulsory free deliveries of products to the state, and so on, agriculture was made to contribute capital towards the expansion of other activities. In industry itself great emphasis was placed on the production of capital goods, items required for building up productive capacity still further; the production of consumer goods was sacrificed while coal, steel, engineering, and the railways had priority. There have been shifts in emphasis but basically this picture is as true now as thirty years ago. If more had been done to expand consumer goods, then heavy industrial capacity could not be as great as it is now. Preparation for the war, the war itself (1941–45), and post-war rehabilitation made conditions far from ideal, of course, and put the country back eight to ten years. At the same time, partly for strategic considerations, partly to mop up surplus labour, many enterprises were started without a proper economic justification, the assumption being that under Communism a consideration of production costs in different places and the advantages of some areas over others did not matter. At all events the industrial capacity of the U.S.S.R. has expanded impressively between 1930 and the present day. So great has been the progress that Soviet politicians are now talking of overtaking the U.S.A. in production per worker both in industry and in agriculture. Precisely when this will happen and whether it will happen for the whole economy or only for certain branches is not clear. Nor is allowance made for a possible expansion in the U.S.A. itself. In general when a comparison is made between the two countries in Soviet publications it is between things in which for one reason or another the U.S.S.R. may be expected to excel. Steel production in the U.S.S.R. has increased rapidly in the post-war period, in the U.S.A. it has fluctuated considerably. But this could mean that the U.S.A. produces enough, not that it is unable to produce more. Comparison is not made, for example, between the motor vehicles industry of the two countries or road-building achievements.

Assuming that the basic production figures released by the U.S.S.R. since 1956 are reliable [1] then it has not been difficult by carefully choosing the right branches of production and the right periods of comparison with the U.S.A. and West Europe

1. Considerable work has been done on this important question in the West and the view is that, apart from fictitious indices of growth of broad sectors of the economy, recent Soviet figures are accurate. Many sets of figures (e.g. on the engineering industry) are not published at all for security reasons and the procedure is to omit figures rather than to falsify them.

to show the superior nature of the Soviet economy and of socialist methods of industrial expansion. But a few examples will show that the very methods by which Soviet superiority can be proved may also be used against the U.S.S.R.

First of all it must be appreciated that Soviet industrial and mining activities have expanded from relatively modest beginnings in the 1920s, and that a small increase in absolute terms may seem a great increase relatively in the early stages of an industry. The following fictitious example illustrates the method: in a given year there is only one factory producing cycles. It turns out 10,000 per annum. The next year another cycle factory is opened. It also produces 10,000 per annum. The output of cycles has increased in a year by 100 per cent. If another of the same capacity is opened the next year, however, it means that only 10,000 additional cycles will be produced, against 20,000 already being produced in the two previous factories, an increase of only 50 per cent in that year. As times goes on the same absolute figure (in this example, 10,000) comes to represent a smaller and smaller percentage increase.

Using this method, the total industrial production of the U.S.S.R. increased over 40 times between 1913 and 1959, that of the U.S.A. only 5 times. But in 1913 U.S. industry was many times larger than that of Russia. The comparison, therefore, proves nothing unless the absolute amount of production involved is considered. The following shows how an increase apparently in favour of the U.S.S.R. is really in favour of the U.S.A.: between 1950 and 1959 the output of electricity increased nearly 3 times in the U.S.S.R., only twice in the U.S.A., from 91 to 265 and from 389 to 794 (thousand million kilowatt hours) respectively. The increase in the U.S.S.R. was 174 units, in the U.S.A. 305 units. In other words the gap had actually *widened* in one of the industries given top priority by Soviet planners.

There is enormous scope for giving an incomplete picture without falsifying figures. Thus, for example, in the 1950s the rate of increase of steel production both in Brazil and in China was faster than in the U.S.S.R. but this does not prove that their economies are superior. Now that its total volume of production is high, the U.S.S.R. has been stressing the importance of absolute increase.

To prove the superiority of their system, Soviet statisticians would have to show that their own progress exceeded that of capitalist countries over a suitably long *and* comparable period of economic growth. The comparison could be over the same period with countries that started to industrialize on modern lines roughly at the same time as Russia (notably Italy and Japan) or over a different period with countries that started before (e.g. France, U.S.A.) or after (e.g. China). But it would be unfair to select certain branches of the economy that have been specially favoured by Soviet planners without giving proper weight to other branches that have been neglected.

Needless to say, insufficient work has been done on this subject on either side to say anything conclusively, but recently a number of U.S. economists have been working on these lines.[1] The general impression is that over a period of nearly a century, progress in Italy, Japan, and Russia has been remarkably similar if differences in emphasis are kept in mind. The greater volume of production in the U.S.S.R. at present may be attributed to its greatly superior resources, both agricultural and mineral, making higher output per worker possible.

A comparison of pig iron production in the U.S.S.R. and the U.S.A. over roughly similar periods in the industrial history of the two countries (a lag of 55 years) shows the same trend (Table 18). Taking into account changes in population over the periods considered and working out the production *per inhabitant* it can be shown that the rate of growth was roughly similar. The rapid growth of heavy industry in the U.S.S.R. is therefore not something unprecedented. It is worth noting that between about 1840 and 1890 the British output of pig iron per inhabitant also increased at about the same rate, credit, surely, to the pioneers of the modern iron and steel industry, though it should be remembered that this meant the

1. See W. W. Rostow's *The Stages of Economic Growth*, which also contains references to other research.

TABLE 18

U.S.A.				U.S.S.R.			
Pop'n in millions	Total pig iron	Year	Per inhabitant output (in kgs.)		Year	Total pig iron	Pop'n in millions
29	0·7	1858	24	26	1913	4·3	159
34	0·9	1863	26	4	1918	0·6	160
38	1·6	1868	42	2	1923	0·3	140
43	2·2	1873	43	22	1928	3·3	151
48	2·6	1878	54	44	1933	7·1	162
54	4·3	1883	80	88	1938	14·7	168
59	7·2	1888	122	?	1943	?	?
67	8·2	1893	122	78	1948	13·7	175
73	11·8	1898	162	143	1953	27·4	191
80	18·0	1903	225	192	1958	39·6	207
89	24·0	1908	270	252	1963	57·0?	225?

SOURCES OF FIGURES: U.S.A - *Historical Statistics of the U.S.A. 1789–1945*, U.S. Department of Commerce, 1949.

U.S.S.R. – *Narodnoye khozyaystvo SSSR v 1959 godu*, Moscow, 1960.

investment of a large share of the national income and sacrifice of the consumer in a way that has been happening in the U.S.S.R. during the Communist period.

Soviet achievements have already been discussed in Chapter 7, Section I, and again in Section II of this chapter. What follows is therefore only a summary.

Progress has been impressive in most branches of heavy industry, although it looks now as though Soviet planners are regretting the previous emphasis on coal and large hydro-electric power stations. Oil and gas are much cheaper to extract than coal, while the large hydro-electric power stations take a long time to build, and consume a large amount of capital for a limited if thereafter very cheap supply of energy. Great advances have been made in some branches of engineering and the U.S.S.R. is probably more advanced than any other country in rocket construction and electricity transmission. The chemicals industry has, however, lagged behind engineering, while in the engineering industry itself many products such as farm machinery and tractors are of antiquated design or poor quality.

Progress has also been great in education and health. Whatever tricks Soviet statisticians play (such as counting their dentists as doctors and then comparing the number of these with doctors only in other countries), the near elimination of illiteracy, the training of an enormous number of technicians, the rapid lowering of the death rate and of infant mortality and the provision throughout the country of reasonably adequate hospital and other medical services show that the U.S.S.R. has not neglected these aspects of cultural and social development.

When one turns to light industry, housing, agriculture, and transport, the weakness of the Soviet planning system is clearly shown. Consumer industrial goods are more widely available than before the Revolution but many items accepted as necessities or at least within the reach of a large part of the population in Western industrial countries are hardly made at all: cars, plastic goods, electrical appliances. Housing is inadequate in most regions of the U.S.S.R. The war can be blamed to some extent, but lack of interest in the building of flats and houses has been the main reason. Population has not changed much in most rural areas but the fourfold increase in total urban population during the present century has barely been matched by housing construction, and conditions are very bad by Western standards in most towns. Agriculture has suffered most, however, and in spite of greater attention to it since Stalin's death, nothing so far seems to have persuaded the peasants of the collective farms to work on the collective land with the same enthusiasm as they till their diminutive private plots.

The transport system, on which the whole future success of economic growth in the U.S.S.R. depends, has been improved greatly but still appears to be inadequate for current needs. Too few of the railways carry too much of the traffic. A modern system of well-paved roads simply does not exist. To reduce the rapid growth of goods carried in the U.S.S.R., regional self-sufficiency in bulky products has been encouraged, but this is only a partial answer to an overburdened transportation system.

Soviet economic growth has clearly been different from that in other modern industrial countries, but this is understandable in view of the particular features and aims of a centrally planned economy, which differs from an economy in which private enterprise is the main or only force at work, and has its own advantages and disadvantages.

An apparent advantage of central planning is that each branch of the economy can be arranged to cater for the needs of other branches depending on it. Wasteful competition such as the duplication of transport services by road and rail can be avoided. Unemployment can be eliminated because work can be provided for everyone even if the result is underemployment, a widespread feature of the U.S.S.R. and East Europe. Soviet economists stress the rational nature of economic planning, and a plan seems so on paper. But it is no secret that to apply the plan in detail over a vast country like the U.S.S.R. is extremely difficult. Bureaucrats abound, bottlenecks occur, factory managers are more concerned about the volume of their own particular production than about its usefulness for other factories or for the consumer. An army of *tolkachi* (literally pushers) or 'negotiators' exists to reduce the bottlenecks, settle the conflicts between producers, and make things run more smoothly.

Other disadvantages of central planning in the U.S.S.R. may be noted. Until recently there has been little concern about production costs either in agriculture or in industry; the aim was to produce everywhere possible, even if output per worker was low. There appeared to be no clear way of showing which farms or industrial establishments had high production costs (and therefore, theoretically anyway, would, under capitalism, have been pushed out of production). There is now growing interest in this problem. Another danger is for a centrally planned economy to initiate an enormous programme of some kind, only to find at its completion or some way through that it is going to be a failure. This is nicely termed 'campaign-ology' by A. Nove.[1] Examples are the plan to plant protective belts of trees to improve climate in areas of steppe and even semi-desert, almost a complete failure, and the drive to make farmers grow more maize everywhere in the U.S.S.R.; an absurd idea since most of the arable lands are either too cold or too dry to suit this plant.

It is hoped that what has been said about the U.S.S.R. gives a fair if oversimplified picture of progress and present conditions under the Communist Party. During the last forty years the U.S.S.R. has suffered great material losses at the hands of foreign invaders. Furthermore, hostile propaganda from non-Communist countries has helped to creat misunderstandings and to keep the Soviet Communist Party constantly alert to the possibility of further attacks. At the same time it has provided a pretext for maintaining what might almost be called a state of emergency. Under these circumstances it is hardly surprising that appreciable material progress has been made only in certain branches of the country's economic and cultural life.

What have the Russians and the other citizens of the U.S.S.R. gained as a result of forty years of Communist domination? Undoubtedly living conditions are better than they were four decades ago for most of the population, and there is the possibility that very soon they will improve appreciably, because the U.S.S.R. is a country with great mineral and forest resources and it now has a basis of heavy industry on which other branches of the economy can be built. On the other hand Soviet citizens have very little freedom in a political sense; they have been discouraged, if not prevented, from practising any religion; and they have had Communist propaganda preached to them from early childhood. In spite of this, the citizens of the U.S.S.R. do not appear to have become machines; they certainly have not lost their personalities nor their ability to think and to judge about matters for themselves. In spite of what they have suffered both from the Communist Party inside the U.S.S.R. and from aggressors, particularly the German army, from outside, they do not appear to be bitter. The friendliness shown by ordinary Soviet citizens when visiting non-

1. A. Nove *The Soviet Economy*, London, 1961.

Communist countries and the enthusiastic welcome given by the Russians indiscriminately to all foreign visitors to their own country in recent years must frequently have embarrassed the Communist Party members.

IV. COMECON AND CHINA

During the period 1945–9 the Communist world was greatly strengthened, first with the acquisition by the U.S.S.R. of

32. The Communist bloc, showing routes across and round it. Projection: oblique zenithal equidistant. Centre of projection: Alma-Ata, Kazakh Republic, U.S.S.R.

various countries in East Europe, secondly by the emergence of the Communist Party in control in China. To this bloc have been added North Korea (possibly from 1945, but clearly from 1953 following the cease-fire there), North Vietnam from 1954, and Cuba from 1961. The Mongolian's People's Republic also belongs. Excluding Cuba, but counting Yugoslavia, there are thirteen countries. They differ greatly in area, number of inhabitants, level of cultural and economic development, and physical conditions. These so-called socialist countries had in 1960 over one-quarter of the world's land area, over one-third of the world's population and industrial production.

Fig. 32 shows the Communist bloc, and Table 19 some distances between the main concentrations of population, East Europe and European U.S.S.R. at one end and south-east

TABLE 19

By	From	Via	To	Miles
Rail	Moscow	Soviet territory	Vladivostok	5,400
Rail	Moscow	Across Manchuria	Vladivostok	4,800
Rail	Moscow	Across Mongolia	Peking	4,400
Sea	Archangel	Northern Sea Route	Vladivostok	7,100
Sea	Odessa	Suez Canal	Vladivostok	10,800
Sea	Leningrad	Panama Canal	Vladivostok	15,600
Sea	Western Europe		New York	about 3,000
Rail	New York		San Francisco	about 3,000

The table appears in a short article on the subject of Communist bloc sea routes in the *Manchester Guardian*, 21 Feb. 1957.

China at the other (see Chapter 7). The countries of the bloc, excluding Yugoslavia, fall easily into two groups, one dominated by the U.S.S.R. and including the countries of East Europe, the whole integrated economically under Comecon, the other dominated by China. The members of the first group are relatively far advanced industrially, the second are underdeveloped. Of the two principal members, the U.S.S.R. and China, the U.S.S.R. is far better endowed with resources, as Fig. 33 suggests, and under these circumstances China could hardly be expected to model its development on that of the U.S.S.R. or to reach such a high production per inhabitant. In spite of the great difference in size (the U.S.S.R. is nearly

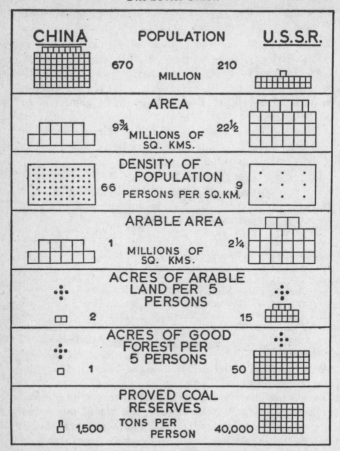

33. A comparison of the population/resource balance of China and the U.S.S.R.

2½ times as large) there have been some similarities in development, as Fig. 34 indicates. In both countries, for example, industry has moved into the interior from the older concentrations.

There are several reasons why the Comecon and China have

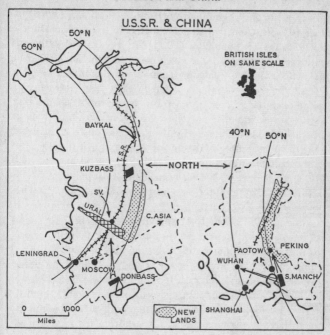

34. A comparison of development in the U.S.S.R. and China.

formed one bloc in world affairs since 1949. The most obvious reason is the presence in power of a Communist Party and an adherence to Marxist and Leninist ideas of economic progress, but political union has not been suggested. For reasons of defence, too, it has been useful to form an alliance, though the U.S.S.R. has made no move at all to supply China with nuclear weapons, a policy that can only delay, not prevent, China's having them. Most important from the Chinese point of view has been the trade between the two parts of the bloc and the technical aid provided by Comecon. China has had to pay for all the equipment and other imports it has received from Comecon, but the help came at an opportune time when the U.S.A. and other non-Communist countries were blockading the country and when China was restoring its existing indus-

247

trial capacity and beginning to expand. Even so, the amount of trade between Comecon and China has not been great. During the 1950s it was about £200–300 m. per year each way (the exchange is approximate), not much more than the trade between the U.K. and New Zealand. It amounted therefore to only a few shillings per inhabitant of China each year, but many of the goods, such as equipment for steel works, engineering works, power stations, and oil-drilling were vital for China in the early 1950s. Chinese exports to Comecon have included such items as rubber and tin, not available in Comecon, but have mostly been food and raw materials, useful but not vital. The U.S.S.R. has, of course, been the main supplier of manufactures to China, but East Germany, Poland, and Czechoslovakia have also contributed.

Although the strength of the bloc should not be underestimated, several weaknesses may be noted. Politically, several versions of Communism, or of the way to build socialism and Communism, have already emerged, and these are quite clearly related to different countries. It is almost worse in the eyes of one Communist country for there to be a different, heretical, version in a fellow Communist country, than for the country not to have Communism at all. Apart from the lone struggle of Tito in Yugoslavia, the two principal camps are represented by the U.S.S.R. and China.

From an economic point of view, trade between Comecon and China has not been so large or so beneficial to China as one might have expected between two such large blocs, connected by an economic alliance. One reason has been that Comecon itself has been short in the 1950s of many of the goods it has been sending to China. Another is simply the combination of distance and inadequate communications between the two main concentrations of population and industry already referred to (see Fig. 32 and Table 19). Several thousand miles of forest, mountain, and desert separate the two concentrations and until 1955 the Trans-Siberian Railway from East Siberia into North China was the only land link between Moscow and Peking. This has been supplemented by a more direct line, only single track, however, across the Mongolian

People's Republic. Another line, also single track, should now be complete between the U.S.S.R. and China across Sinkiang. But these lines are heavily loaded with internal traffic and not suitable for coping with a heavy volume of international traffic. Contrast this situation with about ten transcontinental railways (as well as many roads) across the North American continent. Sea transport is another means of moving goods between the U.S.S.R. and China, but the shorter Northern Sea Route is open only 2–3 months of the year, while the route via Suez, quite heavily used by the Communist powers, is a long one. Moreover, although efficient sea transport is generally much cheaper than rail transport, the merchant vessels of the Communist countries are mostly not large and the port facilities are inadequate, while often an appreciable rail haul at one or both ends requires transhipment and adds to time and cost. For various reasons, seagoing transport in the U.S.S.R., according to Soviet figures, is not actually much cheaper than rail transport per ton-mile. While passengers can fly between Moscow and Peking in a few hours, the journey by land takes over a week on the best trains. The flow of goods must therefore be extremely slow.

If rivalry over Communism and its application have made political relations between Comecon and China far from harmonious in recent years and distance has hindered economic integration of the bloc, there are other reasons why friction may be expected between the U.S.S.R. and China. In the first place the Soviet Union contains along the southern fringes of its Asian territory lands that traditionally belonged, if loosely, to the Chinese Empire. In the second place, the U.S.S.R. is endowed with many resources lacking in China yet is itself not able to utilize them at present. This is particularly true of the forest reserves and minerals of the Soviet Far East. Fig. 35 shows that while the Russians are reasonably well established along the north-western boundary of China they are few in number, a few million, in the valley of the Amur facing northeast China, while here the density of population on the Chinese side (Manchuria) is far higher. Possibly the haste with which the Russians have filled their new agricultural lands in the

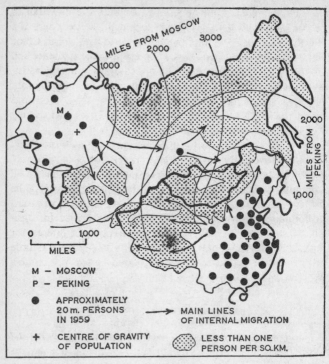

35. Population pressure in the U.S.S.R. and China.

1950s and are now building a third heavy industrial base around the Kuzbass and Lake Baykal is partly due to a desire to demonstrate to the Chinese that they are able to use their natural resources.

If there is scope for rivalry along the frontier zone between the U.S.S.R. and China there is scope outside the bloc as well. Quite clearly there has been a growing tendency for the Soviet and Chinese Communists to compete for the allegiance of Communist Parties in non-Communist countries (e.g. India, Burma) and for the favour of non-Communist regimes in newly independent countries (e.g. Guinea, Ghana). Although they collaborate to weaken and eventually facilitate the downfall of the capitalist industrial countries, behind the scenes there is a duel for superiority in the Communist world itself. Thus China has been active in the traditional Soviet sphere of influence and interference, South-west Asia and North Africa, offering assistance to Iraq, Egypt, the Algerian nationalists, and even Cyprus. The U.S.S.R. in its turn has been busy in China's obvious sphere, South-east Asia, offering aid to Indonesia and seeking a relaxation of tension in Laos.

From the economic point of view China seems more likely than the U.S.S.R. to seek actual territorial gains. Its population/resource balance is so much less favourable, and it may well be more ready to risk a war to acquire new territory. The obvious directions are towards South-east Asia where, unquestionably, large areas remain that could be used for agriculture, and towards the U.S.S.R. India has little of interest for the Chinese since its own population/resource balance is little better, and mountain barriers make movement far in this direction unlikely anyway.

V. THE U.S.S.R. AND THE NON-COMMUNIST WORLD

In the last section the relationship between the U.S.S.R. and China was discussed. In this section Soviet influence on the non-Communist world is considered. As previously stressed, the Soviet Union has a 'sacred' duty to help the 'inevitable' spread of Communism throughout the world. It would use war to do this were it sure of winning and not suffering too serious losses itself. Naturally in the face of great U.S. military strength now and of West European superiority before the Second World War, it has not favoured the outright acquisition of territories by force, though there is nothing against this in Soviet thinking. Russian history in the last few centuries, like that of many West European countries, has been one of expansion, and post-1917 thinking and policy are to some extent a continuation of this; and Russian nationalism and Soviet Communism are not entirely unconnected.

Since 1917 Soviet foreign policy (and internal planning to

some extent) has been partly one of defence against capitalism (e.g. Nazi Germany's attitude to the U.S.S.R.) partly one of attack. The U.S.S.R. was on the defensive in the years following 1917, during the Second World War, and again afterwards, in the face of U.S. superiority in nuclear weapons, and the commonly expressed view in the U.S.A. that a 'Crusade' should be launched to liberate East Europe and to unseat the Communist Party of the U.S.S.R. The Soviet view that capitalism thrives on war is to some extent supported by the boost given to the U.S. economy by the Second World War and even by the Korean War, but in the 1950s West Europe and Japan have both been able both to expand their economy very impressively and to keep unemployment low without a war. At all events, until the late 1950s the U.S.A., by exploiting its superior strategic position, could have seriously crippled the U.S.S.R. in a world war without suffering appreciably itself, but it did not choose to do so. Now the chance is lost. One person, Bertrand Russell, sensed this in 1948: 'Either we must have a war against Russia before she has the atom bomb or we will have to lie down and let them govern us.' (Reported in the *Observer*, 21 Nov. 1948.) Whether anything was seriously contemplated seems doubtful, for military expenditure fell very sharply between 1945 and 1947 and remained low until the start of the Korean conflict in 1950.

In spite of its inferior military position until the late 1950s, the U.S.S.R. has carried on an offensive against the capitalist countries in various ways. At home the Press contains endless articles and cartoons against the West. Abroad it has occurred in the military, political, and economic fields.

As already stressed, actual acquisition of territory by Soviet forces seems unlikely, short of an accident starting off a world war, or possibly a takeover in the U.S.S.R. by military elements anxious to exploit the present strong position both of conventional and nuclear forces there. The East European countries fell to the U.S.S.R., some perhaps unexpectedly, as a result of the Second World War, but remain 'sovereign' states. Since then Soviet forces have not been involved in any major conflict, though arms have been supplied to many (e.g. Korea). Indeed there has been a withdrawal of forces from Austria, Finland (Porkala), and China (Port Arthur). Empire-building is out of fashion and not a thing to indulge in for a country advocating independence for colonial territories in Africa. What is more, the movement of Soviet armed forces into almost any area along its boundary apart from East Europe would be into a country involved in a military treaty with the U.S.A., the U.K., or both.

Since 1945 some success has been achieved by Communist Parties in taking over power in individual countries. In no country has a Communist Party gained an outright majority in a free election (except San Marino); but by building up influence in a government and then taking over power from a minority position, Communist Parties took over Czechoslovakia in 1948 and Cuba in 1961. In the years immediately after 1945 this might have been the fate of France and Italy, and there is always a chance of it happening elsewhere. As for a Communist Party ever gaining a genuine majority of votes, this seems highly unlikely either in the advanced industrial countries of North America and West Europe, or in the backward countries of Africa (witness the difficulty the U.S.S.R. had in organizing its activities in the Congo in 1960–1). But in the many countries at an intermediate level (e.g. Cuba), whether by a genuine election or a takeover, the chance is far from remote. This is not to say that a newly established Communist Party would necessarily model itself on the U.S.S.R. (or China).

Recently, however, the Soviet Union appears to have attached less importance to seeing a new Communist Party in power than to encouraging colonial countries to struggle for independence, whether from political colonialism (Africa, parts of Asia) or from economic colonialism (Latin America). Evidently in the Soviet view this is a step away from domination by capitalist industrial powers towards Communism, via independence.

Currently the most favoured method of extending influence is to trade with and offer aid to non-Communist countries. This is not to say that there are not sound economic reasons for trade, as well as political ones, but basically, on account of its policy of autarky and its great size and resources, the

U.S.S.R. is nearly self-sufficient, and could manage without trading at all. But the unharmonious development of its economy, already stressed, has now given it a surplus of certain items such as steel and oil, while food has been short, and some tropical products, if still a luxury for the ordinary Soviet citizen, have been imported recently. Trade is therefore desirable economically, if not essential, and the number of trading partners of the U.S.S.R. has increased greatly in the last few years. Sometimes, together with its allies in East Europe, it has stepped in to purchase a commodity from a country unable to sell this elsewhere : Egyptian cotton, Chilean copper, Cuban sugar. Often only a token quantity of trade is carried on, but this gives the opportunity for the establishment of diplomatic relations and often an embassy. In some cases the trade has been connected with construction and economic assistance in a country : the Bhilai iron and steel works in India, the new railway system of Iraq.

So far Soviet aid to the non-Communist world has not been appreciable except to certain countries at particular times (e.g. Egypt). At present 95 per cent of the financial assistance of one kind or another received by the developing countries of the world comes from North America, West Europe, and Japan, most of it in the form of government loans repayable over long periods at modest rates of interest, but an increasing amount comes from private sources. The U.S.S.R. also gives loans on favourable terms, but by its own arguments it cannot actually invest money abroad. Until now, however, the Soviet Union and East Europe have not been lavish with their offers of aid and have almost invariably offered credits, not outright grants (gifts) of money. Much has gone to small countries, on which the impact of a limited amount of aid would be felt. The main reason for this lack of enterprise on the Soviet side has been sheer lack of money to offer. It may not be long now, however, before Comecon builds up its economy to such a level that it has enough resources to offer more massive aid and greatly improved shipping services to expand its trade with the non-Communist areas of Latin America, Africa, and Asia.

The world outside Europe and the interior of Asia is for the first time feeling the impact of Russia. On account of its inward looking policy, land-locked nature, and land empire this has not been felt much up to now. Even so there are difficulties. Access to the coast from the great economic 'heartland' of the U.S.S.R. stretching east into Siberia from the Volga is not easy, and most of the ports are somewhat remote from the great shipping routes of the world. But the U.S.S.R. has rapidly developed worldwide interests, exploring the Arctic Ocean, fishing in the North Pacific and Atlantic, exploring Antarctica and establishing permanent bases there, setting up embassies in many African and Latin American countries. As a world power and a world influence it has come to stay. As a trading country and a source of aid for underdeveloped countries it lags far behind North America and West Europe. But with its limited resources it has already made a great impact. China, too, is coming out of its isolation and though on a smaller scale so far, has become a worldwide influence, too. How far it collaborates with the U.S.S.R. and how far it goes its own way will be of enormous importance in world affairs.

Chapter 9

THE UNITED STATES OF AMERICA

I. TERRITORIAL EXPANSION OF THE U.S.A.

THE U.S.A. has been an independent state for not much more than 150 years. In this respect, then, it contrasts with Russia, which, as the Moscow principality, was emerging as a powerful state almost 500 years ago. Yet since 1783 the U.S.A. has passed Russia in industrial and agricultural production, and approached it in population. Both have expanded towards the Pacific, Russia eastwards from an original nucleus in Europe, the U.S.A. westwards from a nucleus on the Atlantic coast, facing Europe, its main source of immigrants.

Although the population of North America is now almost entirely English-speaking, the continent attracted the interest of several European nations after the discovery of America. Until the nineteenth century Florida and what is now south-west U.S.A. were northerly extensions of the Spanish American Empire. England, France, and Holland all approached from the east and annexed territories along the Atlantic side of the continent. In the eighteenth century the Russians entered across the Bering Strait to occupy Alaska and the Pacific coast as far south as Spanish California. In 1700, after a century of colonization, the English settlements in the lowland between the Atlantic and the Appalachians, with fewer than 300,000 inhabitants, did not look like the nucleus of a state destined to extend across the continent to the Pacific coast, but in 1783, when the English colonies had gained their independence from the mother country, they already had more than 3 m. inhabitants of European origin, almost all of them, however, rural dwellers. There were almost no industries in the colonies, and communications were poor.

The period between 1783 and the Civil War (1861–5) was one of great territorial expansion. Fig. 36 shows the main area of European settlement in the U.S.A. in the 1780s, and the various territorial acquisitions up to the 1850s. The purchase of Louis-

36. Growth of continental U.S.A. between the War of Independence and the Civil War. The date of acquisition of each new territory is shown.

iana from Napoleon in 1803 and of Florida from Spain in 1819 enlarged the U.S.A. to more than half its present size. Subsequent expansion up to the Rio Grande in 1845 brought it into conflict with its neighbour, Mexico, and as the result of a war and purchases, this country lost about half (though at the time the more thinly peopled part) of its territory.[1] In the north, an agreement was reached with Britain over the U.S.-Canadian

1. If U.S. history books tend to overlook this example of U.S. military expansion in the best European tradition, the Mexicans do not forget it, which serves as a reminder that though there may be two ways of looking at any question, military superiority counts in the end. A Mexican geographer, Jesús Galindo y Villa, writes thus in *Geografía de México*, p. 114 (Barcelona, 1950): '... but as a consequence of the unequal struggle in 1846 and 1847 against the U.S.A., we lost for ever the vast territory of Texas, which today is the most extensive state in that country, while New Mexico and Upper California were snatched from us as well.'

boundary, and in 1846 the Oregon territory became part of the U.S.A. Continental U.S.A. has therefore had its present form for more than a hundred years. As a result of the U.S. Civil War the future unity of the U.S.A. was assured, and the completion of the first transcontinental railway in 1869 might be taken to mark the final consolidation of modern U.S.A.

During the period of its expansion in North America the U.S.A. took only a small part in affairs outside that continent.[1] In the war with Britain in 1812–15, fighting was confined largely to the Canadian frontier of the U.S.A. and to sea battles in the Atlantic. During the following decade, when the Spanish and Portuguese colonies of Latin America were struggling for independence from Europe, the U.S.A. was satisfied merely to show its sympathy with the new republics by the enunciation of the Monroe doctrine. This opposed any further attempts by European powers to colonize the American continent. Only after the Civil War, which ended in 1865, did the U.S.A. begin to take an active interest in areas outside North America – mainly in the North Pacific and Central America.

In 1867 Alaska was purchased from the Russians for $U.S. 7,200,000, while in the same year Midway Island was acquired (see Fig. 37). U.S. interest in the Pacific at this period was partly a result of the rapid growth in importance of the Pacific states (particularly California), and contacts were established with East Asia. As a result of the short war with Spain in 1898 the U.S.A. acquired the Philippine Islands, a foothold and important interest in East Asia itself, while the Hawaiian Islands, annexed in the same year, provided a vital link in the widely scattered, though territorially small, U.S. Pacific empire. Other small islands were subsequently annexed.

In Central America the U.S.A. had been content around 1850 to extend its frontier only as far as the Rio Grande. The war with Spain in 1898 gave it control over the last Spanish colonies in Latin America – Cuba and Puerto Rico. The former

1. It is interesting to recall, however, that as early as 1803–4, a U.S. naval squadron (forerunner of the present 6th Fleet) was sent to the Mediterranean to combat the North African pirates.

was freed technically, but has always been strongly influenced by the U.S.A. Puerto Rico remained in U.S. hands, becoming a commonwealth in 1952. After 1898, U.S. interest in Central America grew, and when a revolution conveniently occurred in the Colombian province of Panama, the U.S.A. was quick to sign a treaty with the newly formed republic there, thus ending long negotiations with the Colombian government to acquire a concession to build a canal across its territory. The transcontinental canal was opened in Panama in 1914 and at

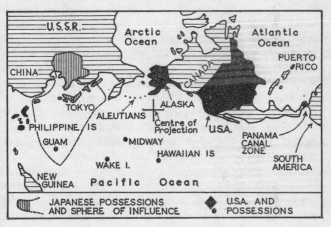

37. United States 'empire' of Central America and the North Pacific. Projection: oblique zenithal equidistant. Centre of projection: 45° N, 160° W.

once became vital to the U.S.A. both strategically and economically, which is why this part of America has on several occasions been the scene of U.S. intervention. Fig. 37 shows the U.S. and Japanese empires on the eve of the Second World War.

Participation in 1917–18 in the war in Europe was followed by a period of isolation, and up to 1941 the U.S.A. attempted to keep out of conflicts in other parts of the world. The Japanese attack on Pearl Harbour in 1941 forced it into the Second World War, and, in spite of some opposition at home, successive post-war governments have committed the U.S.A. by treaty to support, in the event of a war, not only almost all the Latin American republics (Rio Treaty, 1947) but also many of the European and Asian countries in the *inner zone* fringing the Communist bloc.

II. DEMOGRAPHIC AND ECONOMIC EXPANSION

The rise of the U.S.A. to its present position as a leading world power can only be appreciated when the enormous demographic and economic expansion of the country during the last 170 years is taken into account.

In the 1780s the U.S.A. had about 4 m. inhabitants, most of them of European origin. In 1860 it had about 30 m., in 1960 180 m. In the last 170 years its population has therefore increased more than 40 times. During the same period the population of the whole world increased about five times, that of Russia about three times, and that of the British Isles not much more than twice. During the whole of its history up to about 1930, with the exception of a few brief periods, the increase of U.S. population has been more the result of immigration than of natural increase. Since then the larger share of the increase has been accounted for by the natural increase.

Before the 1780s there had been very little industrial development in the North American colonies, most of the population being engaged in farming. Between independence and the Civil War the southern states continued to develop their colonial type of economy and benefited from the rapid expansion of cotton manufacturing in Europe and in the New England states of the U.S.A. In 1794, 17,000 bales of cotton were produced, in 1810, 178,000, and in 1859, 5,400,000. During this period the northern states, and the New England states in particular, were endeavouring to set up large-scale modern industrial establishments on the lines of those in Britain at that period. Cotton spinning by machinery was the first branch to become firmly established, but in the early decades of the nineteenth century the production of iron began on an appreciable scale, and by about 1850 an engineering industry was developing. Already before the Civil War firearms, steam engines, and agricultural implements were being mass-produced.

Although great harm was done to the economy of the southern states as a result of the Civil War, and many still unsettled political and social problems were created, the industrial states, and subsequently the whole of the U.S.A., benefited greatly from experience of various kinds gained during what was the first war to be waged with modern forms of transport and machinery.[1]

During the remaining decades of the nineteenth century U.S. industry expanded rapidly, and new branches of manufacturing were constantly being introduced. During this period it overtook the leading industrial countries of Europe both in absolute production (by 1900 it had more inhabitants than any except Russia) and, in many branches of industry, also in production per industrial worker.

During the present century the U.S.A. has led all other countries of the world in many branches of manufacturing, and has been the largest producer, in absolute terms, and frequently in *per caput* terms as well, of many types of manufacture. Between 1850 and 1900 the number of people engaged in manfacturing rose from 1 m. to 5 m., the latter producing much more per individual than the former. In 1950 there were 15 m. workers in manufacturing, again producing much more per individual than their 5 m. predecessors did in 1900.

1. '. . . the American Civil War of 1861–5, which even in the number of troops involved far surpassed the order of magnitude of the Napoleonic Wars and in which for the first time the railway was used for large troop movements, the telegraph network for messages and a steam fleet, keeping the sea for months on end, for blockade, and in which armoured ships, the torpedo, rifled weapons and monster artillery of extraordinary range were discovered. . . . Amongst the wholly new problems was that of rapidly restoring railways and bridges; the bridge at Chattanooga, for the heaviest military trains, 240 metres long and 30 metres high, was built in 4½ days.' Spengler, O. *The Decline of the West*, Vol. 2 (p. 421 in the English translation by C. F. Atkinson, *Borzoi Books*, New York, 1946).

III. THE U.S.A. AS A WORLD POWER

The Japanese attack on Pearl Harbour in December 1941 might be said to mark the beginning of a third phase in the expansion of U.S. influence, the first two being the growth of the U.S.A. in North America following the War of Independence, and the growth of its North Pacific and Central American empire following the Civil War. Since 1941 U.S. influence, like Soviet influence, has been extended in various ways.

One form of expansion that has played an important part is military expansion. During the war U.S. forces fought in Europe, North Africa, South, South-east, and East Asia. Since the war they have stayed in occupation in certain areas in this *inner zone* including Germany and the Ryukyu Islands near Japan. They have also remained in, returned to, or come for the first time to many other countries of Europe and Asia (including Japan, the U.K., France, and Spain) with the approval of the governments concerned, although the governments in many cases are not formed on U.S. democratic lines and are not necessarily there by the approval of the majority of the population. U.S. financial aid given to allies specifically for military purposes might be included in this form of expansion. U.S. military influence extends therefore to allied countries with (e.g. U.K.) or without (e.g. Pakistan) U.S. bases and to countries (e.g. Saudi Arabia) with U.S. bases but not connected by treaty. It should be noted, however, that the U.S.A. has not permanently annexed any territory as a result of the war. On the contrary, it has granted independence to the Philippines.

A second form of U.S. expansion has been of a political nature. Although opposing the spread of Communism and objecting in theory to any form of government not chosen by the whole population, participating in free elections, the U.S.A. has been much less active than the U.S.S.R. in attempting to spread its particular form of political organization. Assuming perhaps that its own example would be sufficient to guide other nations to the most desirable form of government, it has distributed its foreign aid indiscriminately during the last decade.

Among recipients are Yugoslavia with a Communist regime, Spain with a Fascist one, Saudi Arabia with a doubtful monarchy, France and the U.K., which are colonial powers, several Latin American countries with military dictatorships, and Bolivia with (since 1953) what has been described in the U.S.A. as a Marxist government. It therefore appears that more importance has been attached to limiting the spread of Soviet Communist influence than to replacing Communist and other non-democratic (in the American sense) regimes by an American type of democracy.

The growing influence of the U.S.A. on the rest of the world has been felt most strongly in the present century in the economic sphere. The economic depression of the early 1930s, originating apparently in the U.S.A., affected the whole world with the exception of the U.S.S.R., then enduring its First 5-Year Plan. During the Second World War, U.S. manufactures, perhaps even more than U.S. forces, played a leading part in the defeat of Germany and Japan. Since 1945, U.S. economic expansion has taken place in three main forms: by investment, by increased trade, and by the distribution of credits (loans) and grants (not to be repaid). Fig. 38 summarizes the direction of U.S. foreign investments, trade, and aid, both non-military and military, between 1945 and the late 1950s (source *Statistical Abstract of the United States, 1960*, various tables in Section 32).

Canada and Latin America each have about one-third of U.S. foreign investments, but only 17 per cent of the total return comes from those in Canada, presumably because they are very safe. More than one-fifth of U.S. foreign trade is with Canada (but this represents about two-thirds of Canada's trade) and about one-quarter with Latin America. Thus in foreign investments and trade the U.S. economy is still closely associated with the rest of the Americas, though the proportion is diminishing. On the other hand U.S. aid, both non-military and military, to Canada (for obvious reasons) and to Latin America, has been very slight. This has been resented in Latin America and the situation has changed now.

U.S. investments in and trade with West Europe have been

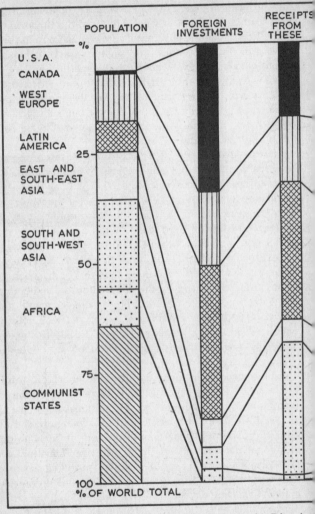

POPULATION   FOREIGN INVESTMENTS   RECEIPTS FROM THESE

U.S.A.
CANADA

WEST EUROPE

LATIN AMERICA

EAST AND SOUTH-EAST ASIA

SOUTH AND SOUTH-WEST ASIA

AFRICA

COMMUNIST STATES

%
25
50
75
100
% OF WORLD TOTAL

38. Influence of the U.S.A. on the rest of the world. Direction

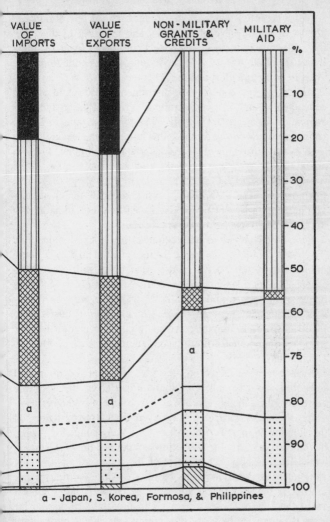

VALUE OF IMPORTS   VALUE OF EXPORTS   NON-MILITARY GRANTS & CREDITS   MILITARY AID

%

— 10
— 20
— 30
— 40
— 50
— 60
— 75
— 80
— 90
— 100

a - Japan, S. Korea, Formosa, & Philippines

J.S. investments, trade, and aid during 1945–58. For explanation see text.

growing recently, whereas the amount of aid has diminished almost to nothing except to Spain, and for most of the 1950s the recipients have been repaying their loans. Even so, more than half of all post-war U.S. economic aid has gone to putting West Europe on its feet again.

Almost all the rest of U.S. investments, trade, and aid are connected with the non-Communist areas of Asia and with Africa. Investments are mainly in eastern Asia and in the oil countries of South-west Asia, the latter giving exceptionally high returns. Investments in Africa are as yet limited. Trade is again mostly with eastern Asia and South-west Asia, while nearly all the aid before 1960 went to Japan, South Korea, Formosa, and the Philippines, countries depending economically and militarily on the U.S.A. Recently aid to India and to South Vietnam has increased appreciably.

Economic connexions with countries in the Communist bloc have been limited almost entirely to some aid to East Europe immediately after the war, aid to and trade with Yugoslavia especially after 1948, and some aid to Poland since 1956. Trade between the U.S.A. and U.S.S.R. is negligible, while in theory it is non-existent between the U.S.A. and Communist China. In other words Communism virtually cuts off one-third of the world's population from any economic contact at all with the U.S.A.

Although the United States has given far more economic aid since the war than all the other industrial countries of the world together, the aid has not always been put to the best possible use and has not always achieved what it was intended to do: to gain support for the West in receiving countries. Again, the amount is currently only a few per cent of the U.S. budget, which itself is only a small part of the total national income, and much of the money has been given on condition that it should be spent in the U.S.A. anyway. What is more, almost all of the U.S. aid, both military and non-military, has so far gone to countries in some way connected with it by military treaty and at the same time of great strategic importance to it. The result is that Communist China has received none, India only a negligible amount, and colonial Africa and Latin

America very little. These parts of the world, which are among the poorest, and which together have more than half of the world's population, have therefore so far benefited little from U.S. aid, which has been just as 'political' and no more philanthropic than Soviet trade and aid discussed in the last chapter.

Chapter 10

THE BALANCE OF POWER IN THE WORLD

I. THE U.S.A. AND THE U.S.S.R.

THE U.S.A. and the U.S.S.R. are widely accepted as being the leading powers in the world today, on whatever basis power is assessed. Their supremacy dates from the Second World War, when the U.S.A. emerged with a greatly expanded industrial capacity, hardly affected by the austerity of this period, with nuclear weapons 'tested' in Japan, and a large bomber striking-force and navy, while the U.S.S.R. finished the war in control of two-thirds of Europe, with the largest land forces in the world, including experienced tank forces and artillery, and a respectable basis of industry in areas not occupied by the Germans. Since 1945 these two countries have gathered others into their orbit and have faced one another in many parts of the world. The U.S.S.R. has been basically on the defensive until the late 1950s on account of its inability to strike back at the U.S.A. with nuclear weapons in the event of a third world war. The U.S.A., on the other hand, by inflicting enormous damage on the U.S.S.R. (which could only retaliate by attacking allies of the U.S.A.) might have gained control of the world militarily without suffering much damage itself.

If this was the situation until recently there has now been a change, for the time is near, if it has not already arrived, when the U.S.S.R. will have powerful enough weapons to cripple the U.S.A., and the means of delivering them; so much so, indeed, that Soviet leaders appear to hold the view that, while they could obliterate the U.S.A., something might even survive in the U.S.S.R. Whether this is so or not, each is now so powerful from a military point of view that nothing more can be done to increase military strength except by way of perfecting the present system. Each has nearly reached a ceiling beyond which it is pointless, even impossible, to go. In this situation of stalemate, then, the U.S.A. and U.S.S.R. will decline relatively as the U.K., France (or possibly West Europe), China, and other countries build up their strength as nuclear powers, because these all have a long way to go to reach the 'ceiling'.

If a world war in which nuclear weapons were widely used occurred, then the world would be so different after it, even if much of humanity did survive, that there would be no point in writing the rest of this chapter. What follows is based on the assumption that a third world war will not occur, but that there will be a struggle between the U.S.A. and the U.S.S.R. and other countries or groups of countries in various non-military fields. Before introducing other contenders in this struggle, a comparison must be made of the two principal powers. Table 20 gives an indication of the level reached in different branches of the economy in the two countries. The first two columns show absolute figures for 1960 if possible, otherwise 1959, for the two countries. In the third column the Soviet total is expressed as a percentage of the U.S. total. In column 4 allowance has been made for the larger number of inhabitants in the U.S.S.R. (212 m. against 179 m.) and the Soviet figure has been divided by $\frac{212}{179}$ or 1·18 to take this into account. Unfortunately the figures are not always exactly comparable, but they are good enough to give a reasonable idea of the differences. The comparability is not discussed, but the sources are quoted at the bottom of the table. Nor is the table explained, since what it shows, and why the Soviet economy is close to the U.S. economy in some respects but lags far behind in others, will be evident from Chapters 7 and 8.

Whatever Soviet and U.S. politicians say, there are undoubtedly many resemblances between the two countries. They do not differ greatly in population, and if the U.S.S.R. is much larger territorially, it still only has about the same area suitable for agriculture. The population/resource balance is good in both countries compared with that in China, India, or even West Europe. What is more, Soviet leaders hope to close the gap between their level of economic development and that of the U.S.A. and to overtake their rival in about ten years' time. Their programme for the period 1960–80 is incredibly ambitious, as has been shown in Chapter 8, Section 11. If there is a continuation of trends in the last ten years, during which time

TABLE 20

1959 or 1960

	Absolute		U.S.S.R. as % of U.S.A. U.S.A.=100	Per caput U.S.S.R. as % of U.S.A. III÷118
	U.S.A.	U.S.S.R.		
Population (millions)	179	212	118	
Area (thous. sq. kms.)	9,360	22,400	240	
Area (thous. sq. mls.)	3,620	8,650		
Cultivated land (th. sq. mls.)	730	790	108	91
Ginned cotton (m. tons)	3·4	1·5	44	37
Cattle (m.)	97	74	76	64
Sheep (m.)	33	136	410	350
Pigs (m.)	57	53	93	79
Coal (m. tons)*	380	435	114	97
Oil (m. tons)	345	148	43	36
Gas (th. m. cu. metres)	325	47	14	12
Electricity production (th. m. kwh.)	840	292	35	30
Energy consumption (m. tons coal equiv.)	1,387	619	45	37
Pig iron (m. tons)	56	47	84	71
Steel (m. tons)	85	65	77	65
Cement (m. tons)	60	46	77	65
Motor vehicles output (th.)	6,675	527	8	7
Cotton cloth (m. metres)	9,559	6,387	67	57
Leather footwear (m. pairs)	561	418	74	63
Radio sets in use (m.)	161	33	21	18
Television sets in use (m.)	50	3	6	5
Railway mileage (th. mls.)	219	77	35	30
Goods on railways (th. m. ton mls.)	575	935	163	148
Surfaced road (th. mls.)	2,083	156	7	6
Goods on roads (th. m. ton mls.)	247	62	25	21
Merchant shipping (m. gross tons)	26	3	12	10

m. = million   th. = thousand

* Soviet lignite × ⅔.

Principal sources: *Statistical Abstract of the United States, 1960* and *S.S.S.R. v tsifrakh v 1960 godu*, Gosstatizdat, Moscow, 1961.

the U.S. economy has not expanded in such a spectacular fashion as it did in the 1940s, then the Soviet aims are not entirely unrealistic; but precisely what catching up means and precisely how and to what extent the U.S. economy might also develop are not taken into account. Growing awareness in the U.S.A. that the Soviet aims to overtake the U.S.A. are not entirely unrealistic has recently stimulated many U.S. economists to investigate the economic race, and many Soviet problems of economic development have been brought to light. What is more, by 1980 the U.S.S.R. (or Comecon by then) might be trying to catch up not merely the U.S.A. but a North Atlantic Community of North America and West Europe.

Whatever the future, the two countries are at present sufficiently large and advanced to make them the outstanding world powers of the mid twentieth century, and it has been easy to explain many of the conflicts of the post-war period in terms of rivalry between the two or between the two blocs led by them. One could fairly convincingly assert that most of the trouble spots were to be found in a zone of friction encircling the Communist bloc and containing the allies and bases established by the U.S.A. in an attempt to confine Communism within Eurasia, one-quarter of the world's land area and a mere one-fifteenth of the whole world's surface. If the U.S.A. kept the U.S.S.R. at arm's length in this way and was itself 2,500–3,500 miles from the nearest parts of the Soviet Union, the U.S.S.R. possesses one advantage: a much larger proportion of the population of the world lives nearer to it than to the U.S.A.

Fig. 39 shows that if lines are drawn at a distance of about 1,500 miles from the boundaries and coasts of continental U.S.A. and U.S.S.R., the former includes large stretches of ocean and no more than a few tens of millions of people in Canada and Mexico, while the latter includes about one-half of the world's population (including most of Europe, India, and China). This would mean that, were not its southern frontiers in difficult mountain and desert country, it would be in a better position than the U.S.A. to reach the main concentration of the world's population.

World events in the last few years have, however, made this relatively simple concept of two major world powers in conflict and of a zone of friction around the Communist bloc, virtually meaningless (see Fig. 46, inset map). In the first place, Communist influence has been felt strongly for the first time far from the periphery of the bloc, in the Congo, in Cuba, and in Antarctica. Secondly, the U.S.S.R. by using nuclear submarines will presumably be able to send its long-range rockets

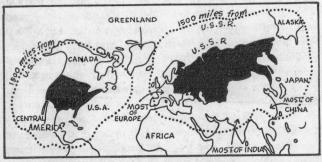

39. Parts of the world within 1,500 miles of the U.S.A. or U.S.S.R.

to the U.S.A. from different directions, so that the assumed direction of attack, 'covered' by the Early Warning Radar Systems of northern North America, can no longer be taken for granted. Thirdly, thanks partly to economic unions of smaller countries, other powers are emerging to challenge the supremacy of the U.S.S.R. and U.S.A. Militarily, if not economically, the two great powers are nearing their ceiling.

II. WORLD POWERS TODAY

The term 'balance of power' is frequently used by historians especially with reference to Europe, and it implies that the strength and influence of countries at any given time is measurable. But assessments of power are usually very approximate and, of course, subjective. In the study of world affairs, however, some kind of assessment is useful, both for understanding present events and for tracing the fortunes of different countries from the past up to the present day and even projecting them into the future.

Broadly speaking, power may be assessed either on the basis of military strength or on the basis of economic capacity. It has been suggested in the previous section that military strength is very much concentrated at present in the hands of the U.S.A. and the U.S.S.R. Any large-scale conflict would inevitably draw in other countries, and two groups would crystallize around Washington and Moscow respectively, leaving the neutrals of Africa, Asia, and Latin America out because in such a struggle their immediate significance, militarily speaking, is negligible. Assuming, however, that such a conflict will not take place, then there is no point in counting up the aircraft, rockets, nuclear submarines, armoured divisions, and so on, belonging to each power. The assessment must be made on the basis of economic strength, a more difficult basis, some of the drawbacks of which are discussed shortly.

A useful starting point for a consideration of the powers in the world today is the list of independent (sovereign) states. In June 1963 there were 111 members in the General Assembly of the United Nations, representing 109 independent countries (the U.S.S.R. on very dubious grounds has three seats). In addition, several important countries are not represented: Communist China, West and East Germany, North and South Korea, North and South Vietnam, and Switzerland. Excluding very small political units like Monaco, there are therefore at present around 115 individual countries in the world, the United Nations itself having about twice as many members now as when it was founded. With the emergence in the next few years of new sovereign states out of existing colonies, the number may rise to about 125.

Apart from the U.S.S.R. and, of course, the non-members, representation in the General Assembly of the United Nations is on the basis of one country, one vote, regardless of population, area, and economic strength of the members. This is not unlike the system of representation in federal countries (e.g. the U.S.A., Switzerland) in which in one house of representatives each internal division (state or canton in the examples given) is equally represented, regardless of the number of inhabitants in it. The Security Council of the United Nations, with its more limited membership and permanent representation of the 'Big Five' of the Second World War, comes nearer than the General Assembly to giving proper weight to the more influential countries.

Even so, the United Nations as organized at present is so unrealistic that it is hardly surprising the more powerful members ignore it if they think fit. Thus Africa, with only about 8 per cent of the world's population, has about one third of

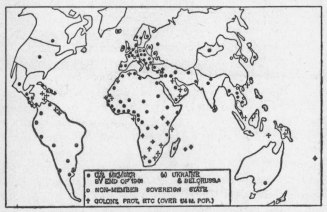

40. Countries of the world in early 1962, showing the 104 members of the United Nations, including Mauritania, the Mongolian People's Republic, Sierra Leone, and Tanganyika, all of which joined in 1961, and Syria, which became a member again after the dissolution of the United Arab Republic.

the seats, while the U.S.A. with nearly the same percentage of the population only has one. China, with nearly 25 per cent of the world's population, has no seat at all. The U.K., with nearly 2 per cent of the population of the world might claim two seats instead of its present one.

Fig. 40 shows the countries of the world at the end of 1961, distinguishing members of the General Assembly of the United Nations, non-member independent countries, and colonies as yet not represented. Fig. 41 shows all political units of the world with more than 1 m. inhabitants (some small members of the United Nations, e.g. Iceland, Luxembourg, and small colonies are therefore omitted) regardless of their status. In contrast to Fig. 40, each circle is drawn in proportion to the population of the country it represents. In West Europe there

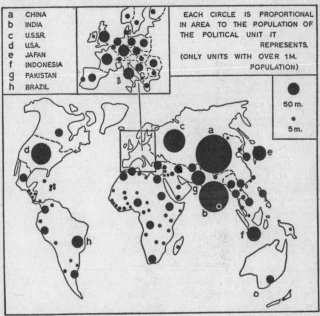

41. Countries of the world with more than 1 million inhabitants. The map includes non-members of the United Nations and colonial territories as well as U.N. members.

are many moderate-sized units, in Africa and Central America many small ones. On the other hand, the four largest (China, India, U.S.S.R., and U.S.A.) together have about half of the total population of the world.

Although population is a fairer basis than representation in the United Nations for an assessment of world power it is still far from satisfactory. Clearly, for example, the fact that

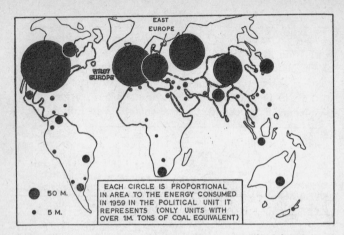

42. Consumption of energy (in tons of coal equivalent) by country. Note: For convenience West Europe and East Europe are taken as single units.

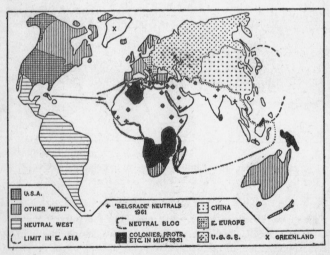

43. Blocs in the world in the early 1960s. The seven blocs are used in Fig. 44. The 24 neutrals attending the Belgrade Conference in 1961 are indicated.

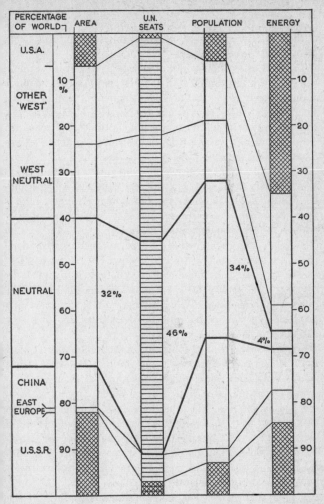

44. World share-out of area, population, consumption of energy, and representation in the General Assembly of the United Nations. Note: For convenience 100 seats are shown. This was the position early in 1961 if Syria, then part of the United Arab Republic, is allowed a place.

Communist China has nearly four times as many inhabitants as the U.S.A. does not mean it is four times as powerful. Other factors must be considered.

The area of a country must obviously be taken into account, since the chances are that a large country will have more natural resources (agricultural land, minerals, forests) than a small one, though only within very broad limits. Economic strength lies not only in resources but also in level of economic development and in ability, technologically speaking, to use them. There is not a simple way of assessing this. Total national income would be a useful measure but for the different ways in which this is calculated in different countries and the difficulty of finding satisfactory rates of exchange to convert different countries to one standard currency for purposes of comparison.[1] More straightforward is an assessment based on the consumption by each country of a particular item of importance in industry, such as steel or energy. For the purposes of this book, total consumption of all sources of energy (converted to coal equivalent) is taken to measure the level of industrial and technological development, since figures are readily available and comparable both for the present and for many decades back into the past.

Fig. 42 shows the distribution of consumption (not production) of energy by countries in the world. Needless to say, it gives a completely different picture from that showing representation in the United Nations (Fig. 40) and from that showing population (Fig. 41). This time only two countries, the U.S.A. and U.S.S.R., together account for half of the world total. In West and Central Africa, only Nigeria and the Congo are worth representing, and even their consumption is diminutive. Obviously, energy alone is no more a fair assessment of power than area or population.

Fig. 44 summarizes what has been discussed so far, showing the share-out among seven countries or groups of countries in

1. See *The Income of Nations*, by Paul Studenski, New York, 1958, for a study of national income and for national incomes in the 1950s. National income figures are also included in the *United Nations Statistical Yearbook*.

the world of area, seats in the General Assembly of the United
Nations, population, and consumption of energy. Fig. 43 shows
the groupings on the world map. The West and countries inclined towards it are divided into the U.S.A., other solidly
Western countries, and other countries of more doubtful allegiance. The Communist bloc is divided into the U.S.S.R., East
Europe, and China. The remainder are classed as neutrals. For
representation in the United Nations to be fair, each country
should have in the other three columns the same percentage of
the world total as it has in the column of U.N. seats. Of course
they do not (see Table 21). The U.S.A. and U.S.S.R., Com-

TABLE 21

	Area	Proportionate U.N. seats	Actual U.N. seats	Population	Proportionate U.N. seats	Energy	Proportionate U.N. seats
1. U.S.A.	94	7	1	180	6	1,387	35
2. Other 'West'	236	17	21	380	13	942	24
3. West Neutral	213	16	23	370	13	222	5½
4. Neutral	439	32	46	995	34	146	4
5. China	123	9	0	710	24	370	9
6. East Europe	10	1	6	100	3	280	7
7. U.S.S.R.	239	18	3	215	7	619	15½
World	1,354	100	100	2,950	100	3,966	100

Actual U.N. Seats shows the number of political units in the area actually
 represented as full members of the United Nations.
Area in hundreds of thousands of sq. kms.
Population in millions (1960).
Energy in millions of tons of coal equivalent (1959).
2. Other 'West': All non-Communist Europe, plus Turkey, Canada,
 Australia, New Zealand, S. Africa.
3. West neutral: All Latin America except Cuba, plus Japan, S. Korea,
 Formosa, Philippines, S. Vietnam.
4. Neutral*: All not included in other groups.
5. China: Communist China plus N. Korea, N. Vietnam, Mongolian P.R.
6. East Europe: E. Germany, Poland, Czechoslovakia, Hungary, Romania,
 Bulgaria, Albania.
 * i.e. in addition to all countries of Africa and Asia not included elsewhere, Yugoslavia and Cuba are included.

munist China, and (among the Neutrals) India are grossly under-represented in the U.N. General Assembly. Both West and East Europe are more or less fairly represented, while Latin America is over-represented and (of the Neutrals) the new African countries are grossly over-represented. By blocs, the Western group is over-represented for its population but not for its energy consumption, the Communist bloc is under-represented for both population and energy, the neutrals are over-represented for population and grossly over-represented for energy consumption.

So much for the United Nations. Obviously at present it bears little resemblance to reality and this is one reason for its failure to cope with most post-war problems. In the early years the West was very strongly represented but recently it has been pushed out of the majority by neutrals. On the strength of this and of the attitude towards the U.K. of these new countries, some British politicians have been short-sighted enough to talk of withdrawing. In fact the whole set-up will have to be modified before it can be expected to achieve anything, and its relationship to world power is remote at present. Some other assessment of this is therefore desirable.

An assessment of the influence of different powers in the world today is a useful exercise if it is appreciated that only an approximate result can be achieved, based on the personal selection of criteria for measuring. One complicated but useful and interesting attempt may be referred to here.[1] Both civil and military factors are taken into account and various sets of figures have been 'corrected' to give a more realistic version of their significance. Thus, for example, not only is working population taken into account, but also its 'technical efficiency' in different countries. The grand totals for the ten leading countries are as follows: U.S.A. 6,459, U.S.S.R. 6,321, U.K. 1,257, China 999, West Germany 663, Canada 498, Japan 410, France 383, India 373, Poland 324.

For the purposes of this book a simple and very approximate assessment is made on the basis of area, population, and

1. F. C. German, 'A Tentative Evaluation of World Power', *Conflict Resolution*, Vol. iv, No. 1, March 1960, pp. 138–44.

consumption of energy. Twice as much weight is given to energy as to either of the other two. For simplicity, the total land area and population of the world are each counted as 250 and the total consumption of energy as 500. Thus, for example, Brazil has 6 per cent of the world's land area or $\frac{15}{250}$, 2 per cent of the world's population or $\frac{5}{250}$, but consumes only 0·4 per cent of the energy or $\frac{2}{500}$. Its total is 22 out of 1000 or 2·2 per cent of the world's economic strength (on this basis). Table 22 shows the leading powers. Slight discrepancies occur owing to rounding of figures. Naturally the results would not be exactly the same if other criteria were taken or even if different weight were given to area, population, and energy. If greater emphasis were given to area, then the U.S.S.R., Brazil, Canada, and Australia would score higher marks; if to population, then Indonesia and Pakistan would, and so on.

Fig. 45 shows the distribution of the leading world powers

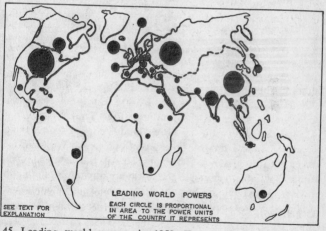

LEADING WORLD POWERS

SEE TEXT FOR EXPLANATION

EACH CIRCLE IS PROPORTIONAL IN AREA TO THE POWER UNITS OF THE COUNTRY IT REPRESENTS

45. Leading world powers in 1959. For an explanation of the 'power units' used, see text.

according to the foregoing assessment, the circles being proportional to the 'power units' given in Table 22 (Column IV). This is the position around 1960 but the picture could be simplified by allowing for the grouping of countries into economic

TABLE 22

	I Area	II Population	III Energy	IV Total (I+II+III)
World	250	250	500	1,000
1 U.S.A.	17	15	174	206
2 U.S.S.R.	41	18	78	137
3 China	17	57	46	120
4 India	6	34	6	46
5 U.K.		4	30	34
6 Canada	18	1	12	31
7 W. Germany		5	24	29
8 Brazil	15	5	2	22
9 Japan		8	12	20
10 France	1	4	14	19
11 Australia	14		4	18
12 Poland		2	10	12
13 Indonesia	3	8		11
14 E. Germany		1	10	11
15 Mexico	4	3	4	11
16 Italy		4	6	10

Others: 9–6 Pakistan, S. Africa, Argentina, Czechoslovakia, Spain.
   5–3 Congo, Nigeria, Sudan, Netherlands, Iran, Ethiopia, Egypt, Venezuela, Belgium, Romania, Colombia, Burma, Turkey.

unions. Thus by adding East Europe to the U.S.S.R. the total (Comecon) rises from 137 to 182. The European Economic Community scores 66, the European Free Trade Association 47, and the Latin American Free Trade Association 62. India is pushed down from fourth to seventh place. All West Europe exceeds China, having 135 points. Clearly the new economic unions that are emerging in the world are already beginning to have an effect on the balance of economic power and their origins, features, and prospects must now be discussed.

III. ECONOMIC UNIONS AND THEIR IMPLICATIONS

Since the Second World War countries have come together in groups in different ways and for different reasons. There have been several important military pacts, some of which (e.g. N.A.T.O.) have persisted while others have changed (e.g.

the former Baghdad Pact). Political union has also taken place on certain occasions but not with much success: the United Arab Republic of Egypt and Syria from 1958 to 1961 proved unsuccessful, while the Communist countries of East Europe retain sovereign status even though strongly influenced by the U.S.S.R. In a sense, too, political ties are being broken by the formation of independent countries from colonial territories. Most widespread and, apparently, successful, is economic union, and this trend towards larger economic units does not seem incompatible with the increase taking place, at the moment, in the number of sovereign states.

Many advantages and disadvantages of economic union have been suggested in recent years. There are various reasons in favour. The principal reason is that many countries are far too small to be viable economic units (e.g. Luxembourg in Europe), and there have been instances of small countries forming economic unions: Benelux, O.D.E.C.A. in Central America, experiments in West Africa. The elimination of the smaller economic units seems inevitable in face of the presence in no more than four units – China, India, the U.S.S.R., and the U.S.A. – of half of the world's population.

The advantages of a larger economic unit and a larger market are related to the fact that many branches of production can be arranged more efficiently and therefore produce more cheaply if they are large than if they are small. There is much controversy regarding this, and certainly many modern industries (e.g. textiles) do not in reality benefit from being in particularly large units of production; others, such as steel production and many branches of engineering, undoubtedly do benefit. At the same time, a large area (a country or group of countries) presumably has a variety of environments and conditions within it, with some places best suited to produce certain goods, others to produce something different. Regional specialization would be encouraged and production costs lowered. Each of the two advantages has evidently been at work in the U.S.A., to the general benefit of its economy. On the other hand, West Europe seems singularly short of areas cut out to specialize for the market as a whole. It has many coalfields but little oil; its agricultural conditions are fairly uniform except for the special Mediterranean areas. There are numerous apparently successful textile districts, motor vehicle works, and so on.

Other advantages of economic union, overlapping to some extent those suggested so far, may be mentioned. Firstly there is opportunity for pooling resources and avoiding duplication. Thus Euratom performs research on nuclear matters in one place for six countries. There is talk of forming an airways system for all the E.E.C. countries. Secondly, and this particularly affects producers of raw materials and foodstuffs, groups of countries may bargain to obtain more favourable conditions of trade and prices for their products. Thus L.A.F.T.A. will have virtually a monopoly of world coffee production. Venezuela and the Middle East countries control nearly all the world's oil exports. Even E.E.C. has been able to force the U.S.A. to bargain over reducing tariff barriers. Thirdly, economic union adds strength to the defensive capabilities of countries. Finally, it may prove to be a step towards political union, though states seem reluctant to renounce their sovereignty in this way.

The form that the new economic units are taking is not similar to the kind of grouping we have been accustomed to in West Europe for the last few hundred years, the sea empire. The great sea empires built up by European powers in the period between about 1500 and 1900 had the effect of bringing together regions with very different physical advantages. Each had the mother country in the temperate zone and at least some territory within the tropics. Various cultural groups, some of them larger both in area and population than the mother country, scattered widely over the world, were brought together under one administration. The sea links required to maintain these empires were often put under great strain during periods of conflict. The existence and cohesion depended on a one-sided administrative set-up, with the dependent peoples having little or no say in their affairs, and on the superior economic and military level of the European mother country. This picture is broadly true even of the British

Empire, the largest in its day of the sea empires, the only one that has endured, in the Commonwealth, as something meaningful into the 1960s. Although the Russian Empire grew up in the same way as the sea empires it has two vital differences: firstly it is compact, and secondly there is a larger number of Russians and other Slavs than of conquered non-European peoples. This second feature is true, of course, also of former colonies of the British Empire, notably Canada and Australia, and the U.S.A.

The various sea empires were economic unions with an exchange of goods between different parts, but trade was mainly of manufactured goods from the mother country to the colonies and of food and raw materials in the opposite direction. The widely dispersed sea empires are no longer satisfactory economic units not only on account of the dominant position of one country but also because they are not compact. The new kind of economic union is made up of countries of equal status, situated close to one another. There are exceptions such as Cuba which, contrary to the general trend, now carries on most of its trade with Comecon, and Australia and New Zealand, which are closely tied to distant West Europe. For these latter countries economic integration with South-east Asia would be a logical step but unthinkable at present.

Which are the large markets at present and which countries may be expected to join reasonably soon? The following may be suggested:

1. The U.S.A., probably with Canada.
2. Comecon (the U.S.S.R. and East Europe) with synchronized development plans and increasing economic interdependence. There have been moves in 1962 to strengthen the economic links in this unit.
3. China, probably with its less powerful Communist neighbours.
4. India.
5. European Economic Community (with or without the rest of non-Communist Europe).
6. L.A.F.T.A., most of the countries of Latin America.

Other groupings seriously considered but not far advanced are the Arab countries, West Africa, East Africa, and South-east Asia (so far only Malaya, Thailand, and the Philippines). Japan would presumably link up with South-east Asia. Although the six groups listed have about three-quarters of the population of the world, many smaller countries remain un-committed, either because they consider it disadvantageous to join a large group (e.g. Bolivia) or because they have some political reason for not doing (e.g. 'neutral' Switzerland) or even because they do not readily fit into any particular group (e.g. Iran) or are not wanted (e.g. Spain). The 1960s will be a period of great economic adjustments, even if political sover-eignty is not renounced by many countries. Indeed new sover-eign states are bound to emerge from the remaining colonies (see Fig. 40), but by the late 1960s there should be about ten large economic unions in the world, containing nearly every country in the world. If present trends continue, two will be Communist, Comecon and China, and in view of the very small trade between them and the desire of the Chinese Communists to pull themselves up by their own efforts, they should be quite separate. Two will belong to the West without any doubt, North America and West Europe. Latin America and South-east Asia with Japan will presumably be more Western than neutral. The remainder, South Asia (India), the Arab world, and 'middle' Africa will be neutral. Southern Africa, with its appreciable proportion of Europeans, will not fit easily into an African bloc, while Australia and New Zealand also occupy a difficult position.

In Section 1 of this chapter it was suggested that in the post-war period the principal events in world affairs could be re-lated to a zone of friction on the periphery of the Communist bloc. This oversimplified picture, even if useful for the decade following the war, is misleading and unrealistic now. Many conflicts in the world in the late 1950s had no connexion at all with the struggle between the U.S.A. and the U.S.S.R. or be-tween capitalism and Communism. The existence of Israel and its relationship to the Arab countries, for example, have little to do with this struggle. The controversy over the mutual boundary of India and China, Indonesia's claim to West New Guinea, even the Berlin crisis, are basically local questions, though it is always possible that they could become part of the struggle between East and West. At present, however, it is important to bear in mind the possibility that there is not merely one zone of friction around the Communist bloc but a zone of friction between each of the large emerging economic unions (compare inset map and main map in Fig. 46). This is a much more complex view and it is not easy for people to accept at present but it does lead to a more realistic view of present trends in world affairs. On this basis, friction is just as likely between Comecon and China as between (say) the Arab world and middle Africa or between North America and Latin America.

The ten or so large economic unions, moreover, seem a logical stage between about 100 sovereign states and the final stage of world government. The time has not yet come for the United Nations (or any single power) to take over the whole world. In Fig. 46 areas are suggested in which adjustments if not conflicts are likely to occur as the economic unions crystallize and become consolidated. In particular, two areas, South-west Asia and South-east Asia appear to lack a nucleus for an economic union. Turkey (unless it is accepted into E.E.C.), Iran and Pakistan (unless it joins India) do not seem to fit easily into any group. Burma, Indonesia, and former French Indo-China are in a comparable position. In Africa it is too soon to suggest how the situation will sort itself out but it may be assumed that the absurdly small new countries will come together, perhaps at first into several groups rather than into one. Outside these areas many countries do not fit easily into one particular bloc. Even if all the non-Communist countries of Europe come together, Yugoslavia still remains a problem. Again, even if every republic of Latin America (excluding Cuba) eventually enters L.A.F.T.A. it is still difficult to see this Association welcoming the overpopulated British West Indies, yet logically this is where they belong. In Africa, the Sudan has both Arabs and Negroes, and the emerging Arab and 'middle' Africa blocs could divide it. Israel is a misfit hindering

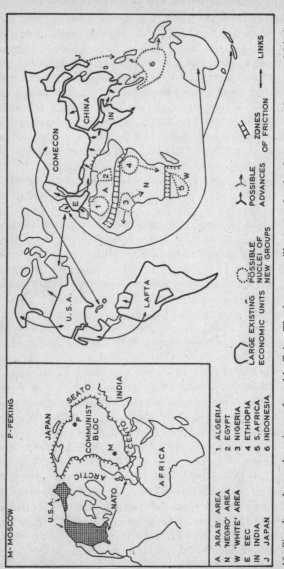

46. Simple and complex views of world affairs. The inset map illustrates the simple concept of a zone of friction around the Communist bloc. The main map shows the complex view of zones of friction around emerging economic blocs as they become consolidated. See also text.

A 'ARAB' AREA
N 'NEGRO' AREA
W 'WHITE' AREA
E EEC
IN INDIA
J JAPAN

1 ALGERIA
2 EGYPT
3 NIGERIA
4 ETHIOPIA
5 S. AFRICA
6 INDONESIA

LARGE EXISTING ECONOMIC UNITS

POSSIBLE NUCLEI OF NEW GROUPS

POSSIBLE ADVANCES

ZONES OF FRICTION

LINKS

M - MOSCOW
P - PEKING

consolidation of the Arab world, but it could perhaps join E.E.C. Between the U.S.S.R. and China the Mongolian People's Republic and North Korea occupy an ambiguous position. Enough examples have been given to show that the 1960s are likely to be a period of complicated adjustments, but it is already a fact, not a matter of opinion, that most of the population of the world is now within six large markets, all of which are reasonably compact, without distant detached parts. Admittedly some are large in area (Comecon, L.A.F.T.A.) or unwieldy (L.A.F.T.A. again, E.E.C. if Turkey, Israel, Scandinavia, and former French colonies are brought in).

As time goes on, the members of each large economic union will presumably exchange goods more and more among themselves (as already happens among the various regions of such large countries as the U.S.A. and U.S.S.R.). They will come to depend more and more upon the resources within their limits and at the same time will do everything possible to achieve industrial self-sufficiency. In this way, more and more areas will become industrialized and less and less food and raw materials will enter world trade. On these grounds the future looks bleak for West Europe, and for Japan unless it links up with less-developed countries in South-east Asia. Surpluses of food, raw materials, and energy will be sought more and more vigorously by industrial areas of the world.

The success of each particular economic union will depend partly on its level of technology at any given time, partly on its ability to organize its economy, but, as the gap narrows, ultimately more and more on the resources it has (and the way they are distributed territorially), measured against the population; that is, on the population/resource balance, which is itself changing, of course, both because of population changes and because technology allows more and more resources to be utilized. A useful exercise to conclude this section is to compare in very general terms the emerging economic unions of the 1960s. The comments in Table 23 are not based on any careful statistical assessment though some of the features taken into consideration do lend themselves to calculations. The purpose is merely to give a very rough idea of the viability,

TABLE 23

	Size	Compactness	Language cohesion	Transport system	Agricultural possibilities	Mineral and energy resources	Population increase	Influence in world	Population/ resource balance
1 North America	Large	Moderate	Very good	Very good	Very good	Very good	Average	Declining	Very good
2 Comecon	Large	Moderate	Poor	Moderate	Good	Very good	Average	Increasing	Good
3 West Europe	Small	Good	Moderate	Very good	Poor	Poor	Slow	Declining fast	Poor
4 China	Medium	Good	Good	Very poor	Very poor	Moderate	Fast	Increasing fast	Very poor
5 Latin America	Large	Very poor	Good	Very poor	Moderate	Good	Fast	Increasing	Moderate
6 South Asia	Medium	Good	Poor	Poor	Very poor	Poor	Average	Little change	Very poor
7 Arab area	Medium	Poor	Good	Very poor	Poor	Moderate	Fast	Little change	Poor
8 Middle Africa	Large	Moderate	Poor	Moderate	Moderate	Moderate	Average	Increasing	Moderate
9 Southern Africa	Medium	Moderate	Moderate	Moderate	Moderate	Good	Average	Little change	Moderate
10 South-east Asia	Medium	Moderate	Poor	Very poor	Moderate	Poor	Fast	Little change	Moderate
11 Australia	Medium	Moderate	Very good	Good	Moderate	Good	Average	Little change	Good
12 Japan	Very small	Very good	Very good	Very good	Very poor	Very poor	Slow	Declining	Very poor

natural endowments, and prospects of the units. In Fig. 47 three large units, which happen to be roughly equal in area and population, are compared in map form in order to show the kind of comparison envisaged in the table.

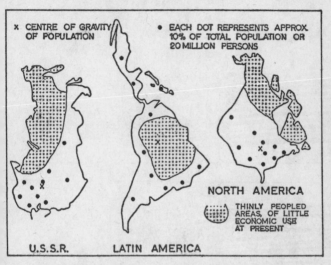

47. A comparison of three large units with special reference to distribution of population.

IV. THE CHANGING BALANCE OF WORLD POWER

In the two previous sections a rough assessment of the relative importance and influence of world powers at present (around 1960) was made and the probable form of the world powers of the future was described. It is now possible to make a study of changes in the last few decades and to project present trends a little way into the future. A simple method of assessing the relative importance of world powers was explained in Section II. By using the same basis of calculation (but remembering that the total of 1,000 points represents something larger in each successive year) Table 24 shows the share-out of points in selected years over the past few decades and also the expected

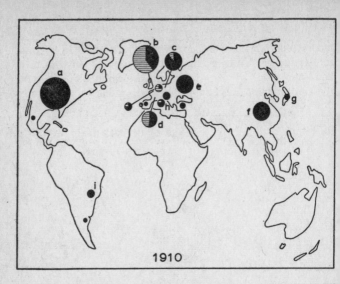

1910

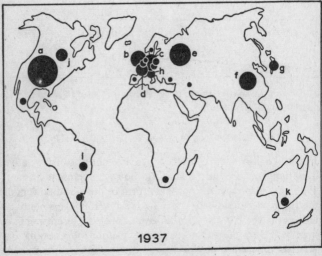

1937

1910	g Japan
a U.S.A.	h Italy
b British Empire	i Brazil
c German Empire	
d French Empire	1937
e Russian Empire	b, d without Empires
f China	j Canada
	k Australia

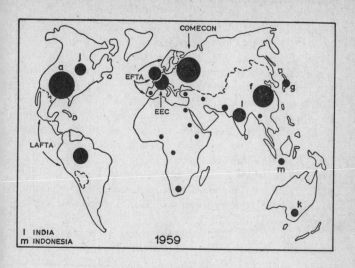

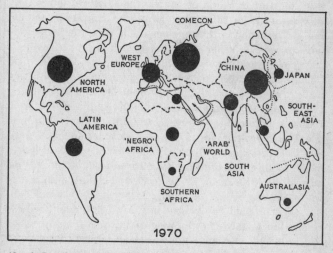

48a–d. Leading world powers in 1910, 1937, 1959, and 1970. See text for an explanation of the method of assessment used.

distribution in 1970. The data for four different years, *c*. 1910, 1937, 1959, and 1970 are mapped in Fig. 48 a–d. Fig. 48c (1959) differs from Fig. 45 in Section II only in that four major economic groupings, Comecon, E.E.C., E.F.T.A., and L.A.F.T.A. have been taken into account and the points for the member countries added together. Fig. 48b (1937) is straightforward, but Figs. 48a and 48d need some explanation. In Fig. 48a (1910) sea empires of that time are added to the strength of the mother country, but are shaded on the circle, not black (this is reserved for the mother country only). Thus the circle for Britain is boosted by the large population of India and by the large area of Canada, Australia, and so on. A straight comparison with 1937 is therefore not possible.

For convenience Fig. 48d (1970) shows likely groupings of countries a decade hence and naturally the calculations are only approximate. No change in area apart from that resulting from the amalgamation of countries is envisaged, but allowance is made for differential growth of population and of energy consumption. It is assumed that population will continue to increase at the same rate in each area as it has been doing over the 1950s. Thus, for example, the population of China may be expected to increase much more rapidly than that of West Europe, the former from 710 to 910 m. in the 1960s, the latter from 350 to 380 m. During this period West Europe's share of the world total will drop, China's share will rise. The energy total for 1970 is also calculated on the assumption that the increase will be by as much in the 1960s as it was in the 1950s. Thus Comecon's total rose from 400 to 900 m. t.c.e. in the 1950s or by 125 per cent, and it is assumed that it will again rise by this percentage to about 2,020 m. in 1970. Since China's total was so small in 1950 on account of the long conflict up to this date, the rate of increase from 20 m. to 370 m. would give an astronomical total for 1970. A more sober estimate, based on possibilities of development, has therefore been used.

In Table 24 only the leading world powers are shown and allowance is made for grouping of countries in 1959 and 1970

TABLE 24

WORLD POWERS 1910–70

NOTE: Appropriate changes have been made to allow for new groupings in VI–VIII. For explanation of points awarded, see text. Owing to discrepancies and small omissions the figures in VII and VIII do not add up to 1000 as they should.

	I 1910	II 1910	III 1937	IV 1949	V 1959	VI 1959	VII 1959	VIII 1970
U.S.A.	247	247	245	246	206	206	237 (N. America)	198
U.S.S.R.	79	79	107	114	137	182 (Comecon)	182 (Comecon)	219
China	88	88	75	79	120	120	125[1] (China +)	162
India				50	46	46	65[2] (S. Asia +)	65
U.K.	(212)	86	62	51	34	47 (E.F.T.A.)	135 (W. Europe)	104
Canada			35	38	31	31	to N. Am.	
Germany*	(84)	77	67	29	29	66 (E.E.C.)	to W. Eur.	
Brazil	18	18	19	22	22	62 (L.A.F.T.A.)	70 (Latin Am.)	76
Japan	12	12	26	20	20	20	23[3]	22
France	(62)	33	32	25	19	to E.E.C.	to W. Eur.	
Australia			18	18	18	18	22[4]	20
							51[5] (Africa)	53
							26[6] (S.E. Asia)	29
							26[7] (Arab Area)	26
							15[8] (Southern Afr.)	15

* West Germany in 1949 and 1959 (v).

I. 1910 showing sea empires.
II. 1910 without sea empires.
II–v. May be compared.
VI. Allows for Comecon, E.F.T.A., E.E.C., and L.A.F.T.A.
VII. Further grouping for comparison with supposed line-up in 1970.

1. China + Mongolian P.R., N. Korea, N. Vietnam.
2. India + Pakistan, Iran, etc.
3. Japan + S. Korea.
4. Australia, New Zealand, New Guinea, etc.
5. Africa excluding northern (to Arab area) and southern parts.
6, 7. As defined elsewhere in this book.
8. 'White-dominated' area in south.

as well as for empires in 1910. The figures in Columns II–V are roughly comparable areas, as are those in Columns VII and VIII. It must be stressed, once again, that the basis of calculation is completely arbitrary and that different results would be obtained if different criteria were used. Nevertheless, in the view of the author any reasonable assessment would give approximately the same results. Some tentative conclusions with considerable bearing on world affairs are therefore drawn from the figures. The figures up to 1960 (once allowance has been made for some discrepancies and for rough calculations) represent facts, and those for 1970 are reasonable, if approximate, estimates for a decade hence. It is up to the reader to interpret the facts in the way he or she chooses.

The most striking fact in 1910 is that the U.S.A., economically speaking, was by far the most powerful single country. Russia, China, and Britain and Germany without their empires, were all about one-third as powerful as the U.S.A. Britain is greatly boosted by the addition of its empire, however, and approaches the U.S.A. in magnitude. Apart from the U.S.A. and China (only on account of its large population and area) there were no powers of any great consequence outside Europe. In Europe, Britain, Russia, Germany, and France were all major world powers. Outside Europe, only Brazil (for its size) and Japan (for its population more than for its industry, as yet) were of moderate importance, while in Europe, Austria-Hungary, Belgium, the Netherlands, and Italy were all powers of some consequence.

Back in 1870 the concentration of power in Europe was more striking still, and Britain, then accounting for about half of the world's energy consumption, was the leading power in the world, even without taking into account its empire. But the comparison is less valid so far back, since energy played a very much smaller role in the economic life of countries then than by 1910. Britain, however, was at its peak (in relation to the rest of the world) between about 1850 and 1870 and has been declining ever since. Germany reached its peak during 1900–10 and has also declined since. The U.S.A. has maintained itself with about one-quarter of the total world power between 1900 and 1950, since which time it has started to decline. The fate of France has been similar to that of Britain. Japan, on the other hand, reached its peak in the 1930s. Russia has long been a formidable power on account of its large population and size, but because of its slower economic development it tended to stagnate over the period 1850–1930 when the powers of Western Europe had reached their peak and started to decline, but since 1930 it has improved its relative position greatly, while the addition of the East European countries (see Column VI) means that Comecon now has more than twice as large a share of world power as the Russian Empire had in 1910 (see Column II). China has for various reasons been so long out of world affairs that the figures shown for it mean very little. Its impact has begun to be felt only since about 1950, but during the 1950s it has greatly improved its position, largely on account of the rapid industrialization that has taken place.

It so happens that the U.S.S.R. and China are the only two major powers that have increased their share of world total power in the 1950s and are likely to continue doing so in the 1960s. Latin America seems likely to strengthen its position somewhat too. The relative importance of India, Japan, Africa, the Arab countries, and Australia does not seem likely to change over the period 1950–70. Finally, both North America and West Europe will have declined sharply in relative importance over this period.

Looking at world history over a longer period still, the present appears as part of the twilight of near world-domination by Europe. Apart from Russia, which has been able to transform its empire into one of the great powers of the present day, the rise and fall of Europe is almost complete. Spain, the Netherlands, Sweden, Austria-Hungary, all great powers in their day, count for nothing. The U.K., France, and West Germany survive as world powers on their reputations. But it needs little perception to see that the former powers of West Europe now have to unite to maintain themselves as a major force in world affairs. Few people appreciate that, if present trends continue, even West Europe will have difficulty in maintaining itself as a major world power, let alone individual countries in it. But look at its probable position even in 1970.

The reader will already have discovered various shortcomings in the figures used for this assessment of world power and will have questioned some of the oversimplified conclusions drawn so far. Certainly the picture presented needs many qualifications. The choice of consumption of energy as the measure of economic development and strength happens to flatter the Communist countries since they have all given energy priority in their programmes of economic growth, and the progress and expected progress over the period 1945–70 is not matched by similar rates of growth in other branches of the economy. China is coming up particularly fast because both its population and its energy consumption are increasing rapidly, but it seems unlikely that the rapid expansion of energy production achieved in the last few years can continue for long, simply because the demand for the energy cannot be expected to grow so fast. Latin America can be expected to gain relatively thanks to its rapidly increasing population and ambitious programme of expansion of heavy industry for the 1960s. For various reasons, however, the immediate prospects of the neutral countries of Africa and Asia do not seem bright.

The apparent decline of North America is due largely to the fact that a very high standard of living and consumption of energy has already been achieved, and the demand for energy is not increasing so rapidly as in Comecon. The same is true to some extent of West Europe, but this region is less fortunate than North America because it depends largely on outside sources of oil for the future increase of energy consumption, while the rate of increase of its population is also slight.

Whatever reservations one puts on Communist development, however, one outstanding trend simply cannot be ignored. Before the First World War no country had a Communist Party in power. In 1917 the Communist Party took over in Russia. In the late 1930s the Soviet Union already had over one-tenth of the power in the world. In 1950 the Communist bloc had more than one-fifth. By 1970 it will have nearly two-fifths even assuming that no new countries are drawn into the bloc; and it is calculated in the Soviet Union that by 1980 the Communist powers will have about 65 per cent of the total industrial capacity of the world, compared with only 20 per cent in 1950. During 1910–70, on the other hand, the share of the West (North America and West Europe) will have declined from about two-thirds to one-third of the world total. The residue of the power lies with countries of varying shades of neutrality, including, in particular, Latin America and Japan, which currently are inclined towards the West.

Thinking on these lines, the Soviet argument is very simple. If between 1920 and 1960 the Communist share of total world power increased from nothing to nearly one-third, then it is reasonable to assume that by 2000, two-thirds of the world will be Communist-dominated even without a war, and this virtually would mean the end of capitalism. Such an argument sounds naïve, but if the Communist countries could win over all the neutral countries they could outstrip and gradually bring about the downfall of the capitalist countries by peaceful means such as depriving them of their sources of food and raw materials. Even the loss of Africa, Latin America, India, or Japan to the Communist bloc would be a disaster for the West.

It is an inescapable fact that owing to the great industrial expansion of the U.S.S.R. in the 1930s, to the addition of new area, population, and industrial capacity in the period 1945–50, and to continuing, top-priority expansion of energy consumption over the period of 1950–70, the Communist world has been gaining rapidly in relative importance in the world, economically speaking. What is more, the Communist powers can more easily regulate their economies and the use to which their industrial capacity is put, because the consumer can more easily be sacrificed.

It is also an inescapable fact that the West is declining, relatively speaking, at least so long as consumption of energy is taken as a measure of economic strength. But if some other item such as motor vehicles produced were taken, then the picture would be quite different. It already has generally high living standards and therefore has the capacity to help the underdeveloped neutral countries, even if it has to slow down the rate of growth of its own living standards to do so. There is plenty of slack to take in; there are links with the neutral countries in the form of traditional trading connexions and shipping services; language is not a great problem in most cases. Comecon for various reasons will not be in such a strong position to influence the uncommitted countries perhaps for another decade, China perhaps for two decades.

The only chance the West appears to have of saving itself and preventing the further spread of Communism is to consolidate the rest of the world, Latin America, Africa, and non-Communist Asia, before the economic impact of Comecon and of China is felt in a big way. This has to be done in the next decade.

Chapter 11

THE EARLY 1960s

I. LATIN AMERICA

FIG. 49a shows some of the areas in Latin America that have been most disturbed in recent years. Of these, Cuba is the most important and deserves special attention.

Cuba is of particular concern both to the U.S.A. and to the U.S.S.R. Its loss to the U.S.A. as an economic sphere of influence has in itself been serious, since large American investments have disappeared. The U.S.A. is also apprehensive about the influence of Cuba on other Latin American countries. The U.S.S.R. is concerned because it cannot now abandon a new socialist country, yet cannot risk too much to defend it. Recently, Comecon has been supplying more aid to Cuba than the U.S.A. has to all the rest of Latin America, and is being forced to import sugar and tobacco, which are not essential to it. Two features of Cuba seem likely to affect its future in Latin America. Firstly, it is an island, and this reduces both the possibility of infiltration from outside and the possibility of sending agitators into other countries; Cuba can, of course, broadcast to other Latin American countries. Secondly, the revolution is now clearly over and Cuba is unlikely to revert to its previous regime without strong outside pressure, which could only come from the U.S.A. If left alone, it can at least feed itself and carry on as it is. Cuba has had a different background from other Latin American countries, with few of the elements (army, landowners, church, and so on) that normally step in to oppose a social revolution, and the Cuban type of revolution need not necessarily be expected to succeed elsewhere in Latin America.

Even so, the situation is very unsettled in many other Latin American countries. Other islands of the Caribbean have great pressure on agricultural land, soil erosion, and in most there is no outlet for emigration. Perhaps the worst country is Haiti, with 3½ million ex-African slaves, very little good agricultural land, and a dictator set against change. Hurricane Flora did enormous damage there in 1963, almost without attracting any attention outside. Jamaica and Trinidad, independent from Britain since 1962, appear to be improving, thanks to the exploitation of bauxite and oil respectively, and the introduction of industry and tourism. This still leaves many smaller islands in a very bad position.

In mainland Central America the six countries are slowly moving towards economic union, and trade between them is increasing. Individual countries, however, could become problem areas. Guatemala claims British Honduras. Nicaragua still has a dictator, and Honduras a dubious government. But, Panama seems the most difficult country in view of the leasing and granting of virtual sovereignty in perpetuity to the United States in 1903 of a zone 10 miles wide for the construction of the canal; this zone extends across the isthmus, cutting Panama into two parts.

In South America conditions are more stable but there are many problem areas. In Venezuela, which depends so heavily on oil, the installations of the oil industry are very vulnerable to sabotage. What is more, the great wealth of the country is very unevenly spread among the population at present. But if Venezuela can survive the next few years it could advance rapidly, thanks to its large revenues from oil, and could serve as a kind of laboratory for development projects, which could later be applied in other Latin American countries. Its neighbour, Colombia, is expanding and diversifying its economy steadily now, but is afflicted by groups of bandits, not necessarily political in their aims, who have for many years hindered inter-regional movements. Further south in the Andes, Peru and Bolivia have encountered many difficulties in their attempts to develop new resources in the post-war period. A major problem in Peru is the presence in the Andes of several million predominantly agricultural Indians whose plight has been made worse by frequent droughts and unsatisfactory land tenure. Bolivia has come to depend very heavily on U.S. aid, but has recently been approached by Comecon countries. It is pressing for a piece of territory on the Pacific coast in Chile.

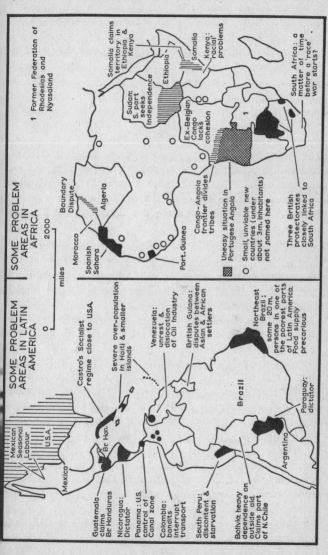

SOME PROBLEM AREAS IN LATIN AMERICA

Mexican Seasonal Labour

U.S.A.

Mexico

Guatemala claims Br Honduras

Nicaragua: Dictator

Panama: U.S. control of Canal zone

Colombia: bandits interrupt transport

South Peru: discontent & starvation

Bolivia: heavy dependence on outside aid. Claims part of N.Chile

Castro's Socialist regime close to USA

Severe over-population in Haiti & smaller islands

Br Hon.

Venezuela: unrest & dislocation of Oil Industry

British Guiana: disputes between Asian & African settlers

Northeast Brazil: some 20 m. persons in one of the poorest parts of Latin America. Food supply precarious

Brazil

Paraguay: dictator

Argentina

SOME PROBLEM AREAS IN AFRICA

0   1000   2000

miles

Boundary Dispute

Morocco

Spanish Sahara

Algeria

Port. Guinea

1 Former Federation of Rhodesias and Nyasaland

Somalia claims territory in Ethiopia & Kenya

Sudan: S. part seeks independence

Ethiopia

Somalia

Kenya: 'racial' problems

Ex-Belgian Congo lacks cohesion

Congo-Angola frontier divides tribes

Uneasy situation in Portuguese Angola

Small, unviable new countries (under about 3m. inhabitants) not named here

South Africa: a matter of time before a 'race' war starts?

Three British protectorates closely linked to South Africa

49a–b. Some problem areas in Latin America and Africa.

303

In Brazil, the comparative prosperity and remarkable industrial boom in the south have failed until recently to improve the very poor conditions in the North-east of the country, where some 20 million Brazilians are affected by lack of agricultural land, periodical droughts, and heavy dependence on agriculture. Now a massive project has been started here to improve water supply and agriculture, to build power stations and to introduce industry.

II. AFRICA

Fig. 49b shows some areas in which disturbances may be expected to occur in Africa. In 1962 and 1963 six new sovereign states emerged in the continent: in 1962 Algeria, Uganda, Rwanda, and Burundi, in 1963 Zanzibar and Kenya. As the new countries of Africa begin to settle down, several features are becoming clearer. Firstly, many boundaries are not accepted and most are not clearly demarcated on the ground. They are easily crossed, and this makes it possible for a rebellion in one country to be supported by a base in a neighbouring country. Secondly, disputes between cultural groups (racial conflicts) within individual countries seem likely to become more serious in the future. Thirdly, many new sovereign states and remaining colonial areas are far too small to be viable economic units.

Several boundaries have been the cause of disputes in the early 1960s, usually because they cut across tribal or other cultural groups. For example, Somalia claims parts of both Ethiopia and Kenya because Somali Bararetta tribes live in all three countries. The dispute between Algeria and Morocco over much of their frontier is less clearly based on ethnic considerations; the possibility that minerals may be found in a hitherto thinly populated desert area seems to have been the main cause. The boundary between Angola (Portuguese) and the Congo (ex-Belgian) divides several tribes, which is unsatisfactory enough, but it has become the scene of a much more serious conflict. A rebellion against Portugal, which now has some 40,000 troops in its colony, is being supported by

Angolans trained in the Congo and supplied by arms from Algeria. This support for Africans against Europeans by other African countries foreshadows what may happen in Southern Rhodesia and in the Republic of South Africa.

The presence of non-Africans in various parts of the continent is likely to lead to many bitter conflicts in the next ten or twenty years. There are several possible variations. Firstly, Africans and Arabs face one another or are mixed along a belt of country stretching from east to west about 10° to 15° north of the equator. In the Sudan, which lies astride this zone, the Africans in the southern third of the country have been dissatisfied since 1955. More recently they have started a fight to the finish for independence from the Arabs. Secondly, Africans and Asians (mainly Indians) are found together in several countries. The Asians are mainly traders and professional people, and are more prosperous than the African population. Thirdly, considerable European minorities are also still to be found in several countries. So far no satisfactory way has been found to guarantee the perpetuation of the privileged position of this population against African majorities. Fourthly, given the large number of countries and boundaries there seems plenty of scope for Africans to quarrel among themselves.

Almost half of the new countries of Africa have fewer than three million people each. Given the small *per caput* gross domestic product, the home market of each of these countries is ridiculously small and it is not worth installing large-scale industry to serve them individually. Some (e.g. Libya, oil; Mauretania, iron ore) have an item to export, but others (Rwanda, Chad, Gabon) depend almost entirely on agriculture producing for the home market. Contrast Nigeria which has more than thirty million people, and is already able to develop several large projects which are economical because of their scale. Several remaining colonial areas are also very small. British Gambia seems destined to be absorbed by Senegal, which almost encircles it. Portuguese Guinea is currently in danger of being overrun by its larger independent neighbours. In southern Africa, the British High Commission Territories (Bechuanaland, Swaziland, and Basutoland) all depend heavily on South Africa from an economic point of view and one, Basutoland, is completely encircled by South Africa, which in 1963 offered to administer all three territories. The Federation of Rhodesia and Nyasaland was dissolved in 1963, and independence seems assured for each member in the near future.

At present, Africa is one of the most uncertain areas in world affairs. France and the U.K. seem to be maintaining their influence, and French and English are used widely. But the United States and the U.S.S.R., the latter with very mixed success, are moving in, and even the Chinese are beginning to exert an influence. Only lack of shipping links and funds, and the language difficulty, have so far prevented them from penetrating more. The gradual emergence of economic unions in Africa seems inevitable, but this will not prevent many further conflicts, which are becoming more drastic as more sophisticated arms pour in from many different parts of the world.

III. ASIA

Fig. 50 shows some of the many recent areas of disturbance in southern Asia. Conflicts in this continent seem to depend more on local circumstances than in Africa or Latin America and fall less easily into a straightforward economic and political pattern.

In South-west Asia four areas have been of particular concern in the early 1960s.

For its small size, Cyprus has caused more trouble than almost any area in South-west Asia, since the position of its Turkish minority has not been satisfactorily guaranteed. Any dispute in Cyprus automatically involves Greece, Turkey, the U.K., the British Commonwealth, and N.A.T.O. The position of Israel in the region is still unclear; the latest cause for dispute has been Israel's plan to divert water from the River Jordan, before it reaches Jordan. Turkey, Iran, and Syria may all become involved in the struggle for a greater degree of regional autonomy by the Kurds in Iraq. There are some 5 million Kurds in these four countries and they appear to be irrepressible. The U.S.S.R., which also has a small group of

Asia

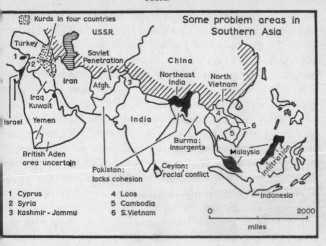

50. Some problem areas in southern Asia.

Kurds, would no doubt like to see these in control of a completely independent Kurdistan. Further south, the future of the Yemen may have considerable bearing on British influence in South-west Asia and the position of many foreign oil companies in Arabia. Early in 1964 the country was still split between republican rebels, supported by Egyptian troops, and royalist forces attempting to recover the country. Egypt, the U.S.S.R., Ethiopia, Saudi Arabia, and the U.K., with Aden and other protectorates in the area, are all watching closely.

South Asia has been characterized by new alignments in the early 1960s, some of which could hardly have been anticipated a few years ago. China's highly successful invasion of Northeast India seems to have been the main cause. India was supported not only by the West but also by the U.S.S.R. Pakistan, seeing its S.E.A.T.O. and C.E.N.T.O. allies offering military support to India, has tried to establish closer links with Communist China. A physical link in the form of a railway or road is difficult to provide, but a regular air service has already been established between West Pakistan and Peking. The dispute between Pakistan and India remains as bitter as ever. The

307

motive of the Chinese invasion of India in 1962 is still no
clear, but it is possible that China eventually hopes for land
access to the Indian Ocean via East Pakistan or even West
Pakistan. As a result of the invasion, Indian unity seems to
have been strengthened, while at the same time somewhat more
tolerance is being shown to cultural groups such as the Naga
tribesmen on the fringes of Indian society.

In South-east Asia, disputes continue both on the mainland
and in the islands. The gradual spread of communist influence
into Laos, South Vietnam, and Cambodia seems inevitable
The enlargement of Malaya in 1963 to form Malaysia brought
with it unexpected consequences. Indonesia claimed the British
colonies on the island of Borneo which, along with Singapore
went to make the new Malaysia. Indonesia has supported its
claim by building roads across the island with Soviet help, and
assembling troops there. Possibly the ease with which Western
New Guinea fell to Indonesia in 1962, after a long dispute with
the Netherlands, has encouraged Indonesia to complete its control of Borneo. The next step would be for Indonesia to claim
the eastern part of New Guinea, now an Australian Protec-
torate. Australia, therefore, is clearly involved in South-east
Asia. China, too, may take a greater interest in the islands as
well as the mainland, given the large and very influential
Chinese element in Malaysia.

IV. U.S.S.R. AND CHINA

For some years now, differences between the Soviet and
Chinese Communist Parties have been noted in the West. In
this section the implications of the dispute will be considered
first for the rest of the world and secondly for the U.S.S.R. and
China themselves.

The independent line of Yugoslavia in 1948 showed that a
Communist party in power in a sovereign state could go its
own way and ignore the Soviet Communist Party. But Yugoslavia was not influential enough to have any permanent
followers. In contrast, now that the Chinese Communist Party
has clearly dissociated itself from Soviet influence, many Com-

munist Parties in the world, whether in power or not, have been forced to choose whether to look to Moscow or to Peking for leadership; a few have not chosen or condemned either.[1]

In countries which already have a Communist regime, proximity to Moscow or to Peking seems to explain the alignment of the Communist Party. Thus, in East Europe, six follow the U.S.S.R., one (Albania) follows China and one (Romania) is uncommitted. There is a Polish joke that the optimists learn Russian, the pessimists Chinese. In East Asia, both North Korea and North Vietnam support Peking, but the Mongolian People's Republic, which lies between the U.S.S.R. and China, is pro-Soviet, while Cuba, which is far from both, again is not committed. In non-Communist countries proximity to one or the other again seems to be a major consideration in determining alignment. There are virtually no pro-Chinese Communist Parties in the Americas, Africa, South-west Asia or West Europe. On the other hand, Peking has many supporters in South and East Asia. The Chinese hope that eventually their supporters will take over in as many Communist Parties as possible and that China will lead the world Communist movement. The Russians can hardly view this prospect with much enthusiasm. As it is, China itself, together with India, Japan, Pakistan, and Indonesia, which all tend to be pro-Chinese, have between them nearly half of the world's population, though much less of its military and industrial strength.

Fig. 51 has been drawn instead of a map to show the relative distance of selected countries of the world from Moscow and from Peking. A map would not show all the distances involved correctly. On the diagram distance increases from Moscow from left to right and from Peking from bottom to top. For convenience, distances are measured between capitals, which can be, of course, misleading; Afghanistan, for example, actually touches both countries, yet Kabul is far from both Moscow and Peking. In very general terms the diagram shows satisfactorily the position of different countries in relation to Peking and Moscow, and the likely pull of each of these, as well as the distance from either and the likelihood of their

1. See a very interesting map in the *Scotsman*, 16 November 1963.

being affected by Communism through being near one, or the
other, or both.

Finally, a few words about the relationship between Moscow
and Peking. There is now little trade between the two countries,
the amount of Soviet aid is negligible and some Soviet-spon-
sored projects in China have been abandoned. The situation is
such, now, that although a military conflict between the two
countries over their frontier is unlikely, tension is growing.

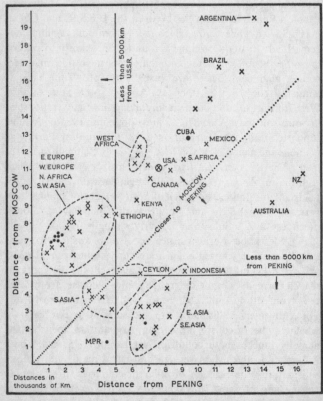

51. Distances of selected countries from the U.S.S.R. and China.
See also Table opposite.

310

The Russians would certainly not allow Chinese to enter as workers on a temporary basis. Nor would they readily give up territory to China. The Soviet press (e.g. *Sovetskaya Rossiya*, 22 September 1963) has blamed the Chinese for transgressing the frontier and has reminded them that this kind of thing is just not done between socialist countries. Soviet apprehension over the Chinese invasion of India can easily be appreciated.

Fig. 52 shows areas between the U.S.S.R. and China over

Under 5,000 Km. from both Moscow and Peking			Under 5,000 Km. from Peking but over 5,000 Km. from Moscow		
	MOSCOW	PEKING		MOSCOW	PEKING
Afghanistan	3,300	4,100	N. Korea	6,300	800
Pakistan	3,600	3,800	S. Korea	6,500	900
India	4,300	3,800	Formosa	7,300	1,700
Mongolian P.R.	*4,500*	*1,200*	Japan	7,400	2,000
Nepal	4,800	3,100	*N. Vietnam*	*6,800*	*2,300*
			Philippines	8,200	2,700
Under 5,000 Km. from Moscow but over 5,000 Km. from Peking			Burma	6,500	3,200
			Thailand	7,000	3,300
			Malaysia	8,100	4,300
Finland	900	6,200			
Sweden	1,200	6,600			
Poland	*1,200*	*6,900*	**Over 5,000 Km. from both Moscow and Peking**		
Czechoslovakia	*1,600*	*7,400*			
Yugoslavia	*1,600*	*7,300*	Nigeria	6,200	11,300
Bulgaria	*1,800*	*7,300*	Kenya	6,400	9,200
Turkey	1,800	6,700	Congo (Leop.)	7,000	11,200
W. Germany	2,100	7,700	Canada	7,000	10,300
Italy	2,300	8,000	U.S.A.	7,700	11,000
U.K.	2,300	8,000	S. Africa	9,200	11,600
France	2,400	8,000	Indonesia	9,300	5,200
Iran	2,400	5,500	*Cuba*	*9,500*	*12,700*
Egypt	2,900	7,400	Brazil	11,300	16,700
Algeria	3,300	9,000	Argentina	13,500	19,500
Sudan	4,500	8,300	Australia	14,500	9,000

The table contains 40 selected countries. The diagram contains 61. Countries in italics have a Communist regime.

which disputes might be expected (see also *The Times*, 10 September 1963, p. 11). The Chinese are apparently moving in large numbers into Sinkiang (the Uighur Autonomous Region).

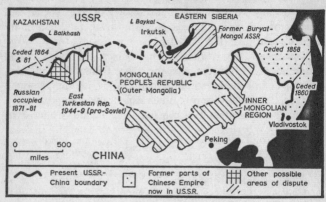

52. The Soviet–Chinese frontier.

If the Russians were gradually to yield territory to China they would probably do so in this order: sacrifice the Mongolian People's Republic first, the Vladivostok area second, the Amur Valley third, and finally parts of Kazakhstan. They would certainly keep the Lake Baykal area, because it has so many natural resources. Not long ago the Buryat-Mongol A.S.S.R., near Lake Baykal, had its name changed to Buryat A.S.S.R., an indication that the Russians do not want to leave grounds for the Chinese to claim an extension of Mongolia into the U.S.S.R.

V. THE UNITED KINGDOM IN WORLD AFFAIRS

Much of the evidence presented in the previous chapter points to the relative decline of the U.K. as a force in world affairs. This decline is obviously a fact, but how great it has been depends upon what particular weight is given to each possible way of measuring its strength and influence. Whatever measure is used, the U.K. has declined over the last century or so in the face of growing competition from other countries. But in the century up to 1850 it was improving its position in relation to the rest of the world, thanks to the fact that many of the major innovations of the technological revolution were first widely applied in England. Subsequently the advantage of being first has been overshadowed by the greater size, population, and resources of later starters, particularly the U.S.A. and, more recently, Russia.

Owing to the narrowing of the gap between birth rate and death rate in the U.K. over the last few decades the population growth of this country is no longer rapid, but only gradual. In contrast, most parts of the world are now going through a period (how long it will last cannot, of course, be forecast) of 'explosive' population growth. For this reason, by the year 2000 our population will only be about 1 per cent of the world's total compared with about 2·5 in 1900. This in itself is a considerable contribution to the decline of the U.K.

More spectacular has been the changing form of the British Empire and, recently, the disappearance of many colonies in Asia and Africa. In fact, even ignoring the independence of the U.S.A. in the eighteenth century, the process has been under way for nearly 100 years, starting with the granting of dominion status to Canada (1867). In the first decade of this century, Australia, New Zealand, and South Africa all received a large measure of independence. The difference between these former colonies and the ones achieving independence after the Second World War is that the former are populated predominantly by Europeans (except South Africa) while the latter are non-European. All but Ireland, Burma, and South Africa have chosen to remain within the British Commonwealth, however, and it should not be overlooked that this is larger in area now than the British Empire was a hundred years ago (most of Africa not yet having been colonized by Europeans). Clearly the Empire has made an important contribution to the economic and even military strength of the U.K. in the past, providing among other things a large market for the manufactured goods of this country and a source of food and raw materials. Whether recently the remaining colonies have been an asset and not a liability seems doubtful. Lack of an empire in recent decades has not prevented Germany from becoming as great an industrial power as Britain and France. At all events, the transformation of former British colonies into either sovereign states within the Commonwealth or into entirely foreign states is proceeding fast, and in the eyes of the world Britain's strength is assumed to be diminishing as well.

As already suggested, the position of the U.K. is rapidly weakening owing to the spread of the technological revolution to many other parts of the world. Over the last century our share in the total world production of every industrial item has declined. In reality, of course, our own production has increased, but the world total has increased much faster. Figures in Table 25 show our changing share in the total world production of certain important items over the last hundred years. Although the relative position of Britain as an industrial power began to decline in the 1860s, decline as a political influence in world affairs dates more noticeably from the First World War. The decline has continued in both industrial strength and world influence up to the present and seems likely to continue owing to the failure of this country in recent years to increase its industrial capacity appreciably.

TABLE 25
Share (percentage) of Great Britain in World Total

	1870	1910	1960
Coal	70	26	11
Pig iron	50	15	6
Steel	50	11	6
Shipbuilding	n.a.	62	16
Cotton spindles	n.a.	40	11

n.a. = not available

From what has been said, it indeed seems surprising and gratifying that the U.K. still plays such an important part in world affairs as it actually does. The existence of the Commonwealth, the possession of a nuclear deterrent, the large amount of foreign trade, these, together with the fact that reputation lasts longer than facts justify, have enabled Britain to play the role of a major world power up to the present. Obviously, however, this situation cannot last indefinitely and a time has come when this country must link up with other countries. The choice appears to be between trying to perpetuate the British Commonwealth (somehow strengthening it as a political and economic unit), falling more and more under the domination of the U.S.A., or linking up with other countries in West

Europe. The three are not entirely mutually exclusive, but stronger ties with one would mean, at least temporarily, weaker ties with the other two.

Although the Commonwealth, being a former sea empire with member countries scattered throughout the world, is extremely uncompact, and therefore, presumably, unviable as a unit of economic organization, it has many advantages. It already exists as a trading bloc and most is organized as the Sterling Area. It contains both temperate and tropical countries, highly industrialized and very backward areas, prosperous and poor regions. It has the advantage of a common language in use everywhere at least for official purposes. On the other hand, centrifugal forces are at work. The British Commonwealth countries of West Africa, for example, are obviously much more concerned about their neighbours from the former French Empire than about, say, the fate of Jamaica or Malaya, also in the Commonwealth. Whether it likes it or not, Canada is becoming more and more involved with the U.S.A. both economically and in defence matters. For these reasons it seems unrealistic to expect to perpetuate the existing pattern of Commonwealth trade when more realistic links can be established.

Immediately after the Second World War it looked as though Britain would fall within the economic sphere of the U.S.A. But although it received about $U.S. 6,000 m. in aid, now has numerous U.S. bases, and would no doubt suffer more heavily in a nuclear war than the U.S.A. itself, economic and political union seem very remote. An economic link-up with the U.S.A. into a North Atlantic Community seems more probable *after* Britain has joined with countries in West Europe.

The third possibility for Britain is to enter an economic and presumably subsequently a political union with part or all of West Europe. It should be appreciated that not only the U.K. but also Germany, France, and several smaller countries have declined as world powers in recent decades and, like the U.K., seem destined to decline still further, and are equally compelled to seek union with other foreign countries. The market of West Europe has the advantage of being all in one place and not scattered over the world like the Commonwealth. What is more, recently a growing share of British trade has been with the continent even though it is still overshadowed by our trade with the Commonwealth. But as different areas in the Commonwealth become more self-sufficient industrially (witness the expansion of industry in Canada, Australia, and India) a large new adjoining 'home' market is an obvious attraction to Britain. From the political point of view, the decline of the countries of West Europe means that they can no longer exert great influence individually, but collectively they could still be a major force in world affairs. Within the new West European bloc at least three – the U.K., France, and West Germany – no doubt would like to be the leading policy maker.

Early in 1964 it is still not possible to see what form West European union will eventually take, but it seems that both E.E.C. and E.F.T.A. will continue to exist and consolidate themselves. Whether or not the U.K. and its E.F.T.A. partners link up with E.E.C. in the next few years one thing is certain; a land link in the form of a tunnel or bridge across the English Channel is vital if the best possible access to the Continental market is desired. Any planning in the U.K. affecting the location of new towns, industrial establishments, and motorways should take it into account. The cross-Channel link will be referred to again in the next section.

VI. CHANGES WITHIN THE UNITED KINGDOM[1]

Like most West European countries, the U.K. will depend for its future existence more and more on an efficient manufacturing industry, and the basic need of the country, therefore, is to facilitate and stimulate the development and expansion of manufacturing in every possible way. One way is to broaden our educational facilities to ensure that everyone capable of benefiting from a higher education has the opportunity to do so.[2] Another is to allow industry to expand in those areas in

1. This section was written before the publication of *The South East Study 1961–1981* (H.M.S.O. London 1964).

2. See *The Rise of the Meritocracy, 1870–2033*, by M. Young (available in Penguin Books, 1961).

the country in which production costs are lowest. The expansion of higher education in this country is hardly a matter for discussion in a book on geography, but the highly controversial question of where to put new industrial establishments seems a matter on which a geographer ought to have some views. The remainder of the section, therefore, is devoted to a brief discussion of this problem.

First of all, the contribution of manufacturing to the productive side of our total gross domestic product must be appreciated. In 1961 the gross domestic product of the U.K. was made up as follows:

Agriculture	4%
Mining	3%
Manufacturing	35%
Construction, electricity, gas, water	10%
Others (services)	48%

Manufacturing has remained close to 35 per cent of the total throughout the postwar period. Agriculture (from 6 per cent in 1948) and mining (from 4 per cent in 1948) have declined. The outstanding role of manufacturing is clear; it accounts for almost all of the exports of this country, though services such as transport, banking, and so on also contribute. If, say, one quarter of all the agricultural land in this country were taken out of farming and covered with houses, factories, roads, and so on, this would take away only 2 per cent of the productive GDP or 1 per cent of the total, a setback that could be made up in an economy expanding at 4 per cent per annum in a very short time. In reality, only a few per cent, not anything like a quarter, would suffice to accommodate all the new development likely to be needed for several decades. Yet a terrible fuss is made whenever another field is built on. Why is this?

Before enlarging on why this attitude is absurd, a second feature of the economy must be made clear. Still in 1750 most of the population of Britain was engaged in agriculture; much of the total population was in the south-eastern part of England where much of the best arable land is to be found, and many industries were here too. Shortly after this, coal began to influence the economy as industry grew, and population moved to coalfield areas where industry was developing. This continued through the nineteenth century and by 1900 much of the population was in or near the major coalfields or in Greater London. No one suggested that something ought to be done to reverse this trend and encourage people to move back to rural areas they had left.

Since about 1900, population has shown a growing preference for many places in the Midlands and South-east of England, this time following new expanding branches of industry able to choose sites away from coalfields and to use electricity. Most of the coalfields have declined in relative importance. Now there is an outcry about this, and moves at least to check the drift of people away from old industrial areas if not to get them back there. In a country in which almost all manufacturing industry is still in private hands, and in which the industrialist and business man have been held in such high regard for so long, why should this instinctive move to the apparently more favourable parts of the country for many industries be interfered with?

The following are among the main objections to further concentration of industry and population in the Midlands and South-east.

1. Why develop industry on new land, presumably taking it from agriculture, when there are plenty of sites in the older coalfield areas?

2. Why abandon existing coalfield industrial areas when they still have our main source of energy, coal, and a surplus of labour, much of it skilled, and accustomed to working in industry of some sort, as well as houses, schools, shops and so on.

3. If much further development takes place in the Midlands and South-east, these areas will be stifled by excessive building and traffic.

4. Strategically it is desirable to have industry as dispersed over the national area as convenient and not all concentrated in a few localities.

In answer to the first point, it has already been made clear that a very large area could be taken out of agriculture without having more than a very slight effect on our total national production. Admittedly much of the most attractive land might be spoilt in certain areas, but the preservation of nature and rurality is a secondary consideration compared with providing the best sites for new industry. It might be argued, however, that the value of the land would perhaps be high and development cost prohibitive in the places chosen in the Midlands and South-east. Again, however, speculation in land is a luxury that should not be allowed to stand in the way of national interests. As for the quantity of land likely in reality to be required in the next few decades, it is not very large. The *whole* population of the U.K. could be rehoused in the single county of Devon with a density of ten houses per acre (quite a generous piece of land for each family) and there would still be land to spare. In fact it will probably be necessary to house in completely new areas only a few million people in the next few decades. Ten million people could comfortably be rehoused in an area the size of Bedfordshire. Five hundred miles of new motorway would only take up some 20,000 acres, roughly the size of one Rural District. New factories could not possibly need more than, say, 100,000 acres. The housing, motorways, and factories could all be accommodated in an area the size of Leicestershire and would reduce our agricultural output *only by a few per cent*. This is likely to go up fast anyway as new farming techniques spread.

The three remaining points may be answered as follows. Firstly, for reasons that are not altogether obvious, certain new industries find the South-east advantageous. Why not allow population to drift gradually away from the older coalfield areas rather than try to get it back there, when these areas have little to offer except their surplus labour? Imported oil and gas are gaining in relative importance and these arrive by sea. Coal can be converted to electricity and now transmitted economically as such at least several hundred miles. The older industrial areas have factories, houses, and roads that are largely inadequate anyway and need renewing. Surely it is better to build in completely new areas in settlements planned for the motor age

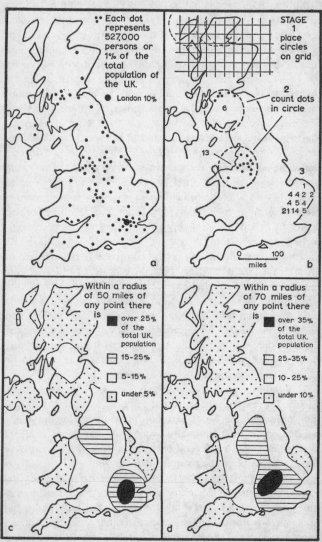

53a–d. Distribution of population and potential market in the U.K.

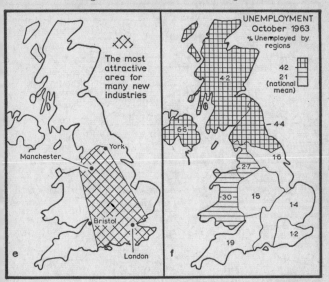

53e–f. Attractive area for many new industries, and unemployment, in the United Kingdom.

than to rehabilitate the old areas. Secondly, it is feared that Greater London and the Birmingham and Black Country areas in particular will be choked out by more development. But these occupy only a tiny area in the Midlands and South-east, and with reasonable imagination and foresight new roads and towns could be planned and built elsewhere, without any danger of congestion. Thirdly, in another world war it would matter little whether industry was spread over the country as a whole or was mainly in the Midlands and South-east.

From what has been said, it will be clear that in the view of the author the best planning policy for the next few decades is to facilitate the development of new industrial centres in the Midlands and South-east rather than to rehabilitate the older industrial areas. These should not, of course, be abandoned overnight, but should gradually be dismantled.

Fig. 53 a–f shows, very inadequately, the way in which some of the conclusions presented in this section were reached.

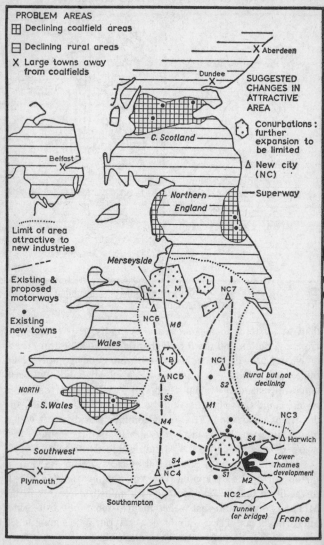

54. Replanning the United Kingdom in the next fifty years.

Fig. a shows the distribution of population in the U.K., each dot representing 1 per cent of the total population. If a circle with a radius, of, say, 50 miles were put down with its centre on Aberdeen, the circle would include only about 2 per cent of the total population of the country. If the same circle were put down on Liverpool it would include about 13 per cent; on the centre of London it would include nearly $\frac{1}{4}$ of the population. Increasing the radius to, say, 70 or 100 miles would increase the number of people in each case, but London would still include correspondingly more than Liverpool or Aberdeen. Figure b gives a general idea of the procedure followed in applying to the country as a whole this concept of differing numbers of people within a given radius of different places. The circle is put down at regular intervals (stage 1) and the number of people falling in it counted (stage 2). Values are recorded at the centre of the circle each time it is put down on an intersection in the grid (stage 3) and isopleths are drawn (Figs. c and d). Figs c and d give a visual impression of the distribution of most and least favourable areas for locating new factories *with a view to having as many people as possible within a certain radius*. Only radii of 50 miles (Fig. c) and 70 miles (Fig. d) are shown. This means, for example, that in Fig. d, within a 70-mile radius of any point in Scotland and Northern Ireland there is less than 10 per cent of the total population of the U.K., whereas within that radius of places north-west of London and in the south-east Midlands there is over 30 per cent. Of course other radii could be taken, and the population of the Continent could also be taken into account. Further, population could be weighted according to purchasing power, and so on, but lack of space makes it impossible to develop the procedure further. On Fig. e is shown the area (shaded) in which a reasonably large part of the national market is within a reasonable distance of any point chosen. This is the area to which many new industries are attracted. Is it chance, too, that unemployment is lowest here? (See Fig. f.) What has been shown could be worked out in several different ways, but these cannot be indicated here.

The reader may not agree that the obvious attraction of the

Midlands and the South-east to many industries depends only on the fact that more of the national market is within striking distance of places here than of places towards the periphery of the country. Many industries require bulky raw materials and prefer to be near ports; many others export a large part of their production and likewise are attracted to a port. Certainly the advantage of having a large port with good shipping connexions not too far away should not be overlooked. London, Liverpool, and Southampton are probably the most attractive. One further possible attraction must be remembered. An increasing share of our exports seem destined to be sold on the Continent. The opening of a Channel tunnel or bridge would make the extreme South-east of the country very attractive to some industries.

In conclusion, Fig. 54 is included to show the kind of developments needed in the view of the author in the next fifty years.

1. Measures to curtail further expansion in or near Greater London, Birmingham, and the Lancashire and Yorkshire conurbations.

2. A superway round London at about 20 miles from the centre to enable traffic to pass easily round. No further development within this ring road.

3. The establishment of several new cities between $\frac{1}{4}$ and $\frac{1}{2}$ million people each. For example, one in East Kent (NC2) near the cross-channel link, one in North-east Essex (NC3) to be associated with links to the Rhine mouth, one near Southampton (NC4) to exploit the worldwide shipping services in the English Channel, one, say, in Rutland, to serve as a new centre for the national government of the country (NC1), and so on.

4. New superways to link these new cities with other parts of the country. The superways (S2 and S3) could be within the favoured part of the country (see Fig. e) yet away from the already very busy London–Birmingham–Merseyside axis.

An integrated plan of this kind should be worked out on a national basis, not on the basis of fictitious economic planning regions. It should be thought out for some decades ahead, not redesigned for each new general election. It requires an enormous amount of research. The scheme should be designed by a team of planners not prejudiced by now meaningless concepts relating to our previous industrial growth nor concerned with furthering the interests of one particular region at the expense of others.

VII. SOME MAJOR TRENDS IN WORLD AFFAIRS

This concluding section is intended merely to draw the attention of the reader to some of the principal processes affecting human activities at the present day. The ideas have all been discussed, if briefly, at some stage in the book.

In the first place, we are all the time faced now with the possibility of a nuclear war in which so much harm would be done to the human race that, even if reasonably large groups of people remained unaffected, world affairs would follow a completely different course because the greatest sufferers would be the currently most advanced and influential countries. In *The War in the Air*, H. G. Wells painted early in this century a picture of the chaos he imagined would follow such a disastrous conflict. Assuming that such a nuclear war does not take place, then some trends may be suggested.

The population of the world has been increasing for at least a century at a more rapid rate than it apparently ever has done in the past, and seems likely to be at least two or three times as large as it is now before the increase stops. Of course there is no way of forecasting when it actually will stop, and the possibility that a rapid population increase is associated with a particular stage in the economic development of a country cannot conclusively be proved by present trends, though many instances at different periods in the last hundred years (France, England, U.S.A., now Italy, Japan, urban U.S.S.R.) suggest that when a certain level of industrialization and urbanization is reached, smaller families become more common.

Fortunately the technological revolution has made it possible to increase food production and utilize new resources, thus making the increase of population on (of course) unchanging land area feasible. Moreover, the technological 'explosion' is likely to continue for a long time to come. The two are obviously closely associated, but what their relationship is cannot precisely be shown. Increased productivity in agriculture and improvements in medical facilities have in many parts of the world enabled an increase of population to take place. Sometimes the newly introduced medical facilities alone have done this without material production keeping up. On the other hand, it may initially have been pressure of population that tested man's ingenuity and started the industrial revolution. Certainly many countries have recently taken steps to improve agriculture and to industrialize in order to cope with growing population. In the end the resources of the world are limited, whatever level the technological revolution reaches. To utilize the resources of other planets in this solar system would require a super-technology as yet far beyond man's reach. The great problem for humanity for many decades to come, therefore, is to ensure that the increase of population stops before the pressure on resources grows too great for a reasonable standard of living to be achieved for everyone.

Turning to more immediate trends, two are of particular importance. Firstly, there is a trend towards larger economic, and presumably, in due course, political, groupings. Those small countries (e.g. Bolivia, Switzerland) that for one reason or another feel that independence is preferable to loss of identity among larger neighbours, should appreciate that they are going against the trend. This trend has been discussed at some length in the previous chapter, and the way in which many countries are forming groups for the purposes of trade has been emphasized. Here one other more sinister feature may be stressed: the growing tendency for countries or groups of countries to forbid overflights by other countries. This often entails a great increase in the distance flown compared with the shortest possible (great circle) distance between points. Three examples are given in Fig. 55. The first shows the recent inconvenient diversion of flights by South African Airways between West Europe and South Africa, the second the detour made by flights between West Europe and Japan to avoid the U.S.S.R. and, the last, the U.S.S.R., faced with the problem it has caused so many other countries, forced to start a new non-

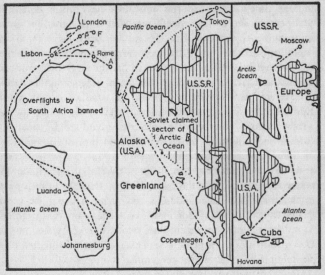

55. Forced detours on intercontinental air routes.

stop jet flight from Moscow to Havana without flying over any
other country.

Secondly, there is a struggle between capitalism and Communism. Although the U.S.S.R., and probably China, too, have
abandoned the idea of starting a major world war to facilitate
the further spread of Communism and are indeed apparently
far from agreement on many matters, let it not be thought that
either country has abandoned the idea of achieving worldwide
Communism by other means: witness the highly aggressive
remarks on the front page of *Pravda*, 17 October 1963. The
headlines glorify the October Revolution and the opening of a
new era in history, and herald the (literal) wreck of capitalism
and confirmation of Communism. In practice the struggle
amounts largely to a competition between private enterprise on
the one hand and state enterprise with a centrally planned
economy on the other, to show which is the more efficient way
of developing an economy, if we ignore the fancy Communist

327

theories on evolution towards the ideal society under socialism. State enterprise, though widely regarded with alarm, plays an important part even in the U.S.A., the great stronghold of capitalism. At the other extreme, there is a private sector in the sale of agricultural products, even in the U.S.S.R.; and in Poland and Yugoslavia there has been a reversion towards private peasant agriculture from collectivization. In West Europe many important branches of the economy are in the public sector: for example, electricity and coal-mining in Britain, the railways in most countries, much of the oil industry in Italy. It is absurd to take the view that one system is perfect and the other hopelessly inefficient. The fabulous setback to material production in the depression of the inter-war period in the major capitalist industrial countries has not been repeated, but is too near to ignore. Nor is there any reason to be complacent about the present high rate of unemployment in the U.S.A. and the failure there to achieve a steady increase in production. The Swedish economist, Gunnar Myrdal, considers this unsatisfactory situation in the U.S.A. the greatest single problem in the world.[1] At the same time, under socialism in the U.S.S.R. there has been constant inefficiency on account of the stresses in a centrally planned, state-owned economy, not to mention the massive self-inflicted setback of collectivization, from which Soviet agriculture has never recovered. Whether or not it is better to have one system or the other, or to have a combination of the two, each watered down, as in West Europe, it seems that in the world as a whole state enterprise is gradually gaining at the expense of private enterprise. This is because for one reason or another, in many of the 'neutral' countries now starting to industrialize, the state is the chief source of capital. Even in the U.S.A. there is growing interest in the successes of the partially planned economies of France, Italy, and Japan, and some concern at the worship of private enterprise and the neglect of anything that is run by the federal or state government, such as education, even if it is something that can be done much better by state than by private enterprise. J. K. Galbraith warns that this is one of the great problems

1. G. Myrdal, *Challenge to Affluence*, London, 1963.

facing the U.S.A.[1] On the other hand it seems very unlikely that the Communist countries would ever move far in the other direction, and certainly, even if farmers are allowed more freedom in producing and selling goods as they like, the private investor, deriving an income from money invested in a nonstate enterprise, is unthinkable.

In view of the military stalemate and the obvious desire of both sides to avoid a nuclear war if possible, the struggle between capitalism and Communism is likely to be carried on more and more intensively in the economic field, with four great powers at work, North America, West Europe, the U.S.S.R., and China. While West Europe has already been making an impact on the world for the last four hundred years, the other three are relative newcomers. Much of the discomfort felt in West Europe in general and in Britain in particular is due to the fact that the other three are trying to move in where West Europe has been withdrawing.

1. J. K. Galbraith, *The Affluent Society*, London, 1958, Penguin Books, 1962.

POSTSCRIPT

In Chapter 10, p. 277, mention is made of 100 members of the United Nations General Assembly. The number by mid-1964 was 112. The following countries have become members since 1960: in Africa, Algeria, Burundi, Kenya, Mauritania, Rwanda, Sierra Leone, Uganda, Tanganyika (now Tanzania); in Asia, Kuwait, Mongolia; in Latin America, Jamaica, Trinidad.

Further modifications in the pattern of states in the world include the dissolution of the Central African Federation, from which Nyasaland and Northern Rhodesia emerged as independent states named Malawi and Zambia respectively. The small British colony of Gambia achieved independence in 1965; it has little more than 300,000 inhabitants and joins the already large number of absurdly small new states in Africa. Zanzibar and Tanganyika united in 1964 to form Tanzania. By mid-1965 there were still no signs that Portugal would give up its colonies in Africa. In Asia, Malaysia, formed from Malaya, Singapore, and British possessions in Borneo, has been struggling to establish cohesion in the face of complicated cultural differences in its own population and threats from its neighbour Indonesia. Indonesia withdrew voluntarily from the United Nations in 1965, the first nation to do so up to now.

In view of the considerable amount of new material now available from censuses taken in various parts of the world around 1960, it has been possible to work out with more precision recent growth trends in the world and in different parts of it. In view of the references made to these trends in various parts of this book (see particularly Chapter 4, Section II and Chapter 10, Sections II and IV) it is interesting to quote here data from a United Nations source (*Unesco Courier*, February 1965) which predicts on the basis of continuing recent trends a population for the world of 7,410 million in the year 2000, compared with around 3,000 million in 1960 and 6,000 million widely accepted for 2000. But the rate of growth is expected to differ greatly among major regions, with the fastest rate in Latin America and rates well above the world average in

330

Postscript

Africa and South Asia (including India). Europe excluding the U.S.S.R., on the other hand, is only expected to have a gradual increase and its share of total world population should drop from around 14 per cent in 1960 to less than 8 per cent in 2000. The United Nations has no monopoly of prediction, of course, and like so many other forecasts, the figures here for the year 2000 may turn out to be quite wrong. But short of a disastrous world war there seems nothing to stop the present fast rate of increase continuing in many parts of the world at least for some decades.

	1960 Population millions	% of world	Expected percentage of world 1980	2000	Expected rate of growth 1960–2000 (1960=100)
North America	199	6·7	6·1	5·3	195
Oceania	16	0·5	0·5	0·4	207
Europe	425	14·2	11·1	7·7	134
U.S.S.R.	214	7·2	6·6	5·4	188
Latin America	212	7·1	8·6	10·2	357
East Asia	793	26·5	25·3	24·2	228
South Asia	858	28·7	31·6	35·0	302
Africa	273	9·1	10·2	11·6	315
World	2,990	100	100	100	248

As far as we are concerned in the West, perhaps the greatest single mystery in world affairs at the moment is the dispute between the U.S.S.R. and China. One cannot help feeling that if these two powers were in agreement over their aims in world affairs they could form such a powerful influence that the U.S.A. would not be participating so easily in various conflicts around the world as it has been doing recently (e.g. Vietnam, Dominican Republic). While it is pretty clear that the U.S.S.R. would like a solid communist camp, with itself of course as leader, or at worst as senior partner with China, there seems little sign that China wishes this at all; indeed China seems more interested in becoming the leader of the underdeveloped (or developing) countries, regardless of the aims or wishes of the U.S.S.R. Whatever the true aims of China, some notes on recent economic developments there must be added to what has been said in Chapter 7, Section III.

Postscript

The population of China apparently continues to grow as quickly as or perhaps somewhat more quickly than world population, by about 2 per cent per year; this is not so high as in many countries but the sheer number involved is impressive: about as many additional people each four years as the whole population of the U.K. One figure puts the population of China at 735 m. in 1964, though this may include Taiwan and the Chinese living elsewhere in South-east Asia. China continues to have 22–23 per cent of the total population of the world, while the age structure is such that there is a large proportion of people of potential child-bearing age.

Since the successes of the late 1950s, industrial expansion has failed to continue at rates hitherto achieved and expected in plans. Agriculture suffered from unfavourable conditions of various kinds. After several years of stagnation and in some cases decline, there appear now to be improvements in the economy. In agriculture, although work is mostly organized in large communes, the interest of peasants appears to have been stimulated by the establishment of very small private plots (1/24 of an acre, half the size of a modest-sized suburban garden in the U.K., per family) and the existence of a free market in some agricultural products. A little benefit may have been derived also from the development of irrigation in Sinkiang by the Chinese army and technicians. Although there was no great improvement in grain harvests in 1962 or 1963, the 1964 harvest is reported to have been good, reaching 190 m. tons of grain, of which 82 m. tons were paddy.

Progress in industry has been held up through lack of capital, unrealistic planning, the withdrawal of Soviet technicians from some key projects, and lack of suitable goods to export in exchange for equipment from foreign countries. The need to pay back Soviet loans and to buy grain from Australia, Canada, and elsewhere has been an added difficulty. There was some progress in industry in 1964, when China produced about 10 m. tons of steel, which however still gave it a production per inhabitant of only about 3 per cent of that in the U.K. Oil production was up to about 7 m. tons in 1964, enough for China's limited needs. There appears to have been a tendency to direct the efforts of industry more than previously to help-ing to raise farm production. But the 3 m. tons of fertilizers produced in 1964 still gives a consumption of about 1/10 of the Japanese level. Other branches in which developments are being made include oil refining and the manufacture of farm machinery. Certainly China has not turned out to be the great industrial power it might already have become if trends in the 1950s had continued. Nevertheless it has found enough money and technicians to design and explode a nuclear device by October 1964.

At the moment, China appears ready to trade with any country that it finds convenient as a partner, and the amount of trade with the U.S.S.R. and East Europe is three or four times less than it was around 1960. But it is hard to see what China can spare to export at all, whereas it obviously needs many kinds of equipment, as well as raw materials such as timber, scarce at home, and foodstuffs, at least in bad years. While noting the improvement of Chinese relations with a number of non-communist countries (e.g. full diplomatic rela-tions re-established with France, a direct air service to Pakis-tan), it seems pointless to speculate as to the aims of its leaders, even in the next few years, since it is quite possible that they themselves have no clearcut policy, at least until confidence is restored in the economy and more impressive progress achieved. Perhaps the new five-year plan, promised for 1966, will reveal something.

Tables 26 and 27 are included to provide more recent figures for population and some key items of industrial production for the larger countries of the world and may be used particu-larly in connexion with Chapter 4. They are self-explanatory. On the basis of sets of figures of this kind for some or all of the countries of the world, correlations have been suggested in this book and of course in many other publications dealing with world problems. For example, such general statements are made as: poor countries have a high birthrate, in highly urbanized countries the non-agricultural sector of the economy tends to account for a large share of the national income, small

TABLE 26

	I Area	II Pop'n	III Density of Pop'n	IV Steel	V Coal (to nearest million) tons)	VI Oil
1 China	9,561	720	75	10	420	7
2 India	3,046	450	148	6	61	2
3 U.S.S.R.	22,402	222	10	84	430	224
4 U.S.A.	9,363	187	20	113	396	425
5 Indonesia	1,492	98	66	*	*	24
6 Pakistan	947	97	102	*	1	1
7 Japan	370	95	257	39	54	1
8 Brazil	8,512	75	9	3	2	5
9 W. Germany	248	55	220	37	176	8
10 U.K.	244	53	219	26	201	*
11 Italy	301	50	167	10	1	3
12 France	547	47	86	20	52	3
13 Mexico	1,973	37	19	2	1	18
14 Nigeria	924	37	39	*	1	5
15 Spain	505	31	61	3	14	*
16 Poland	312	30	97	8	10	*
17 Philippines	300	29	98	*	*	*
18 Turkey	781	29	37	*	4	1
19 Thailand	514	28	54	*	*	*
20 Egypt	1,000	27	27	*	*	7
21 S. Korea	98	26	265	*	7	*
22 Burma	678	23	34	*	*	1
23 Argentina	2,777	21	8	1	*	15
24 Iran	1,648	21	13	*	*	84
25 Ethiopia	1,184	21	18	*	*	*

I Area in thousands of sq. km.
II Population in millions, 1962 or nearest.
III Persons per sq. km.
IV Output of steel in millions of tons in 1964.
V Output of coal in millions of metric tons, with lignite converted to hard
coal equivalent in 1962.
VI Output of oil in millions of metric tons in 1964.

Sources: I–III, V *United Nations Statistical Yearbook 1963*, New York, 1964.
IV British Iron and Steel Federation. VI Petroleum Information
Bureau.

* (cols IV–VI) less than ½ m.

countries are unviable, and so on. For the most part such conclusions have been reached intuitively. It is not difficult, however, using fairly simple and straightforward statistical techniques, to state the degree of correlation with more certainty
after the application of statistical tests to appropriate data.
One possible test is briefly explained here, more to show a
method than to draw any surprising conclusions from its
results.

The thirty-five countries of the world with the largest number of inhabitants are listed in Table 28. The test to be ex-

TABLE 27

	I Energy consumption	II Electricity consumption	III Population change	IV People per doctor
1 China	561	42	20	4,000
2 India	161	64	23	5,300
3 U.S.S.R.	3,046	1,836	17	550
4 U.S.A.	8,263	5,636	16	794
5 Indonesia	117	13	22	50,500
6 Pakistan	75	29	21	9,050
7 Japan	1,388	1,608	9	950
8 Brazil	367	357	34	2,780
9 W. Germany	3,884	2,657	13	705
10 U.K.	4,948	3,223	8	947
11 Italy	1,410	1,407	6	619
12 France	2,591	1,947	12	958
13 Mexico	916	357	31	1,840
14 Nigeria	45	17	19	33,900
15 Spain	987	830	8	1,030
16 Poland	3,278	1,204	13	1,100
17 Philippines	169	132	32	7,430
18 Turkey	281	132	26	2,960
19 Thailand	77	34	30	8,250
20 Egypt	284	151	26	2,690
21 S. Korea	328	81	29	3,380
22 Burma	50	22	30	11,830
23 Argentina	1,194	565	16	710
24 Iran	354	58	19	4,020
25 Ethiopia	10	7	16	100,500
26 Yugoslavia	933	710	11	1,570
27 Romania	1,640	621	9	695
28 Canada	6,015	6,519	21	945
29 N. Vietnam	55	21	34	29,800
30 S. Africa	2,437	1,812	26	2,100
31 E. Germany	5,191	2,766	3	800
32 S. Vietnam	55	25	37	29,800
33 Colombia	576	321	22	2,480
34 Congo (L.)	93	187	24	66,500
35 Afghanistan	17	11	31	37,200

I, II *per caput* consumption of total energy (in kilograms of coal equivalent) and of electricity (in Kwh) in 1962 or nearest year.

III Average annual population change during 1958–62, per million increase or decrease.

IV Number of inhabitants per physician. Note that in certain countries dentists are considered in total.

Sources: All figures direct from or derived from *United Nations Statistical Yearbook 1963*.

plained could equally be applied to a smaller or larger number of countries, to the complete list of sovereign states, or to a sample selected randomly from this. In column A, the countries are ranked in descending order of total population, in column B, according to total area, in column D, according to *per caput*

TABLE 28

	A Pop'n	B Area	C Density of pop'n	D Energy consumption	E Electricity	F Pop'n change	G Inhabitants per doctor	F/G d	dª
China	1	3	15	17	26	17	22	5	25
India	2	6	7	25	24	22	24	2	4
U.S.S.R.	3	1	31	7	7	14	1	13	169
U.S.A.	4	4	25	1	2	12	6	6	36
Indonesia	5	11	17	26	33	20·5	33	12·5	156
Pakistan	6	16	9	29	28	18·5	27	8·5	72
Japan	7	24	2	12	9	5·5	10	4·5	20
Brazil	8	5	32	19	16·5	33·5	19	14·5	210
W. Germany	9	29	3	5	5	9·5	4	5·5	30
U.K.	10	30	4	4	3	3·5	9	5·5	30
Italy	11	26	5	11	10	2	2	0	0
France	12	21	13	8	6	8	11	3	9
Mexico	13	9	26	16	16·5	30·5	15	15·5	240
Nigeria	14	17	20	33	32	15·5	31	15·5	240
Spain	15	23	18	14	11	3·5	12	8·5	72
Poland	16	25	11	6	12	9·5	13	3·5	12
Philippines	17	27	10	24	21·5	32	25	7	49
Turkey	18	18	21	23	21·5	25	20	5	25
Thailand	19	22	19	28	27	28·5	26	2·5	6
Egypt	20	15	23	22	20	11	18	7	49
S. Korea	21	35	1	21	23	27	21	6	36
Burma	22	19	22	32	30	28·5	28	0·5	0
Argentina	23	7	33	13	15	11	5	6	36
Iran	24	10	30	20	25	15·5	23	7·5	56
Ethiopia	25	13	27	35	35	12	35	23	529
Yugoslavia	26	28	16	15	13	7	14	7	49
Romania	27	31	14	10	14	5·5	3	2·5	6
Canada	28	2	35	30·5	1	17·5	8	9·5	90
N. Vietnam	29	33	8	30·5	31	33·5	29·5	4	16
S. Africa	30	12	28	3	8	25	16	9	81
E. Germany	31	34	6	9	4	1	7	6	36
S. Vietnam	32	32	12	30·5	29	34·5	29·5	5	25
Colombia	33	14	29	18	18	20·5	17	3·5	12
Congo (L.)	34	8	34	27	19	23	34	11	121
Afghanistan	35	20	24	34	34	30·5	32	1·5	2

consumption of all sources of energy and so on. The figures on which the ranking is based can in fact be seen in Tables 26 and 27, though in Table 26 figures are only given for twenty-five of the thirty-five countries concerned. Looking at columns A and B in Table 28, it is not difficult to see that if the country with the largest number of people was also the largest in area, it would be ranked 1 in both columns A and B, if the second largest in area was also second in population it would be ranked 2 in both columns, and so on, down the column; there would then be complete correspondence between the two columns of figures. If, on the other hand, the largest in population was the smallest in area, then its ranking of 1 in column A would be set against a ranking of 35 in B. In short, the closer the agreement between the 35 individual pairs of numbers, the closer the correlation between the two variables, in this case population and area.

A statistical test called Spearman Rank Correlation Coefficient may be applied to two columns of figures like columns A and B in Table 28, and a coefficient of correlation derived in the form of an index (r), falling always somewhere between +1·0 for a complete positive correlation (identical ranking in the two columns) and −1·0 for a somplete negative correlation (inverse order of ranking). An index near 0 (how near depends on the number of objects ranked, in this case thirty-five countries) could easily be obtained by chance, as for example if the numbers were arranged 1–35 as in column A, and then the same numbers taken randomly (say on counters out of a bag) and set down in the order they came out. The formula that obtains the index of correlation is:

$$r = 1 - \frac{6\Sigma d^2}{n^3 - n}$$

(d is the difference in ranking between each pair of numbers, as in columns F and G in Table 28, while Σ means 'the sum of all . . .', in this case the d^2).

A similar procedure can be applied to any pair of columns in Table 28, as for example, A with D (population with energy consumption *per caput*), F with G (population change with availability of doctors), or any other variable for the thirty-five countries in which one is interested. Of course the usefulness and significance of the sets of figures and their relationship should be borne in mind. The calculation is shown worked out manually for columns F and G. One might be led to think, for example, that the rate of population growth tended to be lower in countries in which doctors were plentiful than in countries in which they were scarce (though there might seem equal justification in arriving at the opposite hypothesis). A look at columns F and G gives the impression that although ranking is far from identical, there is some similarity. The column to the right of G, headed d, shows the difference in ranking between F and G. The following column, d², shows this difference (d) squared. The 35 values for d² are added (Σd^2), the total being 2562. Thus the calculation is as follows:

$$r = 1 - \frac{6 \times 2562}{35^3 - 35} = \frac{15372}{42875}$$

$$= 1 - 0.36 = + 0.64$$

which indicates a fairly strong positive correlation suggesting that the fewer people there are per doctor (and therefore in general terms, the better the medical services) the slower the rate of growth of population. This does *not* prove any causal relationship between the two variables but points the way to there being some connexion between the two, perhaps only indirect (as through *per caput* income), not to be explained away by chance. In other words, the probability of the numbers in columns F and G arranging themselves as closely to one another as they did could only have occurred very rarely by chance. As great an index as ± 0.4 would only be expected by chance 1 in a hundred times if 35 numbers were arranged randomly together; the 99 per cent confidence level for n=35 is roughly ± 0.4.

To work out such a correlation coefficient manually (and accurately) takes some time. If the number of things ranked is much greater than 35 (say 80 or 120 sovereign states) then d² can be very large and the calculation laborious. Fortunately it is now possible to have the calculations made by an electronic computer. This has been done for each possible pair of columns in Table 28: A with B, A with C, B with C, and so on. The results are shown as returned from the computer in the form of a matrix. All that the computer has done has been to work out rapidly calculations (in this case requiring a day or two manually) that one might refrain from doing manually as no constructive results are necessarily forthcoming.

		Population *A*	Area *B*	Density *C*	Energy *D*	Electricity *E*	Population change *F*	Doctor *G*
Population (absolute)	A	1·00	0·30	0·29	0·23	0·16	0·23	0·24
Area (absolute)	B	0·30	1·00	−0·75	0·02	−0·00	−0·16	−0·05
Density of pop'n	C	0·29	−0·75	1·00	0·08	0·05	0·27	0·11
Energy consumption (*per caput*)	D	0·23	0·02	0·08	1·00	0·96	0·63	0·91
Electricity consumption (*per caput*)	E	0·16	−0·00	0·52	0·96	1·00	0·58	0·89
Population change 1958–62	F	0·23	−0·16	0·27	0·63	0·58	1·00	0·64
Inhabitants per doctor	G	0·24	−0·05	0·11	0·91	0·89	0·64	1·00

As there are seven variables there are 21 different correlation coefficients excluding each variable with itself, which of course comes out each time at 1·0. F with G comes out at +0·64, as when calculated manually, confirmation that the manual calculation was correct (or that the computer and its programme were functioning properly). Since electricity output is part of total energy output, a strong positive correlation is obtained here (+0·96), as expected. If *per caput* consumption of energy (D) is taken as a substitute for *per caput* income, then, as a gain might be expected, a generally high level of development is closely correlated with availability of doctors (G), a correlation of +0·91. What is also revealed is a fairly strong correlation between high level of development (represented by D) and low rate of population increase, a correlation of +0·63. On the other hand, the correlations between energy consumption on the one hand and size of country, either according to number of people (A), at $+0.23$ or with area (B), at $+0.02$ are so near zero that they could easily have been reached by chance and the general conclusions that size and level of development are not connected, reached in *The Economic Consequences of the Size of Nations*,[1] seems to be confirmed.

In conclusion, the following points may be noted in connexion with the procedure outlined. First, data is lacking for many interesting variables (e.g. national income data for many communist countries). Secondly, greater precision would be obtained if all or most of the sovereign states of the world were ranked, rather than the thirty-five largest in population. Indeed, the results in the matrix apply to the thirty-five countries taken for this exercise and to these only. However, the indices of correlation for the eighty largest countries, arrived at by the same method, were found to be very similar. Thirdly, there is a more precise method of assessing correlations (product moment) as well as one that can be used with even less exact data (chi-square).[2] These are introduced for geographers by S. Gregory in *Statistical Methods and the Geographer* (London, 1963). Fourthly, however, whatever method one uses, the network of sovereign states is an unsatisfactory system for collecting data to make correlations at all, since states differ so greatly in population, in area, and in other ways. Moreover, the geographer wishing to reach more precise conclusions about many aspects of world affairs, or the relationship in fact of any two or more distributions on the earth's surface, will have to give up completely the idea of looking at distributions on flat maps, and will have to devise some reasonably uniform grid covering the land and/or sea surface and collect and process data in the cells of this grid.

1. Edited by A. Robinson, London, 1960.
2. A fuller study of the countries of the world, using more sophisticated mathematical techniques, will be found in the section by B. J. L. Berry in N. Ginsburg's *Atlas of Economic Development*, Chicago, 1961. Here Berry makes a remarkable contribution to 'quantitative' geography.

SELECTED REFERENCES

GENERAL

East, W. G., and Moodie, A. E. (editors), *The Changing World* (Harrap, London, 1956).

Boyd, A., *An Atlas of World Affairs* (Methuen, London, revised edition 1959).

Oxford Economic Atlas of the World (Oxford U.P., London, 1959).

Gourou, Pierre, *The Tropical World* (Longmans, London, 1961).

Pounds, N. J. G., *Political Geography* (McGraw-Hill, New York, 1963).

CHAPTER 1

Hartshorne, R., *Perspective on the Nature of Geography* (Murray, London, 1959).

Steers, J. A., *An Introduction to the Study of Map Projections* (University of London Press, London, revised edition 1960).

Clark, W. E. Le Gros, *History of the Primates* (British Museum, London, 1956).

Barnett, A., *The Human Species* (Penguin Books, Harmondsworth, revised edition 1961).

CHAPTER 2

Grenville, J. A. S., and Fuller, G. J., *The Coming of the Europeans* (Longmans, London, 1962).

CHAPTER 4

United Nations, *Statistical Yearbook* and *Demographic Yearbook*.

Statesman's Year-Book, for notes on the main features of every country in the world.

Cipolla, C., *The Economic History of World Population* (Penguin Books, Harmondsworth, 1962).

United Nations, *World Economic Survey 1960* (New York, 1961).

Times Review of Industry, a monthly publication with much useful information about industrial and technological developments in Britain and elsewhere.

Petroleum Information Bureau (29 New Bond Street, London, W1.) for up-to-date material on all aspects of the oil industry.

British Iron and Steel Federation (Steel House, Tothill Street, London, SW1.) for information on world iron and steel industry.

Selected References

Brown, A. J., *Introduction to the World Economy* (Allen and Unwin, London, 1959).

Myrdal, G., *Economic Theory and Under-Developed Regions* (London, 1957).

Rostow, W. W., *The Stages of Economic Growth, A Non-Communist Manifesto* (Cambridge U.P., London, 1960).

CHAPTER 5

Paterson, J. H., *North America* (Oxford U.P., London, 1960).

James, P. E., *Latin America* (Cassell, London, revised edition 1959).

Butland, G. J., *Latin America* (Longmans, London, 1960).

Stamp, L. D., *Africa, A Study in Tropical Development* (London, 1953).

Boyd, A., and van Rensburg, P., *An Atlas of African Affairs* (Methuen, London, 1962).

Cole, M., *South Africa* (Methuen, London, 1961).

Cumberland, K. B., *Southwest Pacific* (Methuen, London, 2nd edition 1958).

Australia and New Zealand Bank Ltd, *Australia's Continuing Development* and *New Zealand's Continuing Development.*

CHAPTER 6

Hoffman, G. W. (editor), *A Geography of Europe* (Methuen, London, 1961).

Elkins, T. H., *Germany* (Christophers, London, 1960).

The Common Market, A Survey by *The Times* (London, 2nd edition 1962).

Kitzinger, U. W., *The Challenge of the Common Market* (Oxford, 1961).

Oxford Regional Economic Atlas, *The Middle East and North Africa* (Oxford U.P., London, 1960).

Fisher, W. B., *The Middle East* (Methuen, London, revised edition 1961).

Dobby, E. H. G., *Monsoon Asia* (University of London Press, London, 1961).

CHAPTER 7

Baransky, N., *Economic Geography of the U.S.S.R.* (Moscow, 1956). An English translation (made in the U.S.S.R.) of a standard Soviet school textbook.

Cole, J. P., and German, F. C., *A Geography of the U.S.S.R.* (Butterworth, London, 1961).

Selected References

Shabad, T., *China's Changing Map* (London, 1956).

Wang Chun-leng, *A Simple Geography of China* (China Knowledge Series), Peking (Foreign Languages Press), 1958.

Kuo, Ping-chia, *China; New Age and New Outlook* (Penguin Books, Harmondsworth, 1960).

CHAPTER 8

Nove, A., *The Soviet Economy* (Allen and Unwin, London, 1961).

SSSR v. tsifrakh (yearly), Gosstatizdat, Moscow, for latest Soviet figures.

CHAPTER 9

Galbraith, J. K., *The Affluent Society* (Hamish Hamilton, London, 1958; Penguin Books, 1962).

Statistical Abstract of the United States (yearly), U.S. Department of Commerce, Bureau of the Census, for U.S. statistical data.

INDEX

Bold figures denote important references; italic figures, pages where maps or diagrams appear

Index

Index

Index

MORE ABOUT PENGUINS
AND PELICANS

If you have enjoyed reading this book you may wish to know that *Penguin Book News* appears every month. It is an attractively illustrated magazine containing a complete list of books published by Penguins and still in print, together with details of the month's new books. A specimen copy will be sent free on request.

Penguin Book News is obtainable from most bookshops; but you may prefer to become a regular subscriber at 3s. for twelve issues. Just write to Dept EP, Penguin Books Ltd, Harmondsworth, Middlesex, enclosing a cheque or postal order, and you will be put on the mailing list.

Some other books published by Penguins are described on the following pages.

Note: *Penguin Book News* is not
available in U.S.A., Canada
or Australia

APPLIED GEOGRAPHY

L. Dudley Stamp

Geography, literally 'writing about the earth', still means to far too many of us, influenced by school-day memories, the wearisome descriptions of countries in which lists of capes, bays, mountains, rivers, towns, and products play a major part. But its real interest is to describe and reflect the complex, underlying causes – the physical build and the natural resources, the sequence of human occupation and social organization – which have built the world we know, and will change and develop it in years to come. To know and understand these causes and their certain or probable effects is vital in all planning for the future, and this is the field of applied geography. In this book, a pioneer effort in its field, the principles of geographical survey and analysis are applied to the problems of Britain of today.

Two important new Penguin reference books

THE PENGUIN ENGLISH DICTIONARY

Containing more than 45,000 entries and specially prepared for Penguins by a team led by Professor G. N. Garmonsway of London University, this new dictionary places particular emphasis on current usage. Definitions, which include hundreds of post-war words and senses, are as direct and simple as possible, and a new and immediately understandable system is introduced as a guide to pronunciation. In all *The Penguin English Dictionary* makes an unrivalled catalogue of English words as used today in print and speech.

THE PENGUIN ENCYCLOPEDIA

This concise and authoritative new encyclopedia has been geared deliberately for use in the second half of the twentieth century. Articles by specialists, under more than 6,000 main headings, pay particular attention to the rapidly advancing areas of science and technology; but the arts and humanities have not been neglected. These simple, accurate, and intelligent explanations are likely to prove equally handy for the schoolboy, the student, and the family bookshelf. Specially commissioned for Penguins, this up-to-date work is remarkably comprehensive and fully cross-referenced. It will be followed by a gazetteer and a dictionary of biography.